THE **COMPLETE IDIOT'S GUIDE** TO

Human Prehistory

by Robert J. Meier, Ph.D.

ALPHA

A member of Penguin Group (USA) Inc.

This book is dedicated to my wife, Carol, and to my family. We are many, yet we are as one.

International Standard Book Number: 0-02-864421-2
Library of Congress Catalog Card Number: 2003105462

05 04 03   8 7 6 5 4 3 2 1

Interpretation of the printing code: The rightmost number of the first series of numbers is the year of the book's printing; the rightmost number of the second series of numbers is the number of the book's printing. For example, a printing code of 03-1 shows that the first printing occurred in 2003.

Printed in the United States of America

Note: This publication contains the opinions and ideas of its author. It is intended to provide helpful and informative material on the subject matter covered. It is sold with the understanding that the author and publisher are not engaged in rendering professional services in the book. If the reader requires personal assistance or advice, a competent professional should be consulted.

The author and publisher specifically disclaim any responsibility for any liability, loss, or risk, personal or otherwise, which is incurred as a consequence, directly or indirectly, of the use and application of any of the contents of this book.

Most Alpha books are available at special quantity discounts for bulk purchases for sales promotions, premiums, fund-raising, or educational use. Special books, or book excerpts, can also be created to fit specific needs.

For details, write: Special Markets, Alpha Books, 375 Hudson Street, New York, NY 10014.

Publisher: *Marie Butler-Knight*
Product Manager: *Phil Kitchel*
Senior Managing Editor: *Jennifer Chisholm*
Acquisitions Editor: *Mikal Belicove*
Development Editor: *Tom Stevens*
Production Editor: *Billy Fields*
Copy Editor: *Krista Hansing*
Illustrator: *Chris Eliopoulos*
Cover/Book Designer: *Trina Wurst*
Indexer: *Julie Bess*
Layout/Proofreading: *Angela Calvert, Mary Hunt*

Contents at a Glance

Contents

Foreword

Humans have a natural curiosity about their origins. For millennia, societies have invented myths to explain how humans came to be. Today science has provided an alternative story, one that can be tested and one that, with increasing discoveries, is becoming ever more detailed. This scientific story is of interest to everyone, but many find the numerous species, the long names, the detailed differences between one species and another, and the immense depth of time too complex to fully comprehend. Too often the latest discoveries are said to "overturn" our earlier understanding, erroneously implying that the story keeps changing. In addition, feelings of guilt resulting from contradictory religious beliefs dampen the curiosity of others. But this is our story and one of science's epics. The details make a fascinating drama that continues to unfold. It is a story based on fossils, artifacts, genes, and geology. Although new discoveries make us rethink the details, the basic outline remains the same and should stand the test of time. We all share a common origin from an apelike African ancestor, 6–7 million years ago. The advent of stone tool technology approximately 2.6 million years ago set us off on a different trajectory, providing the potential for the subsequent dramatic increase in our cranial capacity and the development of a complex communication system. These events have been key to our evolution, an intelligent species that today has reached a degree of technological development never seen before.

How is it that modern humans have become so successful? We are the most populace large mammal, more than 6 billion individuals inhabit all corners of the globe and our numbers are increasing. We have an extraordinarily complex technology allowing us to produce our own food, build our own houses, cure diseases, and penetrate space and the depths of the oceans. We understand the mechanics of the most complex systems in biology, chemistry, and physics; and we can communicate this knowledge to others. No other species can claim these spectacular achievements. But how successful will we be in the long term? Ultimately will our achievements prove our success or lead to our undoing? We have inhabited this earth for an extraordinarily short time: *Homo sapiens*, appeared fewer than 200,000 years ago. Will *Homo sapiens* have a future that can compare in longevity with the millions of years that so many other species survived?

This book explains the key events in our evolutionary story. It puts us, modern *Homo sapiens*, in the perspective of our evolutionary past, addressing contentious and controversial issues particularly those that have a bearing on our future. Why is it that *Homo sapiens* are so geographically widespread, so destructive of the planet, and so arrogant that we dare to presume that our future is secure? How do our religious prejudices affect our willingness to understand and appreciate our evolutionary past? Why are there so many deadly conflicts between nations and different ethnic groups when we are a single species with a common past? What role will our ability to manipulate our genetic heritage play in the future? It is essential that we face these issues and address the consequences of our current acts as a destructive, acquisitive species. As a bipedal ape with a small brain, for much of our evolutionary history we lived in harmony with the natural world. Today our living habits increasingly divorce us from nature and yet we are still, as before, dependent on its complex web of inter-acting life forms for our own survival. It is thus essential that we develop and nurture the means to ensure the careful stewardship of the earth that we share.

To understand our origins is to better understand ourselves. To put ourselves in the perspective of our past is to provide an awareness of the options for our future. Incredible as it may seem, we now have the ability to control the course of our own evolution and to direct the destiny of other species with which we share this planet. This is a tremendous challenge and one that each individual should shoulder. Let us not destroy the natural world that has nurtured us to this point in our evolutionary history, but instead dedicate ourselves to protecting our planet and its wealth of resources and thus ensure that we have reason to be optimistic for the future.

Dr. Meave Leakey

Dr. Meave Leakey is a standard-bearer of a family of paleoanthropologists who have dominated their field for many decades. For more than 70 years, the Leakeys have been digging in Africa, uncovering fossilized clues to the origins of our earliest ances-tors. Meave's field expeditions and lab work have established her as a visible and dis-tinguished scientist in a highly competitive and male-dominated profession. Her research interests range from human origins to the evolution of monkeys, apes, and East African mammals. Meave is a Research Associate in the Palaeontology Division of the National Museum of Kenya. She was recently named a National Geographic "explorer-in-residence," in honor of the 43-year relationship between the National Geographic Society and the Leakey family dynasty of pioneering fossil hunters.

Introduction

This book is about us. Well, us before we came to be what we are now. It was a rather long journey getting here, stretching back at least four million years. That's a very long time, and a lot happened along the way. We will try to give you a sense of the time it took for us to get here and present the highlights along the way.

Part 1, "Science Underground," provides a history of prehistory and introduces you to some of the more prominent figures of the day. One of these is Raymond Dart, and his work is highlighted in the first chapter. This also is the section where we take up the methods of dating archaeological and fossil sites, and how fossils are named once they are recovered.

In **Part 2, "Walk the Walk,"** we not only cover the earliest major discoveries made in the prehuman fossil record, but we also interpret these finds with regard to our becoming bipedal, hence the title of this part. But we also will deal with our ancestors' teeth as indicators of diet, and this is the place we document the first appearance of stone tools.

Part 3, "Out of Africa," and **Part 4, "Out of Africa, Again?,"** may sound like our early ancestors were on the move, and that is what these parts are about. They trace the initial departure of groups from Africa and into Eurasia, and then what might be a second relatively more recent major departure of later groups, once again into Eurasia.

Part 5, "Out of Asia," carries the travel theme to the next stage, the peopling of the Pacific and the New World. That brings us up to about 10,000 years ago or a little less.

Part 6, "Issues in Human Origins," takes a closer look at the nature of science, what Darwin contributed to evolutionary theory, how his theory has been advanced, but also how evolution has been subjected to certain nonscientific challenges. We end with a look to the future of humankind.

This book emphasizes human variation, in both biology and behavior. And there is an undercurrent of questioning throughout this book. We present factual material, not an overwhelming amount, but enough to support theories and to show why certain questions require continuing study. With questions come controversies, and we devote some space to these. But bear in mind that prehistorians generally agree on the overall picture of human origins and subsequent major biological and cultural developments. Differing viewpoints are really a measure of a vital, active science. Prehistory is still being written. I wouldn't be a bit surprised if some new fossil or archaeological find is made or reported on before this book is published. And I hope, after you read this book, that you will come to see new and old discoveries, in a new light.

Boxes Along the Way ...

To show the way in little packages of information, throughout this book you will find these kinds of sidebars:

Fieldnotes

Here is where you will find additional information on topics covered. These comments are like the notes or logs kept by prehistorians while working in the field, on a fossil hunt or at an archaeological dig.

Anthrolingo

Human prehistory has managed to get by without a huge number of technical terms, yet there are some that should prove useful as we describe the workings of prehistorians. These boxes provide definitions. The terms to be defined appear italicized in the text and in bold where defined in the sidebar.

Paleofacts

At times, misinformation, incomplete information, and, quite frankly, even outright myths have entered into discussions of human prehistory. Look for these boxes to present facts and dispel fictions.

Paleoquest

The study of human origins is a dynamic process. New discoveries are constantly being made. Some answers are in, but many more questions are actively being investigated and reinvestigated. Here you will find boxes that describe questions that require continued research.

Anthropos

Some prehistorians are well known, and some have made major discoveries. Usually, these go together. The work of such prominent prehistorians is highlighted in these boxes.

Acknowledgments

Many thanks to Mikal Belicove, Tom Stevens, Billy Fields, Krista Hansing; and others of the editing and production teams at Alpha Books. I greatly appreciate that Meave Leakey wrote the Foreword. A special thank you to the technical editor, Bruce Hardy. My deepest appreciation to Scott Brish and Leslie Harlacker, for preparing most of the figures and photos. Thanks to my colleagues who provided illustration material and assisted in other ways, including Nick Toth, Kathy Schick, Kevin Hunt, Cheryl Munson, Patrick Munson, Dick Adams, Jeanne Sept, Della Cook, Paul Jamison, and Rika Kaestle. Special thanks to my family and friends for all of their encouragement and expressions of interest in this book.

Special Thanks to the Technical Reviewer

The Complete Idiot's Guide to Human Prehistory was reviewed by an expert who double-checked the accuracy of what you'll learn here, to help us ensure that this book gives you everything you need to know about prehistory. Special thanks are extended to Bruce Hardy.

Trademarks

All terms mentioned in this book that are known to be or are suspected of being trademarks or service marks have been appropriately capitalized. Alpha Books and Penguin Group (USA) Inc. cannot attest to the accuracy of this information. Use of a term in this book should not be regarded as affecting the validity of any trademark or service mark.

Part 1

Science Underground

In this part, we look at the movers and shakers of the field, describe dating techniques that allow us to place prehistoric materials in their proper time sequence, and introduce the art and science of naming fossils. Chapter 1 recounts one of the most significant fossil discoveries in human prehistory, Raymond Dart's discovery of the Taung Child in South Africa and his report in 1925. It serves as our model for introducing the science that goes underground to find its evidence.

Discovery in Stone

In This Chapter

- Prehistorians find a life in the past
- A child is found at Taung
- Darting Dart's discovery
- Lessons from Taung for prehistory

As seekers and keepers of the past, *prehistorians* devote their careers to making discoveries of long ago places, peoples, and events. When the past happens to be millions of years ago, what would you expect to find and find out? Using both simple and highly sophisticated means, prehistorians ply their science into tedious, meticulous, and, at times, eye-straining, back-bending work. And, occasionally, they make exciting eye-popping discoveries. This chapter describes one such discovery, the finding of the Taung Child. It truly is a momentous and rather unique contribution. Yet, it also has many of the elements that generally make up prehistoric research. So the discovery of the Taung Child serves to introduce the overall topic of human prehistory.

Anthrolingo _____

The term **prehistorians** is used here to designate scientists who have devoted or continue to direct at least some of their professional life to studying the past. Many prehistorians, especially those from the earlier centuries, were trained in other occupations that were sometimes quite different from what they practiced. In the next chapter, I discuss related job titles, such as paleoanthropologists, who study fossil remains, and archaeologists, who study stone tools and other such early signs of human activities.

Facing the Past

It was the fall of 1924. Professor Raymond Dart, a teacher and anatomist at the University of Witwatersrand in Johannesburg, South Africa, carefully chiseled away on a chunk of *breccia*, or cemented limestone.

Anthropos
Raymond Dart was born in 1893 in Queensland, Australia. After being educated in Australia, he spent his professional life at the University of Witwatersrand in Johannesburg, South Africa. He established the department of anatomy at "Wits" and achieved much of his professional acclaim from his discoveries and interpretations of early prehumans, or "ape-men." Dart died in 1988, at the age of 95.

Dart had received two crates of breccia from the Taung quarry, which provided stone for building roads. Workers noticed that some of the breccia chunks blasted from the rock quarry had fossils embedded in them. They collected them and then turned them over to Dart for study.

The piece he chiseled away at resembled a goose egg in size and shape, but its surface texture was somewhat roughened. These telltale features indicated to Dart, trained in neuroanatomy, that this was an *endocranial cast*, a prehistoric fossil of some sort.

Anthrolingo _____

An **endocranial cast,** shortened as endocast, forms on the inside of a fossilized skull as the brain is replaced with solidified minerals. This is a natural process. Some researchers produce endocasts by coating the inside of the skull with a flexible material (that later sets up), such as latex or silicon. Technically, these latter examples are molds from which casts are then made.

Raymond Dart looks over the Taung Child.

(John Reader. Photo Researchers, Inc.)

The fossil-bearing rocks blasted from the Taung quarry were estimated to be at least two million years old. In Chapter 3, we take up the matter of dating fossils—no, not that kind of dating, but ascertaining what time period fossilized creatures once lived in. We will try to comprehend the staggering amount of time measured in millions of years. For now, two million years ago might seem unfathomable. But hang on—we will be tripling that number in our quest to find our earliest prehuman ancestors.

Remarkably, the Taung endocast had nicely and naturally preserved in limestone what had been the outer surface of a once functional, thinking brain. But whose brain? A monkey, an ape, or possibly a prehuman ancestor?

Dart knew of earlier such humanlike fossil finds from Germany (a Neandertal) and from Java (an erectus). These prehistoric humans will be more properly introduced in later chapters. He also had heard that a fossil baboon skull had been found at the Taung quarry. This discovery contradicted the prevailing thinking among South African paleontologists that monkey and ape fossils would not likely be recovered from

Fieldnotes

Fossils are formed when tissues and cells of once living creatures are replaced by minerals. Hence, the process is also called mineralization; in the case of wood, it is referred to as petrifaction. Once fossilization is complete, there is a much better chance that animals or plants will be preserved over a long period of time.

the rocky arid regions of South Africa, a couple thousand miles away from forested habitats of these primates today.

Eagerly tackling the question of whose brain this was, Dart began to search his boxes of breccia for more fossil clues. Just then, his quest had to be postponed temporarily when his wife reminded him that he was to be the best man at a friend's wedding that very afternoon. Dart fulfilled that social obligation and then Dart resumed his search, quickly spying a promising chunk. Against high odds, he found another part that fit the endocast. Chiseling continued, with Dart even resorting to using his wife's knitting needles at times. There, in the coldness of stone, appeared a very young humanlike face. To be sure, it was a fleshless face, but it was intact from its chin to its forehead, to now go along with its casted brain. This was truly an unusual and exciting fossil. But what was it? More precisely, *who* was it?

Paleoquest

How old was the Taung fossil when it died? Did children develop at the same rate back in the days of the Taung Child, between 2 and 3 million years ago, or were they on a developmentally faster pace, as found in modern apes? The tentative conclusion is that dental development was on a faster tempo, which placed the Taung child at about three years old.

Anthrolingo _____

A canine **diastema**, or gap, appears in the upper jaw between the upper canine and the first bicuspid (premolar). This allows the lower protruding, cone-shape canine to fit in when the animal closes its jaw. Chapter 6 provides a full description of teeth.

The Taung Child

Relying upon his anatomy background and an avid but little practiced interest in studying fossils, Dart assembled the evidence before him. To his trained eye, this fossil was neither monkey nor ape. For instance, its brain appeared more filled out in the front portion, which Dart saw as a human condition rather than an ape condition. (A correction to this assumption is covered in Chapter 7.) The endocasted brain was, moreover, only a little larger than that of a young chimpanzee.

Then there were the teeth. Chimpanzees, even youngsters who still have their milk teeth, also have relatively large canines that protrude beyond the level of the other teeth. In order to accommodate a fanglike lower canine, a gap, or *diastema*, forms in the upper jaw.

The Taung fossil did not have protruding canines. Hence, a diastema was not needed, nor was it present. All of the milk teeth were erupted, along with the beginning eruption of the first permanent molar. This is popularly known as the six-year molar, in accordance with the usual time of eruption in children today. Based on this fact, the fossil became known as the Taung Child. There was insufficient evidence to hazard a guess as to whether it was a boy or girl. I will provide some information in a later chapter regarding determination of sex of a fossil. Because the child's age was subsequently more accurately estimated to be about two to three years old, it was also called the Taung Baby by some researchers.

Dart thought he had even more convincing evidence of a humanlike creature. Looking at the underside of the skull, he saw that the foramen magnum of the Taung Child was located about halfway back, just as you would find in us humans today. Our skulls are sort of balanced on the top of the spinal column.

The foramen magnum is the large opening that allows the spinal cord to enter the cranium. Dart apparently had not observed its position in monkeys and apes. He wrongly assumed that these quadrupedal primates would have a foramen magnum that opened to the rear of the skull, which would orient their eyes for forward viewing.

> **Paleofacts**
>
> The position of the foramen magnum in primates does not accurately distinguish the mode of locomotion, as in quadrupedalism (four-legged creatures) versus bipedalism (two-legged animals). In monkeys, and particularly in apes, the foramen magnum is located toward the rear of the skull, but on its base or bottom.

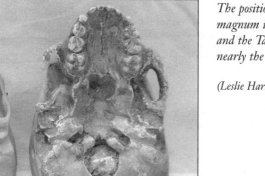

The position of the foramen magnum in the chimp (left) and the Taung Child are nearly the same.

(Leslie Harlacker/Scott Brish)

Especially in the Great Apes (gorilla, chimpanzee, and orangutan), there is a pronounced forward projection of the jaws relative to the rest of the face. This condition is termed *prognathism*, and this might as well give the impression that the foramen magnum exits to the back, as it actually does in some four-legged forms such as dogs.

In apes, the skull is perhaps not so well balanced on the spinal column, but, thankfully, it won't topple off. Any tendency for it to tip forward and droop the jaw onto the chest is countered by massive neck (nuccal) muscles holding it up, a feature pronounced in apes. Maybe you have noticed that gorillas don't seem to have a distinct neck region. Huge shoulders blend right into the head. As discussed in Chapter 5, apes are adapted to an upright posture of their upper body. Obviously, this requires the foramen magnum to be located on the bottom of the skull, just as in humans.

Very likely, the Taung Child was a fully active biped, skipping and hopping much as children do today. But conclusive proof for bipedalism must be based on other evidence (presented in Chapter 5). Conclusive proof for skipping and hopping is not forthcoming anytime soon, if ever.

Faulty assumptions aside, Dart was very likely right. His correct interpretation of the humanlike status of the Taung Child established the first scientific basis of one of our earliest ancestors. How early? Dart had in mind a time period of about one million years, but with much better dating methods, it turns out that the Taung Child lived more than two million years ago.

You probably have noticed that the Taung Child could not have been our actual ancestor, unless sexual maturation was impossibly accelerated back then. Reproductively speaking, the Taung Child could not have produced any offspring to form an ancestral line. In fact, this could be true for all of the fossils discussed in this book, even the mature adults. They may well represent our ancestral line, but currently there is no way to say that they were personally our ancestors. They may have been Uncle Joe or Aunt Flo who had no children themselves.

Dart used the Binomial System of Classification (see Chapter 4) and named his fossil *Australopithecus africanus* in a 1925 published report. Literally, this name translates as, "southern ape from Africa." Does this mean that he was somewhat unsure of its placement in the line of apes or humans? Probably not. It simply means that he considered the Taung Child as an evolved transition between ape and humans. The Taung Child represented a set of fossils (later fossils of adult *A. africanus* would be found in 1936 in Sterkfontein, South Africa) considered a "missing link" or, by another popular appellation at that time, as "man-apes."

Many of the leading scientists of the day, such as Sir Arthur Keith, debunked Dart's claim for *A. africanus* and instead considered the Taung Child to be nothing more than a little ape. They also reasoned that the immaturity of the Taung Child obscured more apelike features that would have developed later during adolescence and adulthood. The interpretation of the little child from Taung became steeped in controversy, which carries on even to this day.

Starting from the earliest stages of embryonic and fetal development, the more closely related two organisms are in an evolutionary sense, the longer they will resemble each other. Hence, all primates (monkeys, apes, and humans) will share some prenatal (prebirth) features and will begin to diverge in appearance as they are born and grow older. Newborn humans and chimps certainly look different. This must be a great relief to most human parents—and maybe even chimp parents as well. But they do resemble each other more closely when they are young than when they are adults. Interestingly, chimp babies change more as they get older and do so more quickly, compared to human babies. Because of this situation, chimps and the other Great Apes (gorillas and orangutans) are called *gerontomorphic* (having an adult appearance much different than their baby appearance); humans are said to be *paedomorphic* (retaining more of the appearance of babyhood into the adulthood). Let's use prognatism as an example.

At the baby stage of chimp and human, the jaws and associated middle face are relatively flat and do not jut forward very much. Yet, the chimp at adulthood has a high degree of prognathism, much more so than the adult human. Of course, all of these terms are rather flexible, so that degree of prognathism can be seen to differ among our ancestors. Generally, because of larger jaws and teeth, prehumans tend to be more prognathic and could be considered more chimplike in this regard. Be cautioned, however, that this does not mean that they are chimps!

Anthrolingo

Gerontomorphic refers to animal forms that grow up to look very different than they did when they were young. **Paedomorphic** is the opposite outcome: Certain features in the young animal are retained into the adult stage.

Beyond Taung

Dart's work on the Taung Child offers a characteristic picture of carrying out prehistoric research. First, of course, is the not-so-little matter of finding a fossil or a stone tool, or some other preserved remains from the past. Then there is the lengthy time spent preparing the study material—in this case, a fossil. In spite of their stony makeup, fossils can be quite fragile. In one incident, although it's not well documented, a valuable fossil skull (aren't they all valuable?) fell from a table and literally splitting off the top of its head. Careful, steady hands are required; in this case, researchers were able to put the fossil skull back together again. Being a careful sort of person, Dart secured the Taung Child fossil in a bed of sand before applying his tools.

A paleoanthropologist cleaning a fossil.

(Scott Brish/Leslie Harlacker)

Basic tools used to clean fossils may be quite ordinary. Dart used small chisel-type instruments; others have employed dental picks, paint brushes, and the like. Obviously, when the teeth are encrusted with tightly bound cemented matrix, cleaning them can be a dental hygienist's nightmare! In fact, it took Dart several years to separate the lower jaw of the Taung Child, thereby exposing the occlusal (chewing) surface of the teeth. Perhaps he was lacking in experience, but not in patience. That's certainly a plus for anyone who wants to be a prehistorian.

Then he entered his task with a very important question, if not a formally constructed hypothesis. He wanted to find out what this unknown fossil was. It seems likely that Dart was motivated by a sense of anticipation and excitement of discovery. In the next chapter, we consider these and other motivations and justifications for conducting prehistoric research. For now, we want to emphasize that all good prehistoric research begins with good questions to pursue.

Dart was interrupted at one point to be in a friend's wedding. Interruptions and delays are likely occurrences in most prehistoric research projects. If you find Dart's reason for interrupting his work somewhat amusing, then humor and lightheartedness can often be a part of prehistoric research as well.

Finally, in the course of doing prehistoric research, Dart got the payoff of an extremely significant fossil find. But as reported, his interpretation initially was not accepted and generated strong objections within his scientific cohort. Of course, not all prehistoric discoveries are of this scientific magnitude. Perhaps operating within prehistoric research is a tongue-in-cheek law that states: "The level of controversy is directly proportional to the scientific impact of a new discovery." Possibly you have read about or seen on television some major discovery of prehistoric bones or stones said to entirely rewrite our existing understanding of some segment of prehistory. What must be regarded as media hype should not detract from the significance that the discovery could well have in modifying our current set of interpretations.

Paleofacts

Based on a discovery of a large assemblage of animal parts (bones, teeth, and horns) in another cave site in South Africa, Raymond Dart speculated that these had been fashioned into weaponlike tools. He further speculated that *A. africanus* was a ruthless hunter, and he applied such terms as "killer apes." Others, perhaps not always in a grateful manner, made reference to the "Dartians." There is little acceptance of the "killer ape" speculations today.

Controversy stirred up by Dart's interpretation of the Taung Child is quite typical of current disputes that permeate and percolate within alternative interpretations of prehistory.

Many examples of differing points of view appear throughout the remainder of this book, usually highlighted in the Paleoquest boxes. Also, in Chapter 21, we discuss a counterpoint that is raised by creationists who deride scientists when they are unable to reach unanimity in their interpretations. Suffice it to say here that controversy and disagreements, when conducted on a professional level, add to the vitality of the science.

Professional outlets are available when researchers present their findings at yearly meetings, through workshops, and through publications in specialized journals. These forms of communication among researchers are imperative for science to progress. Researchers who publish books and articles directed to the general public are also important, as are the media outlets (television/radio, magazines/newspapers)—but without too much hype, please.

To Sum Up

This chapter described the discovery of the Taung Child. Its discovery sets up a general framework for viewing prehistoric research. So, in a literary sense, we now can use this child to lead us along the rocky road of human prehistory. It promises to be full of excitement—not wild and unrestrained, but the kind of enjoyment that comes from wondering when, how, and why we humans came to be who we are today. So fill yourself with wonder and join the walk. No running, please.

The Least You Need to Know

- The small Taung fossil had a big impact on human prehistory.

- Recovery and preparation of a fossil for study requires tremendous effort.

- Major discoveries often lead to major controversies.

- Each fossil or stone tool discovery is unique.

- Collectively, fossils and tools tend to have common and related elements of prehistoric research.

Chapter 2

Introducing Prehistory

In This Chapter

- ◆ Presenting the past
- ◆ Anthropology defined
- ◆ A place for paleoanthropology
- ◆ Historical persons of prehistory

If you tell people that you study prehistory, you are likely to receive a blank expression. But if you say that you are an archaeologist, almost everyone understands what kind of work you do, perhaps with a hint of Indiana Jones in their minds. This chapter discusses the attraction of prehistory as a field of study. It places prehistory in the broader context of anthropology. And it retraces a number of ideas, and some major misconceptions, that prevailed before the development of prehistoric research as a science. Finally, we mention some founders, recognized for the contributions they made in the beginnings of the science of prehistory, which is barely 200 years old. It's a mere youngster in the realm of scientific disciplines.

Why Study Prehistory?

It might sound cliché to say that prehistory is done because it is there. But there is indeed an element of truth in that statement. It may not be a mountain to climb, but it is a trench to be dug by hand. Yes, there are rewards and awards in the works, both personally and professionally. Personal satisfaction may come from carrying out a field or laboratory project well, regardless of the payoff in scientific significance. And you could probably toss in a measure of fame and glory, but not likely a fortune. Product endorsements haven't caught up with fossil hunters yet.

Professional recognition encompasses many entities, mainly within academic circles (faculty/museum staff appointments; publications and presentations; tenure/promotion and salary advancements; research project funding, various bestowed awards and honors, etc.). I do believe, however, that most prehistorians are deeply motivated by a sense of wonder and a quest to discover the unknown. And in that vein, prehistory is studied because it is there to be understood.

> **Paleofacts**
>
> The great popularity of the *Planet of the Apes* movie series seems to indicate that many people enjoy toying with the notion that, contrary to humans reverting to the past, our close primate relatives, the apes, will someday catch up with us. Fantasy can certainly be fun.

Another cliché essentially states that those who don't know their past are destined to repeat it. I am not sure that caution necessarily extends back several million years or so. Could we possibly revert to the "ape-man" stage? I hope not. But then there are lessons from the past that just might help us to better decide our future.

The more we know about where we came from (in the sense of our prehistoric origins), the better we will understand ourselves. As professed by the Greek sages 2,500 years ago, "Know thyself." And that's a pretty good reason to do prehistory.

Prehistory in Context

To this point, I have used prehistory to represent a discernable scientific endeavor. And that is true, to a degree. But now let's delve a little more deeply—excavate, so to speak—into the broader aspects of this scientific field. Sorry, I will stop short of recognizing Indiana Jones!

Anthropology is the recognized discipline that seeks to study all peoples at all times in all places. That's quite an ambitious goal and likely never will be fully realized. It certainly won't be accomplished without some division of labor. These days, anthropologists tend to specialize their training along conventional lines. Here are the four main subfields of anthropological study:

- Physical anthropology deals with biological and genetic aspects of both ancient and present-day humans.

- Archaeology investigates remains of past cultures.

- Cultural anthropology covers social customs and other patterns of behavior of present-day cultures.

- Anthropological linguistics examines connections between language and culture.

Fieldnotes

Some undergraduate programs in this country offer training in all four of the sub-fields of anthropology, considered to be the classic approach. Other programs drop one of the subfields, often anthropological linguistics, but sometimes physical anthropology. Graduate school training focuses on one or perhaps a combination of two of the subfields, and then students select a specialty for dissertation research.

Three of the four subfields emphasize culture in their study. Common usage of this term might suggest a high level of intellectual development, as in a cultured person who attends the opera. And, of course, culture for biologists refers to growing bacteria in a Petri dish. For our purposes, however, culture is learned behavior that is shared between one generation and the next, such as parents and children, and also exchanged between different cultures.

You could say that culture is a lens through which people view their world. It's a lens that can change over time, sometimes very quickly. Cultural anthropologists get to study all sorts of human behavior, be it economics, political systems, religion, and so on. And they may get to go to far-away, exotic places to boot. But what about prehistorians?

Prehistory is directly linked with prehistoric archaeology. Prehistoric archaeologists also might carry out their research in exciting foreign settings, even in exotic far-away lands. Then, too, like their colleagues in cultural anthropology, archaeologists have a major goal of describing and understanding the culture of ancient peoples. Of course, they cannot directly observe how people carried out their daily activities.

Paleoquest

Do primates, such as monkeys and apes, have culture? They certainly pass along learned behavior. This has been documented in a number of studies of primates living in captivity and in the wild. Ongoing research hopes to better understand the nature of primate cultural abilities and limitations.

In fact, they are restricted by what was once produced by a culture and then preserved after long periods of time, possibly under highly destructive forces. For the earliest time periods, there might be only stone tools as cultural *artifacts* in the prehistoric record.

As more kinds of artifacts appear in the record along with other lines of evidence, prehistorians try to build broader pictures of cultures from standpoints of social organization, *subsistence* activities, and ritual. Since prehistoric archaeologists might deal with cultures that persisted over centuries, there is an opportunity to study how well cultures adapted to change and to trace their migrations and interchanges among different ancient cultures.

Fieldnotes

Archaeologists recover cultural materials from field sites that they excavate carefully and thoroughly. This kind of research project is often referred to as a "dig." Sometimes a collection of materials is done on the surface that has been exposed due to erosion.

The material culture record (that part of culture that is preserved) diminishes the farther back you go in time, all the way to the very origins of stone tool manufacturing. This is the stuff that prehistoric archaeologists have to work with. Well, there are also those fossils, or bony remains, such as the Taung Child.

Anthrolingo

The term **artifact** refers to any object that has been made or modified by humans or human ancestors. In a sense, these objects are artifacts of human cultural behavior. They are the products of what people have thought about and then made. Prehistoric artifacts are mostly stone tools, since they preserve so well.

Subsistence refers to activities devoted to making a living—how people get their food, what they eat, and whether divisions of labor between men and woman are present.

Here is where physical anthropologists, specializing in human paleontology, enter the scene. Their background training is in skeletal and dental (tooth) anatomy and paleontology, and they are grounded in evolutionary theory. Their principal task is to discern the proper place for newly discovered fossils within an ever-expanding array of fossils already assigned to human evolution. Prehistoric archaeologists reconstruct past cultures, and physical anthropologists reconstruct evolutionary relationships of past populations.

This academic division of labor sorts out prehistoric archaeologists who specialize in stone tool study from human paleontologists who specialize in the study of fossils. Another job title used for the past decade or so has gained a solid foothold among professionals: paleoanthropologist. No, this does not refer to an old anthropologist!

Paleoanthropology recognizes the very close connection between behavior and biology. Indeed, these are integrated to the extent that inferences can be made about behavior from biology (for example, inferring *bipedalism* from leg bones). And biology can be inferred from behavior (for instance, knowing what the diet is helps to infer the nature of the teeth and the corresponding jaw anatomy and musculature). These topics are discussed in subsequent chapters.

Paleoanthropology is a combined biobehavioral approach that actually includes a team of researchers. Although they are individually trained in many related areas, they combine their specialties to maximize the scientific value gleaned from stones and bones recovered from prehistoric sites. Indiana Jones wouldn't stand a chance against this formidable team! Okay, he probably would have more exciting adventures.

Anthrolingo

Bipedalism is the evolved capacity to habitually stand and walk on the hind limbs.

A paleoanthropologist examining a fossil.

(Leslie Harlacker/Scott Brish)

When Does Prehistory Begin and End?

It might be helpful to make a distinction here. Prehistoric archaeology is different than historic archaeology primarily in terms of professional training, and obviously, with respect to time period of study.

At present, the earliest evidence of stone toolmaking is at about 2.6 million years ago in East Africa. This could be used to signify the beginning of prehistoric cultural activity. Then, too, the earliest dates of fossils that are believed to be our ancestors go back at least another two million years. And it is fully expected that new discoveries of stones and bones will continually push back these dates. So prehistory has an indefinite beginning. The same can be said for when prehistory ends.

Let's just say that prehistory is customarily considered to be that time before recorded history. This can be arbitrary and variable, since recorded history, as evidenced in written documents, differs across cultures. Indeed, some cultures have not developed written language, yet they have managed by other means to effectively remember and transmit important knowledge to succeeding generations.

> **Paleofacts**
>
> Cultures without written languages readily transmit knowledge through oral tradition, as practiced by the Griots (men) and Griottes (women) of West Africa. They are the keepers of historic knowledge, which is passed along verbally and is accompanied by their music.

The division between history and prehistory is sometimes quite clear. For instance, writing appeared in ancient Egypt around 3100 B.C.E. For this book, we do not need to make such a precise distinction. We simply trace the origins and developments of humans up to the time of their spread across the world. This takes us up to several thousand years ago.

Pioneers in Prehistory

But first, let's take some baby steps back in time to review historically key persons, ideas, and events that initially hindered and ultimately helped to shape the development of prehistoric research as it is conducted today. Our brief review spans the past 350 years. This was a time when Earth and its living inhabitants were thought to be relatively static and very young. These ideas were then replaced by the notion of a dynamic Earth that had an immense time depth and that housed continually evolving life forms.

> **Paleofacts**
>
> A new perspective on time can be seen in recent estimates of origins. The origin of the universe is estimated at 12 to 14 billion years, roughly 2 million times older than the date of creation calculated by Archbishop Ussher. The age of our planet Earth is approximately 4.6 billion years, and life on Earth was present about 3.5 billion years ago.

In 1650, Archbishop James Ussher, an Irishman, set the date of Divine Creation at 4004 B.C.E. He arrived at this precise time by relying on historical records, astronomical cycles, and, importantly, on the genealogies or family trees that appeared in the Christian Bible. Later calculations even established the exact day and time for creation.

Archbishop Ussher's date would mean that Earth truly was young. It would have allowed little opportunity for massive changes in Earth's appearance, except through catastrophic events such as floods, volcanoes, and earthquakes. Life forms would also not have had much chance to change. But this notion of "fixity of species" fit nicely with prevailing views that corresponded with biblical accounts in Genesis.

A prominent proponent of this notion was a mideighteenth-century Swedish natural-ist, Karl von Linne (latinized to Carolus Linnaeus). In 1735, Linne published *Systema Naturae*, which presented his basis for taxonomic classification. In Chapter 4, we con-sider Linne's contribution to present-day classification. Essentially, Linne devised a system for uniquely naming all of the life forms (or species) that had been created by God. Linne held the notion that the number and kind of species were constant since the time of creation as calculated by Archbishop Ussher.

Rumblings of change in the air confronted these ideas of a young static Earth and no major changes in plants and animals. One such proposal was unleashed in the late eighteenth century.

Georges Cuvier, putative father of vertebrate paleonotolgy, observed turnovers in ancient life forms at different levels in deposits beneath Paris streets. He boldly declared that these changes in species were due to "serial creation" that occurred fol-lowing major extinctions of life forms caused by upheavals on Earth. This, of course, countered both the "fixity of species" and the static Earth ideas. It meant that not only did the Earth undergo drastic alteration, probably due to worldwide floods, but there was near extinction of all life forms, leaving behind a few remaining survivors to again populate Earth. Cuvier referred to these events as "periodic revolutions," but they are better known as "catastrophies," a term that Cuvier did not prefer. While Cuvier's proposal did explain his observations, it did not advance understanding of natural processes of geologic or biological change.

Breaking into the nineteenth century also meant some major breakthroughs in thinking about time and change with respect to our earthly home.

Changing Times and Life

In 1830, Charles Lyell, an English geologist, published *Principles of Geology*. In it he argued that, contrary to catastrophies or geologic revo-lutions, the causes and time frames of geologic change that were currently taking place had always been there far into the past. This is known as *uniformitarianism*.

Anthrolingo

Uniformitarianism is not a religion that is based on a strict dress code; it is a doctrine that states that the geologic processes that we see in action today are the same ones that operated in the past. Slow change may occur in rivers cut-ting canyons, but at times, violent and more rapid change happens during flooding, earthquakes, and erupting volcanoes.

Lyell's observations convinced him that immense periods of time were required for Earth to undergo any substantial modification. Mountains were not built or destroyed overnight. This would be so even if there were occasional relatively rapid and spectacular events like volcanoes.

From one Charles to the next: Charles Lyell provided Charles Darwin, a close friend and colleague, the time depth that Darwin needed for postulating his theory of evolution. In 1859, Darwin, an English naturalist, published *Origins of Species* (shortened title). This work, which Darwin considered but an abstract, contained his extensive compilation of empirical evidence documenting changes in species due to natural selection. Known as the "mutability of species" idea, it really means that life forms experienced continual evolutionary change. And from one or perhaps a few forms arose the great multitude of species that either were still living or had become extinct. Darwin had the notion that biologic change, like geologic change, was mostly gradual. This meant that for all of the species to be formed, a great deal of time would have passed. Enter Lyell's contribution to Darwin. Darwin's work is more fully covered in Chapter 20.

Fieldnotes

James Hutton (1726–1797), from Scotland, is credited with founding modern geology and was an early and highly dedicated proponent of uniformitarian principles. He strongly opposed catastrophism. He felt that the slow but steady processes of weathering and erosion could explain Earth's features as long as there was enough time.

By the end of the nineteenth century, the stage was set for placing all of life within a constantly changing world, which, in turn, spurred on changes in plants and animals. In sum, humans, as one of these forms, could now be viewed in an evolutionary light. But before these historical developments came puzzling discoveries of stone tools in association with extinct animals. There were also fossils of early prehumans that were initially not accepted for what they were.

So let's take another brief jaunt back into history to recount the contributions of some early prehistorians as they built a foundation for their new science on newly discovered stones and bones of ancient ancestors.

The First Rock Stars

The earliest discoveries of ancient tools and fossils are hidden in the deep recesses of time, inaccessible even to the best of excavators. We do know that, for millennia, inquisitive persons collected tools fashioned from *flint*.

Their antiquarian interests sought flint tools for personal enjoyment, for aesthetic purposes, and possibly in admiration of the ancient toolmaker's skills. Count me among those who stand in awe of their technical abilities.

In the mid-1600s, flint tools were called thunderbolts, signifying their fantastic production by lightning and thunder. Fantasy ruled back then, and these tools were also thought to be made by fairies and elves. Fantasy tends to be more constrained today.

Displaying all of the formal pioneers of prehistory becomes problematic, but at the very least, the following persons and discoveries are noteworthy.

Anthrolingo

Flint is a preferred raw material for making stone tools. It breaks or fractures in predictable fashion, and there tends to a lot of it around the world. Flint was probably also traded because of its value.

Frere Finds Flint

In 1797, John Frere found flint tools in Hoxne, England. This find was significant because the artifacts were buried under 10 feet of soil, below a layer of earth that contained bones of extinct animals. This means that the bones were probably "sealed off" from the upper layers and thus must be at least as old as the extinct animals.

Layers of Time

In 1815, William Smith, an English surveyor, established the use of stratigraphy, based on his observations that there was an ordered layering of earth deposits, rather like layers of a cake. So time was ordered since the oldest layers or strata were on the bottom and the youngest were at the top. Stratigraphy became the workhorse for geologists and prehistorians in establishing a dating method for the artifacts recovered from an *archaeological site*. Hence, strata are basically layers of time. Stratigraphy is discussed in the next chapter.

Anthrolingo

An **archaeological site**, or simply site, is a place where people once lived and left behind artifacts. Sites can represent different kinds of cultural activities, such as camping, butchering animals, making tools, and burying dead.

In 1824, Flint tools were found in association with extinct animal bones at Kent's Cavern, England. The significance here is that the tools were sealed in stalagmite, virtually ensuring that the tools were of the same age as the extinct forms of rhinoceros and elephant.

Setting the Stage

In 1836, Christian Jurgensen Thomsen devised a three-age system for organizing a guidebook to exhibits in the Danish Museum in Copenhagen. The system arranged materials made from stone to bronze to iron, which implied their temporal or historical sequence of development, and a progression of tool-making technology in terms of difficulty in manufacture and of usefulness and durability of the tools.

Anthrolingo

The **skull** consists of the cranium and the mandible, or lower jaw. If the cranium is missing its face and bottom portions, then it is called a **calvarium**, or sometimes a skullcap. This is not to be confused with certain types of headgear.

Paleofacts

The spelling of Neandertal without the *h* is okay when referring to the fossil. But when using its scientific name, it should be *Homo sapiens neanderthalensis.* The scientific name came before a later change in a German spelling rule of "valley" from *thal* to *tal.*

You Neandertal

In 1856, a prehuman fossil skull (actually, just the upper part, called a *skullcap* or *calvarium*) was found in the Neander Valley in Germany. The Neandertal fossil was found by some boys who chased a ball that they were playing with down into a cave opening. They gave the fossil to their teacher, who then turned it over to a scientist for study.

Earlier such fossils had turned up in Belgium and on Gibralter but were not so thoroughly studied as the Neander Valley specimen. This skullcap was as large as that of modern humans, but it had heavy bony development over the orbits where the eyes would have been.

In spite of the mounting evidence, there was reluctance to accept the antiquity of humans, so the Neander Valley skull was mostly judged as pathological, or just possibly a member of an extinct human race. These and other contemporaneous fossils found in Western Europe will be classified as *Homo sapiens neanderthalensis* when we again present them in Chapter 10.

Discovered in 1856 in the Neander Valley, Germany, this is the first recognized fossil of a premodern human.

(Leslie Harlacker/Scott Brish)

Stones Break the Silence

In 1859, Boucher de Perthes, a French Customs official who had made systematic searches for flint tools and found them back in 1836, was joined by Sir John Evans and Sir Joseph Prestwich to visit the Sommes deposits near Abbeville, France. As in earlier discoveries, this site contained stone tools in association with extinct animal remains. What was different here is that Sir Joseph, a geologist, addressed the Royal Society of London and claimed that de Perthes's collection of tools, and also the earlier discovered Frere's tools, were solid evidence for the great antiquity of humans. With this public announcement made by a highly respected scientist, there was now a firm basis for correctly interpreting human prehistory. Note that the date of Sir Joseph's address was 1859, coincident with the publication of Darwin's *Origin of Species*. Could this be the adolescent growth spurt of prehistory? Well, we are still waiting for prehuman fossils to be accepted.

Fossils from Java

In 1891, Eugene Dubois, a Dutch physician, traveled to Southeast Asia with the express purpose of discovering a "missing link." That he did. After a couple of unsuccessful attempts and a series of mishaps, he made his momentous find on the Island of Java. More precisely, it was along the Solo River near to the town of Trinil. Similar to the Neander Valley discovery, the find was a skullcap (originally mistaken for a turtle shell or carapace) that turned up initially. Subsequently, many more skulls were discovered, along with a thigh bone or femur that indicated upright posture to Dubois. Was this the "missing link"? Dubois named it *Pithecanthropus erectus*, or "upright apeman," which apparently answers that question for him, at least. In Chapter 9, this fossil will be renamed *Homo erectus*. We will continue to appreciate the significance of Dubois's discovery as the first of this kind or species.

Dubois initially considered "Java Man" to be a missing ape-human link. Later, perhaps because of a continuous barrage of negative comments to this proposal, Dubois placed his Java fossils in a vault and denied access to anymore scientists. Much later, in 1935 (shortly before he died in 1940), he wrote a report in which he compared "Java Man" with the gibbon, a Southeast Asian ape.

Paleofacts
Some have said that Dubois claimed that "Java Man" was a giant gibbon, but this is incorrect. He always maintained that it was a transition, first calling it a "human-ape" link and then settling for "ape-human" link.

Dart Revisited

We are once again on familiar ground. In 1924, Raymond Dart discovered the Taung Child and, like Dubois, proposed the existence of an ape-human transition. Also like Dubois, we should recognize Dart's significant contribution of discovering the first representative of a new kind of prehuman—in this case, *Australopithecus africanus*. Finally, like Dubois, Dart suffered the slings and arrows of dissenters. It's a controversy that still persists.

The Least You Need to Know

- Understanding the past, and thereby better understanding ourselves, is a strong motivation for doing prehistoric research.

- Anthropology is the home discipline of prehistorians, who in North America are usually known as prehistoric archaeologists.

- The scientific foundation for prehistorians and paleoanthropologists is built on ancient artifacts of past cultures and fossils of once living prehumans and humans.

- Before the development of prehistoric study in the mid-nineteenth century, humans were viewed as unchanging and of recent origin.

Chapter 3

Telling Time

In This Chapter

- ◆ Comprehending deep time
- ◆ Layering the past
- ◆ Time catches up with Piltdown
- ◆ Chemical clock at Olduvai
- ◆ Plio/Pleistocene and Paleolithic time charts

As you might imagine, time is of the essence in prehistory. More precisely, deciphering prehistory depends on determining reasonably accurate dates of when events occurred and when our earliest ancestors lived and died, or even died out. This chapter looks into some widely used methods of dating the past, with examples that help to illustrate how the methods are applied. Unnecessary technical terminology is avoided. Be warned that if you go online to find out more about any of these dating methods and search on keywords that include "dating," you will very likely get a listing of websites well outside your intended interest.

Four Score and Seven Years Ago ...

This, of course, leads off Lincoln's Gettysburg Address delivered on December 8, 1863. And Lincoln was indeed referring to Independence Day of 1776, some 87 years earlier. If you didn't know already, you probably figured out that a score equals 20 years. I start off with this historically significant example for several reasons. First, dates of this sort are very familiar to us. History as taught in our schools is anchored with such dates. The nightly news programs and daily newspapers are constantly reminding us of this or that date in our history or of some other nation in the world. So we are familiar with telling time according to the standardized Gregorian calendar.

Fieldnotes

Calendar dates can be designated in different ways. You might be familiar with the use of A.D. (meaning "anno domini" or "year of the Lord") and B.C. ("before Christ"). There has been some effort to covert A.D. to C.E. ("common era") and B.C. to B.C.E. ("before common era"). However, since the time period we will be dealing with far exceeds the past 2,000 years, we will simply use either B.P. ("before present") dates or refer to a date of B.Y.A. ("billion years ago"), M.Y.A. ("million years ago"), or K.Y.A. ("thousand years ago").

How do we comprehend a period of time that is beyond our personal experience? Coincidentally, we might well appreciate the four score and seven years length of time because that is within our possible lifespan. Methuselah notwithstanding, the oldest human on record lived to be around 120 years old. Thus, we can never expect to directly experience fairly recent historical periods of time, let alone the immense amount of time recorded on the geologic clock.

Geologic time is usually measured by the gradual processes of rivers carving out canyons and mountains eroding to the sea. Soils and sediments are deposited across eons of time. Then, too, there are nature's forces of relatively rapid change. Earthquakes, volcanic eruptions, and tsunami tidal waves are among the most spectacular of these. The eruption of Mount St. Helens in Washington in 1980 is one of those events that helps us to understand the periodic fastness and fury of natural forces. But for the most part, geologic change comes in much longer time-consuming doses. I think we are generally pleased about this.

Paleofacts

Methuselahs of the living world are bristlecone pines growing in the White Mountains of California. When one tree's annual growth rings were carefully counted, it turned out to be more that 4,600 years old!

In the preceding chapter, I gave origin dates of the universe (12–14 B.Y.A.), Earth (4.6 B.Y.A.), and life on Earth (3.5 B.Y.A.). My mind boggles in an attempt to comprehend these numbers. It is with some sense of relief that we will be dealing with dates that are much more recent, geologically speaking—only in the range of millions, not billions, of years. But wait a minute—a New York minute, if you like. It is not much easier to comprehend millions, or thousands, or even hundreds of years of elapsed time.

Relative Dating

Speaking relatively, this is a fundamental way of reckoning past-time periods. Prehistory utilizes several methods for determining *relative dates.*

Stratigraphy

We have already mentioned stratigraphy as the workhorse for archaeologists. Unless they have been disturbed, layers, or strata, of a site's deposit are essentially layers of time. The lower strata are older than the upper strata, conforming to the *law of superposition.*

Anthrolingo

Relative dating uses methods that place events in their proper chronological sequence, such as before/after, younger/ older, and early/middle/late. These sequences are "floating in time" without a more precise dating method.

The **law of superposition** is named for Nicolas Steno, a Danish geologist and anatomist (and currently being considered for sainthood), who in the seventeenth century observed that in a sequence of sedimentary beds, the oldest beds were on the bottom and the youngest were on the top. That seems obvious now, but apparently it hadn't been formally recognized before Steno.

Earth's layers remain cakelike and in their proper age sequence unless they are disturbed. Natural events such as floods can alter once-ordered beds. Burrowing animals have been known to disturb natural stratigraphy and move artifacts around in a site; they even have taken up residence inside human skulls. And human activities like road-building and excavating for buildings can markedly change the original layering of soils. Obviously, prehistorians must be able to recognize and deal with disturbed strata.

Depth of a deposit can be used with caution for relatively dating a site, but this method is not always reliable. Layers of soil are not built up in a uniform manner across widely separated regions, nor are they eroded away at a constant rate. This means that some very deep sites are actually younger than older sites that have thinner or fewer strata.

The cakelike layers of an archaeological site.

(Patrick Munson)

Biostratigraphy

The Taung Child was dated partially on the basis of stratigraphy. However, cave deposits can be very tricky to date in this manner, and, of course, stratigraphy alone would not tell us how long ago the Taung Child lived. An extension of stratigraphy was therefore used. Associated finds with Taung included fossil baboons, which were used to date Taung with the *biostratigraphy* method.

Anthrolingo

Biostratigraphy is a dating technique that uses fossils that have been accurately dated at one site to date comparable species of fossils at another site. Fossil baboons from East Africa, where precise dating is possible, were used to date the South African Taung Child who was found associated with fossil baboons.

Biostratigraphy is widely used to date fossils from the many cave sites in South Africa, since there has been little success in using any of the more precise dating methods. Biostratigraphy yields fairly rough estimates of age. Hence, the Taung Child is usually considered to be between two million and three million years old. Prehistorians have learned to live with this level of imprecision, especially in the earliest time periods.

Paleoquest

Biostratigraphy assumes that the compared fossil species from the different sites evolved in the same manner. This assumption is subject to continued testing.

Fluorine Dating

The final relative dating method to describe here was instrumental in clearing up what probably is the most celebrated hoax in human prehistory. This is the infamous Piltdown forgery. Piltdown quarry, in

Sussex England, was the site from which bones and teeth were recovered in 1912 by Charles Dawson. The find was dubbed another "missing link" and was scientifically named *Eoanthropus dawsoni*, or "Dawson's dawn man."

To be sure, the cranium, housing the brain, was quite modern, while the lower jaw or mandible was decidedly apelike. You might realize that this made Piltdown just the opposite of the Taung Child "missing link." The Taung Child had a mixture of traits that included a small apelike braincase coupled with humanlike canines. Perhaps because of certain expectations of how human evolution should have occurred, combined with a less than thorough study of the bones and teeth, Piltdown was accepted as authentic by some prehistorians for 40 years. In 1953, it finally was declared a deliberate hoax.

> **Paleofacts**
>
> An important caution in recovering materials from a site is that their physical association, being found together, does not necessarily mean that they belong together or are even related to each other. That is an important lesson presented by the Piltdown hoax.

Someone, perhaps Dawson himself, had deliberately "planted" or "salted" the quarry with the bones and teeth along with a expectation that they would be found and given serious consideration in light of human evolution. How true that was. But how was the hoax ultimately exposed? First, there was a more careful examination of the materials. They were found to have been "doctored" to appear older in age. They had been broken to remove helpful diagnostic features, and teeth had been filed to appear more humanlike. And then fluorine dating came into the picture.

Over time, bones that are buried closely together take up or absorb the same amount of minerals found in the ground water of the soil. One of these minerals is fluorine.

Thus bones of the same age should have about the same concentration of fluorine. Well, it turned out that the Piltdown skull (actually, parts of two skulls were found) had more fluorine than the Piltdown mandible. The mandible had about the same amount of fluorine as fresh specimens. (I wonder what fluoridation of water supply has done to change our current level of fluorine in our teeth and bodies?) So the cranium and the lower jaw were not of the same age—in fact, they were not even of the same species. The jaw was that of a modern orangutan, while the cranium was indeed a human

> **Paleoquest**
>
> "Missing link" has been and continues to be an appealing way to designate the transitional form between ourselves and our apelike ancestors. Paleoanthropologists don't search for a vital "missing link," but rather for a series of fossil forms that connect us with our past ancestry that we shared with apes.

from an earlier time period. We return to the Piltdown hoax in Chapter 21 for other cautionary tales that it raises.

Not So Absolute Dating

Relative dating is indeed relative, but absolute dating is not absolute. For that reason, there has been a shift to using the term *chronometric dating* ("metrically measured time") as a substitute. At least a dozen chronometric dating methods can be used, depending on situations found at a site. We have already noted that the South African cave deposits are not favorable to chronometric dating. But it turns out that sites in East Africa are ideal. We will describe only one such method that have been used extensively and that continues to be applied to the prehistoric record: potassium-argon (K-Ar) dating.

Anthrolingo

Chronometric dating includes methods from which dates of archaeological sites have been precisely determined, usually given in terms of years before the present time, such as 2 M.Y.A.

When does a volcanic eruption become a friend of prehistorians? When it resets a radioactive clock to zero hour. Another answer to this question will be given when we discuss the famous footprints of Laetoli. But for dating purposes, volcanic rocks become molten, forming rivers of hot lava. This very high heat releases all of a gas called argon from the molten rock. That would be the zero point of the radioactive clock. But where would more argon come from? It is produced as an unstable form of potassium loses its energy, known as radioactive decay. Thus, over time, radioactive potassium becomes stable argon gas.

With the clock set a zero, new argon begins to accumulate in the cooling bed of lava. Next, what needs to be known is how long it takes for a given amount of argon to form from potassium. It took physicists a while to figure this out, but they determined that radioactive potassium will decay at a rate such that half of its radioactivity is lost every 1.25 billion years. There I go again, with those huge numbers. But this, too, is a friendly number because it means the K-Ar clock runs at the right speed for dating prehistoric sites in the range of millions of years. Enough of the argon gas becomes trapped in the rock over millions of years to be measured accurately. Too soon after a volcano, there wouldn't be an adequate amount of argon for reliable dating.

Let's go to one of those sites in East Africa where K-Ar was applied very successfully: Olduvai Gorge in Tanzania. Called the Grand Canyon of East Africa, the gorge was formed over time by rivers cutting their way through the layered beds of long past volcanic eruptions. This place that caught the attention of prehistorians Louis and Mary Leakey, who spent decades searching for evidence of our early ancestors. In 1959, success visited Mary. While Louis lay ill with flu back at camp, Mary (and her Dalmatian dogs) combed yet one more rocky slope. There in the bright July sun, she spied a partially exposed skull and teeth. The find was initially called *Zinjanthropus boisei*, but currently it is classified as *Australopithecus boisei*. Common names tend to be more fun. "Zinj" was also named the "Nutcracker Man" in honor of the huge molar teeth he (presumed to be a male) possessed.

Anthropos

Mary Douglas Nicol Leakey, archaeologist by early training but heavily involved with discovery and interpretation of fossils, was born and educated in England. Along with her husband, Louis, she was instrumental in establishing human origins research in East Africa beginning in the 1930s. Among her major discoveries was the first fossil ape skull in 1947, the Zinj skull in 1959, and, with her staff, the Laetoli footprint trails in 1978–1981. (More on these footprints later.) Mary Leakey died in 1996.

But how old was the fossil? Louis Leakey felt confident that Zinj was at least 600,000 years old. This was based on previously dated animal fossils found in association with Zinj. But a great surprise was in the works. The layered beds of Olduvai were subjected to K-Ar dating. The bed that dated Zinj proved to be 1,750,000 years old! At the time of the discovery, this date was truly astonishing and led some to once again propose Zinj as another "missing link." It is now believed that Zinj actually belonged to a dead-end side branch of our evolutionary tree.

Most of the dates cited in subsequent chapters are based on K-Ar testing. In some instances, other chronometric methods are mentioned because they help to place the fossils or stone tools in a proper time frame.

Dividing Time

A time framework is standard for tracing major happenings in prehistory. In fact, two frameworks commonly are used, and unfortunately, they do not entirely overlap. One refers to divisions, called epochs, of the Cenozoic era; the other is based on cultural development and evolution. A quick way to summarize these is through a chart.

The Pliocene geologic epoch marks the time period when prehuman fossils were first discovered and thus signifies our origins. The earliest of these is dated at around 6 M.Y.A. and is

---

Paleofacts

Paleolithic means "Old Stone Age," but this term is not used very often anymore.

---

described in Chapter 5. The earliest evidence of stone tools dates back about 2.6 M.Y.A., during the Lower Paleolithic. This monumental material is covered in Chapter 8.

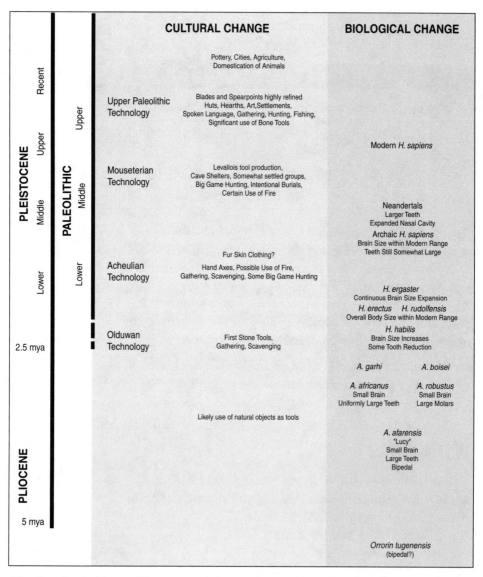

Timelines for the Pliocene/Pleistocene and the Paleolithic. Major cultural and biological changes.

(Scott Brish)

The time chart will be our guide as we discuss major fossils and stone tools. You do not need to memorize it since it won't be on the exam. Correction: There aren't any exams at all.

The Least You Need to Know

◆ Comprehending vast periods of time is difficult.

◆ Relative dating methods, especially stratigraphy, are very helpful to prehistorians.

◆ Chronometric dating methods are even more helpful, but they are also more limited in where they can be applied.

◆ Divisions of the Pliocene/Pleistocene and of the Paleolithic are both used as time frameworks of prehistory.

Chapter 4

Name Calling

In This Chapter

- ◆ The living world according to Linne
- ◆ Classifying by the numbers and shape
- ◆ Not all hominids are human
- ◆ Trends in primate evolution
- ◆ Evolution in tree form

A tree by any other name is still a tree. But a fossil really doesn't exist until it has been assigned a valid scientific name. Naming organisms, both plants and animals, has been practiced for unknown years into the past. Very likely, human language, when it first developed, named the living creatures of the world important to them as food, friend, or foe. Most cultures today maintain a "folk taxonomy" that represents an understanding of the living world and connections between life forms, although sometimes mythical. This chapter considers a formal taxonomy that serves our need to not only keep track of individual fossils, but also to trace their evolutionary relationships. The focus here is on setting up a system for naming our ancestors.

Father of Taxonomy

In Chapter 2, we cited the significance of Karl Linne as he established a taxonomic or naming system in the eighteenth century. His purpose for doing so was decidedly religious. He felt that if he could name all of the kinds of plants and animals in the world, the completed classification would reveal the underlying design of the Creator.

Anthropos

Karl von Linne (Carolus Linnaeus) is known as the father of taxonomy. His most famous book is *Systema Naturae*, which published in 1735 his classification of species. He recognized the similarity between the Great Apes to us and named the chimpanzee—*Homo Troglodytes* ("cave man")—and the orangutan—*Homo sylvestris* ("forest man"). The gorilla wasn't known to him and wouldn't be discovered by the Western world until 1799.

Linne's highly ambitious task was perhaps made a little easier than what we might think, since he subscribed to the notion of "fixity of species." This meant that no new species had been formed and none had died out since the time of creation. Even so, it seems an incredibly difficult endeavor when we consider that new species are still being named 250 years later.

Linne's system of classification is an example of an "inclusive" hierarchy. First, this means that there are stepwise levels or categories into which the animal forms are arranged. Then each higher category includes all of the animals from the lower categories. In contrast, an "exclusive" hierarchy is used by the military or church organization in which an individual can be a member of only one category and is then promoted through the ranks or grades. You can be either a private or a general, but not both at the same time. Whether as a private you can ever be a general is another matter.

Paleofacts

How many living species are there? No one has a final answer. Perhaps in the tens of millions. Insects have the highest number of species.

We are classified as primates, along with apes and monkeys. In a higher category, we are also classified as mammals, which not only includes primates, but also all the other mammals, such as horses, bats, and whales. Here is a summary of our taxonomic classification:

Kingdom animalia

    Phylum vertebrata

        Class mammalia

            Order primates

                Superfamily hominoidea

                    Family hominidae

                        Genus Homo

                            Species sapiens

Basic Rules

Linne published a much revised edition of his taxonomy in *Systemae Naturae* in 1758. This is the starting point of modern scientific classification of species. Any names given before that date are not accepted. Linne devised a Binomial System of Nomenclature, which consists of both a genus and a species name. Hence, our name is *Homo sapiens* ("wise man"). It is customary to italicize scientific names. And we can certainly hope that we live up to that "wise" part of our name.

Naming a new species today is governed by *The International Code of Zoological Nomenclature* ("The Code"). It's not a thrilling read, unless you thoroughly enjoy browsing dictionaries. The Code requires that new names follow consistent criteria. For Linne, that meant grouping or classifying animals entirely by their *morphology*, or anatomical similarities. This resulted in a few problems. Linne wrongly classified sea mammals (such as whales) as fish. He also included mythical creatures such as the satyr in his classification as some form of human. But then he was trying to name each and every species that ever had been reported, but not necessarily observed and verified.

In addition to morphology, modern taxonomy is expected to reflect evolutionary relationships of the classified animals. This does not always work out so well. But that's what happens when you consider that a classification is a static and purposely stable system that has been imposed on a dynamic process of *evolution*. Evolutionary

Anthrolingo

Morphology is used in paleoanthropolgy to refer to the shape and structural features of animals. For example, when we described prognathic faces in Chapter 1, this referred to a feature of facial morphology. Morphology sometimes also indicates size, as a robust morphology means large, pronounced features.

Anthrolingo

Evolution is a process of change over time in living forms. Sometimes a distinction is made between evolution that takes place within a given species (called microevolution) and what happens when new species are formed (called macroevolution).

Paleoquest

An ongoing question speculates whether species are just names given by taxonomists or whether they really do exist in nature. We do know that cats can't mate with dogs, and generally living forms that can't successfully interbreed are recognized as different species. This rule can't be directly applied to fossils. So naming of fossil species becomes even more controversial.

relationships are fluid, and, of course, as more discoveries are made from the fossil record and from living forms, classifications become obsolete. Yes, changes in classification can be made, but this is not encouraged; otherwise, there is too much confusion regarding what classification system is current. This chapter gives examples of classifications and evolutionary relationships, represented by treelike structures, later.

As an illustration of how a classification is stabilized, once a name, is given it can't be changed even though it is no longer accurate. For example, Raymond Dart gave the Taung Child the name *Australopithecus*. He thought it could be the transition between apes and us. But now it is considered fully within our family, so why shouldn't its name be changed to *Australoanthropus*? This was tried some years ago but was not allowed by The Code.

How do new names become valid in a classification? There is a three-step procedure that involves first thoroughly *describing* the fossil, then *comparing* the fossil to all existing similar fossils, and finally *publishing* a report on the new fossil. After these steps, a newly proposed species can be considered—and argued about—among interested paleoanthropologists. Time will tell whether it will receive full acceptance.

A few more details are embedded in these three simple steps. For instance, the published report must be in a journal that is likely to be read by other researchers. It can't be a handout at the local pub. This ensures that new scientific knowledge is actually shared. And the name must be latinized—that is, spelled as a Latin equivalent. Once again, this relates to stability and communicating effectively across languages and nations. If Latin is considered a dead language, then what is more appropriate than to use it to name fossils?

Our Proper Name

Up to now, you probably noticed that I used "prehuman" to signify our ancestors. This needs clarification. First, what is meant by "human"? Second, if some of our early ancestors were not yet human, what do we call them?

Let's answer the second question first. The name that is commonly used to designate all of our ancestors, as well as us, is hominid. This is derived from the classification of our Family Hominidae. Thus, hominid refers to our well-extended family. We define what constitutes a hominid in greater detail in the next chapter, but for now, it refers to primates who are in the process of becoming adapted or who already have adapted to upright walking or bipedalism.

That's the easy part. Now, what is a "human"? I am pretty sure you already have a definition that includes attributes usually associated with being humane. Kindness and compassion are characteristic qualities that come to mind. We normally do not grant these to other animals or nonhumans in part because they cannot be clearly demonstrated in their behavior. There's the rub when it comes to documenting humane behavior in prehistory. What evidence would it take? Most likely, convincing evidence is not preserved in the prehistoric record. Hence, it is not clear whether early hominids were human.

There is often reference to early hominids being *primitive*, and nonwestern peoples have been called primitives. Usage of this term in anthropology designates a cultural activity that is less technologically advanced or a biological condition that appeared earlier and then developed into a more advanced or *derived* condition.

> ### Paleofacts
>
> The earliest hominids were customarily given a name including "man"—for example, Java Man. The term *man* generally refers to mankind. Sometimes *man* is still being applied today (later we refer to Millennium Man), but the term is being replaced by *humankind*.

> ### Anthrolingo
>
> **Primitive** traits observed in fossils are those that are also found in ancestral forms. **Derived** traits are those that evolved later, after splitting off from the ancestor. For example, the fact that we have five fingers is a primitive mammalian condition, but also because we have highly flexible fingers, this is a derived condition that took us away from most other mammals.

If we argue that our closest primate relative, the chimpanzee, does not possess humane qualities, then we can infer that our common ancestor also lacked these qualities. Furthermore, inference tells us that our humaneness was developed sometime after our evolutionary line split from that of the chimpanzee. In spite of the uncertainly of documenting humans in the fossil record, there has been some conjecture that hominids of the Middle and Upper Paleolithic did show compassion toward injured or impaired individuals. This proposal is discussed in Chapter 11.

What this little tangle (or maybe "tango" is a better way of saying it) means is that becoming human is a process that took place over a long course of evolution. Thus, there will not be a sharp marker between prehuman and human—only shades of development that are very imprecisely preserved in the prehistoric record. You have heard the saying, "To err is human." So perhaps some of the hominid fossils that have been found are remains of those individuals who used poor judgment and blundered into their demise.

Trending Toward Humans

As mentioned already, a taxonomic classification is quite static. It fixes names on a dynamic evolutionary process. These names are not only helpful; they're also necessary for good and, at times, heated exchange among paleoanthropologists. But if we want to review the major changes that characterize our evolution, something more can be added. That something is *evolutionary trends*.

Anthrolingo

An **evolutionary trend** refers to discernible adaptive changes that show stages of development rather than appearing fully completed. An important trend covered in Chapter 7 is the increasing brain size in hominids that spanned some two million years.

Anthrolingo

Prosimians are primates, including lorises, lemurs and tarsiers, that generally are regarded as more primitive or more like the earliest evolved primates than the more derived primates, including monkeys and apes.

Major trends in earlier primate evolution are the forerunners to our becoming human. They set up the stages for our later development. Thus, we need to have a look at primate trends to better understand where we came from. Two trends of particular interest relate to our eyes and to our hands. And if eye-hand coordination comes to your mind, that's intended.

The Eyes Have It

The ability primates have in seeing is derived from their adaptation to living in trees—that is, their arboreal adaptation. Tree-living in a three-dimensional world that primates have mastered involved this list of attributes of their vision:

◆ Stereoscopic vision or depth perception

◆ High visual acuity (seeing fine detail)

◆ Color vision

These visual qualities are less developed in the *prosimians* (such as lemurs), who retain more of the conditions found in the earliest evolved primates. *Prosimians* are sometimes regarded as Lower Primates.

In the Higher Primates, including monkeys, apes, and us, all of these visual adaptations are well developed as derived conditions. This trend can be termed *visualization*.

Anthrolingo

Visualization refers to a primate evolutionary trend in which the eyes, and associated areas of the brain, became increasingly adapted to living in the arboreal or tree environment.

Hand to Mouth

Living in trees is partially secured with eyes that can see what's up and down. It also is aided by hands that can grasp the situation, most often tree limbs. This grasping ability is combined into an arboreal adaptation of primates where, once again, the Higher Primates developed greater degrees of flexibility of fingers and toes (which in monkeys and apes are really fingerlike).

Paleofacts
While all primates have flexible fingers on their hands, a distinction often is made between the use of these fingers for grasping, called a power grip, and the ability to pick up small objects from a flat surface, called a precision grip. Humans are especially well equipped with a precision grip, but they don't match up as well with other primates, particularly the apes, when it comes to power grasping.

But there is a bit more to the story: Flexibility of fingers not only allows for grasping tree limbs, but it also aids in feeding activities. This is where hand-eye coordination gets a second, complementary application. Hands, along with highly mobile arms and legs, place the primate in a position to reach out and grab its food, and then bring it to its mouth. Higher Primates probably packaged eye-hand coordination into a highly efficient system for both moving among the trees and eating directly from the fruit, nuts, and leaves of their home. This trend of hand or manual dexterity might be referred to as *manualization*.

Anthrolingo

Manualization refers to a primate evolutionary trend in which the forelimbs and hands became increasingly adapted to feeding and moving around in the arboreal or tree environment.

*A juvenile gorilla munching
on some tasty food.*

(Robert J. Meier)

These trends in primate evolution, which actually began some 65 million years ago, set the stage for continued development of our hominid line. Beyond these two trends, here's a list of what's ahead in our trending toward humans, arranged in their order of evolutionary development:

Prehominid trends:

- Visualization

- Manualization

Hominid trends:

- Erect bipedalism

- Dental reduction

- Brain expansion

These trends indicate the *process* of becoming human. What we eventually call human was not attained in a single neat package. It came in parts and parcels, along with some compromises, as we shall see.

Family Trees

A certain descriptive device is useful for displaying the ongoing process of evolutionary change. It is called an evolutionary tree, with a variant name of *dendrogram*.

A dendrogram is based on taxonomic classification, which we said earlier should try to reflect evolutionary relationships. It is somewhat comparable to a genealogy or pedigree that more precisely indicates ancestors and descendents of a family. Appropriately, that is called a family tree. The following figure shows an example of a dendrogram based on primate evolution.

Anthrolingo

A **dendrogram** is a graphic treelike display of evolutionary relationships between species. The shorter the branches are on the tree, the closer the species are—or, in other words, the more recently they split off from their common ancestor.

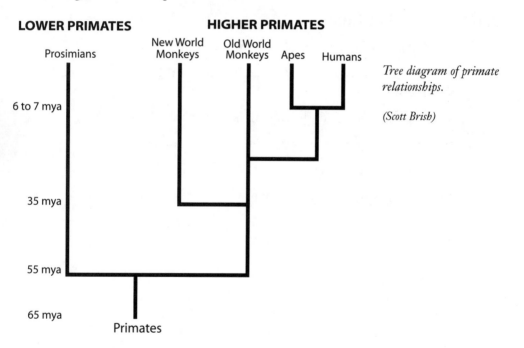

Tree diagram of primate relationships.

(Scott Brish)

The trunk of the primate family tree splits into two major branches of the Lower Primates and Higher Primates. Lower Primates, or prosimians, include lemurs of Madagascar (Malagasy Republic), and lorises and tarsiers from Asia. They retain some traits that are believed to have been present in the earliest primates. Higher Primates consist of the monkeys, those who live in South America (like the "capuchin" or "organ grinder" monkey), and those from Africa and Asia (like the Rhesus macaque, which has been used extensively in medical research), apes (gibbon and orangutan from Asia, and chimpanzee and gorilla from Africa)—and us humans, from around the entire world.

Paleofacts

Common usage often confuses apes with monkeys. This usually takes the form of calling chimps as monkeys in movies, cartoons, and even in political campaign ads. They are really quite different kinds of primates.

In depicting evolutionary relationships, a dendrogram is really an interpretation or someone's reconstruction of what these relationships are. A consequence of different and conflicting interpretations means that several dendrograms of hominid evolution exist. They don't always coexist very peacefully. Time may reveal which are more accurate. We will keep the number of dendrograms to a minimum and then indicate what the major disputes are.

The Least You Need to Know

- Karl Linne was the founder of modern taxonomic classification.

- Rules for classifying are found in the International Code of Zoological Nomenclature.

- All humans are hominids, but not all hominids were human.

- Early trends in primate evolution led the way to humans.

- Evolutionary trees, or dendrograms, show relationships among species.

- Primates are highly variable, from prosimians to people.

Part 2

Walk the Walk

In this part, we begin with a hallmark of hominids, bipedalism (walking on two feet), and we offer alternative explanations for how and why this happened. The most important hallmark of hominids, however, is the brain. For advanced clues about brain development, we look at toolmaking.

Nevertheless, the hard evidence for interpreting human evolution consists of bones and teeth. Teeth preserve well and are useful in sorting out dietary patterns.

Chapter 5

Standing Up

In This Chapter

- ◆ Hominids in Ethiopia 3.5 million years ago
- ◆ Footprints at Laetoli
- ◆ Models to explain adaptation to bipedalism
- ◆ Watery origins for hominids?
- ◆ Evidence for even earlier hominid origins

Humans are featherless bipeds. That distinguishes us from our bird friends, who, likewise, have taken to walking on their hind limbs. There is little likelihood that we and birds came to this form of locomotion for the same reasons. Certainly, we didn't arrive at erect bipedalism from a common ancestor that we shared. Bipedalism also was certainly a momentous development in our becoming human, closely vying with our large brain as a hallmark of our being. This chapter describes the earliest indisputable evidence of bipedalism in hominids and also gives some space to late-breaking news on this topic. It indicates how variable our becoming human is, since we became bipedal before our brains got larger and our teeth got smaller. Indeed, we probably walked before we talked. What are the advantages in being able to move about on hind limbs? And did our ancestors go through an aquatic stage before landing on land? Walk this way to find out.

Lucy, a Diamond Discovery

In paleoanthropological circles, there is a Lucy more famous than Lucy Arnaz, a.k.a. Lucille Ball. Lucy, as in fossil form, was discovered by Donald Johanson in 1974 in the fossil site at Hadar, Ethiopia. K-Ar dating has placed this site at 3.5 million years ago (M.Y.A.).

Anthropos
Donald Johanson was born in Chicago in 1943. Likewise, he received his doctorate from the Anthropology Department at the University of Chicago. Johnson has mounted several paleoanthropological expeditions to East Africa, most notably at the Hadar site in Ethiopia. He was the founder and is currently the director of the Institute of Human Origins, affiliated with Arizona State University.

Johanson reports that on the day of the discovery, he and a colleague were about to cease surveying and search for fossils as the noon sun pushed temperatures well above 100°F. In a final detour to a small gully, Johanson spied a fossil fragment that looked to him like a piece of a hominid arm. That was rather bold and hasty in pronouncement, but the first impression was increasingly verified as the two researchers continued to find more bits and parts of what later turned out to be skeletal remains from a single individual.

The skeleton of Lucy.

(John Reader. Photo Researchers, Inc.)

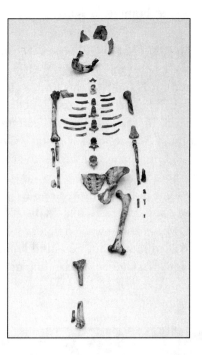

The skeleton was nearly 40 percent complete! This truly was a gem of a discovery, rare and highly valuable. Was it merely a coincidence that over the long evening hours back at camp, while the entire research group mulled over the significance of the find, the Beatles hit "Lucy in the Sky with Diamonds" blared from a tape recorder? Yes, it probably was, but it was from this song that the general public would come to recognize Lucy as the earliest hominid.

Johanson closely followed the requirements for naming a new species, as covered in Chapter 4. Lucy, along with subsequently discovered fossils of her kind, are classified as *Australopithecus afarensis* ("*australopithecine* from the Afar region in Ethiopia").

> **Paleofacts**
>
> The value of fossils and also cultural artifacts is not determined by their monetary worth, but by their usefulness in making scientific interpretations. Sale of fossils and artifacts on the open market is frowned upon and may even be illegal.

What else do we know about Lucy? Well, that she was a she. The preserved pelvic region showed the tell-tale size and shape for possibly carrying and delivering a baby. Whether she did can't be determined. *Sexual dimorphism* is displayed in pelvic differences seen in men and women.

Anthrolingo

Sexual dimorphism describes the differences seen between the sexes, most obviously in those morphological traits related to the reproductive capability of females. It also can generally refer to other features that tend to separate the sexes in terms of overall size of the skeleton and the degree of muscle development seen from bony landmarks on the skeleton. The canine tooth also shows sexual dimorphism, with males having a larger canine.

We also know that Lucy was an adult. This was determined by her teeth: The third molar tooth had already erupted. This tooth, called a "wisdom" tooth, erupts in modern humans usually sometime during the 20s. But, as in the case for adjusting the age of the Taung Child with its first permanent molar, some adjustment likely is needed for Lucy as well. Perhaps she was a late teenager at the time of her death.

Lucy was clearly a child-size adult, estimated to be only about 3 feet tall and weighing around 60 pounds. For comparison, that would make her about the size of a five- or six-year-old child of today. Remember, we are looking for an evolutionary trend toward increased body size of hominids. Clearly, that trend doesn't appear to have started yet with Lucy.

The most scientifically significant aspect of Lucy was that she walked. How do we know this for sure? Evidence for erect bipedalism is spread throughout the entire skeleton but the best proof comes from the knee joint. Quite simply, erect bipeds have angled thighbones (femur) from the knee to the hip joint. Yes, we are "knock-kneed." But apes, from which a distinction must be made, have thighbones that are straight up and down from knee to hip.

The chimp (left) has a vertical thighbone, but humans have a thighbone that's on an angle.

(Leslie Harlacker/Scott Brish)

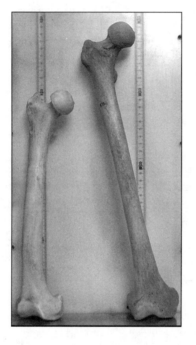

Having the angle from knee to hip allows us to carry our upper body weight through the hip and into the leg, ankle, and feet, while maintaining a good sense of balance while standing upright. When we start to walk, we basically shift our weight forward, setting us off balance. Then we must get the next foot planted before we fall flat on our face. Walking could be considered controlled falling.

Paleoquest

An ongoing discussion and continued research among paleoanthropologists speculates about details of Lucy's walking behavior. Did she have exactly the same striding pattern or gait that we now have? Maybe not. But there seems little doubt that she, and the entire group she represents, were well adapted to erect bipedalism. And they may also have been quite adept at climbing trees.

Great Apes (chimps, gorillas, and orangs) can and do stand and move about on their hind legs. This is called facultative or compensatory bipedalism. Their walking does not come with ease or with good balance.

Swingers

Apes are adapted to moving around in the trees by means of arm swinging, or *brachiation.* Brachiation is done by young apes and less so by large adults; tree branches may not be strong enough to support their body weight. But even as adults, they regularly support themselves in the trees with their long, heavily muscled arms and grasping hands with curved fingers.

Knuckling Down

When they are on the ground, African apes (chimp and gorilla) are basically quadrupedal—they walk on all fours. They make sort of a fist and support their weight on the back of their hands, in the knuckle region—not with flattened palms, as seen in monkeys and also in human babies when they are learning to creep and walk.

Paleofacts

A number of animals practice facultative or compensatory bipedalism, with about the same results. Horses and elephants can "walk" for short distances, but with rather unsteady balance.

Anthrolingo

Brachiation is the mode of locomotion involving the repeated grasping of a tree limb with the hand of one arm, swinging the body forward to then grasp the tree with the hand of other arm—hence, arm swinging.

Paleoquest

Active research is being done to find out whether early hominids actually went through a phase of knuckle-walking before becoming erect bipeds.

From Hand to Foot

The bones of Lucy's foot look almost like ours, but with relatively longer toes. One distinct feature of our foot, and seen in Lucy, is the way that the big toe lines up with the other four toes. It does not extend out to the side, like a thumb does and like the big toe in the ape does. This thumblike position, of course, allows the foot to work like a grasping hand. So it looks like Lucy was using her feet for walking and less so for grasping. Supporting evidence for the shape of Lucy's foot came in a most spectacular way in a site located just to the south of Olduvai Gorge.

Footprints in the Ash

In 1976, Mary Leakey and her team were doing fieldwork at Laetoli, where prehistoric research had gone on for four decades, with limited success in finding hominid fossils. Then one day, while the team was taking a break and playfully throwing dried elephant dung Frisbee style, one of the members noticed peculiar impressions in the exposed ash layers of a stream bed. He rightfully assumed that they were the ancient indentations of fossil animals. However, it wasn't until more impressions were found the next year that serious attention was given to them. That was when Mary Leakey and her team discovered trails of impressions that convinced Leakey at least that hominids had once walked here.

Footprints in time. Look for the way the big toe lines up with the other toes.

(John Reader. Photo Researchers, Inc.)

Initially, not all who saw the impressions were so sure. But the footprints have stood the test of time, so to speak. They generally now are regarded to be a long sequence of foot impressions made by two or possibly three hominids as they traveled across a wet ash layer some 3.7 million years ago, as dated by the K-Ar method. Why were they that close to a recently active volcano? Where were they going or coming from? These are questions that stimulate the researcher's mind.

Lucy and the Laetoli footprints established clear-cut evidence that bipedalism evolved in forming the hominid line more than 3.5 million years ago. Since the evidence was so solid, any division or split between hominids and apes must have occurred even earlier, and less clear differences should be expected. Later we discuss newly discovered fossils that address this matter.

Mosaic Patterns

In our prehistoric development, walking came before talking and a lot of other uniquely human traits. This patchy pattern has been described as *mosaic*. In this sense, our modern self was a picture in progress millions of years ago, with bits and pieces to be added along the way. From Lucy onward, we became bigger in body, with greatly expanded brains, somewhat reduced tooth size resulting in flatter faces, and an increasing dependence on cultural behavior for our livelihood.

Anthrolingo

Mosaic refers to evolution in humans that occurred over a sequence of steps, not all at once. For example, bipedalism took place before brain expansion and tooth reduction.

These Feet Are Made for Walking

Now that we have stated the evidence for hominids as bipeds, we need to face a tougher question. Why did hominids take to walking on hind limbs? Two major scenarios usually are proposed: Either they were forced to, or an opportunity that came along. A combined mixture of necessity and favorable circumstances could be a third possibility to explain why our feet are most suitable for walking on. At the same time, our hands don't function so well in that capacity, but they serve us very well for manipulation.

Tool Use Model, Not

Not so long ago, it was fairly well accepted that our ancestors became bipedal in order to free their hands for making and using tools. There was a popular saying at the time, "Tools maketh the man." Well, Lucy, the biped, appeared at least a million years before there is any concrete evidence of stone toolmaking—and, of course, she isn't a man.

This earlier model packaged tool making along with increasing brain size, canine tooth reduction, and, of course, the key ingredient, bipedalism. Since hominids 3.5 million years ago had small brains, relatively larger canines, and apparently no stone tools, that model has been largely discarded. It has been replaced with new platforms to stand upon.

Trees Left the Hominids

The *savanna model* opens with climatic change toward drier conditions that led to shrinking forests in East Africa. Of course, this would mean a loss of habitat and home for prehominids. Whether by choice or necessity, some of these prehominids invaded the more open grasslands or savanna. This invasion then prompted changes in behavior—and, over time, in morphology—for prehominids to become hominids by virtue of bipedal adaptation.

Anthrolingo

The **savanna model** proposes that hominids became erect bipeds as their former homeland of trees were reduced by drier climates and they took up residence in the large grassy savannas of East Africa.

Standing upright would have allowed the hominids to see better over the tall grasses in sighting food, mates, and enemies. This, of course, would enhance their survival. It is also conjectured that hands freed from locomotion could perform a number of survival-promoting behaviors such as carrying and caring for babies. And more babies means higher success measured in evolutionary accounts.

Fieldnotes

Successful reproduction is important for a species' survival. But two strategies receive continued investigation. One is based on having as many offspring as possible, but with little investment of the parents. The other is to restrict the number of offspring produced but expend much parental care of each of them, as to increase their chances of survival.

Hominids Left the Trees

This scenario, referred to as the *tree-dwelling model*, likely posed more freedom of choice for prehominids in taking up bipedalism. To a large degree, it presumes that prehominids, by virtue of living in trees, were already adapted a long way for standing up when they hit the ground walking. Our modern relatives, the apes, regularly sit upright. So, once on the ground, standing up is not so much of a stretch. Or perhaps it was this stretch position on the ground that allowed prehominids access to tree food (fruits and nuts) just out of their reach.

Kevin Hunt, from Indiana University, follows this line of reasoning in promoting what he calls the "postural feeding hypothesis." He has spent many years making first-hand observations of chimps feeding in their natural habitat in Uganda, East Africa.

His work established that chimps were essentially bipedal both on the ground as they reached for fruit hanging from the lower tree limbs and, significantly, also when they stood and ate on higher branches. To maintain balance, they did use one arm to support themselves. His conclusion is that bipedalism was not initially evolved in hominids for walking, but as an aid to eating. In this example, the chimpanzee is used as an analogy from which to understand early hominids.

Anthrolingo

The **tree-dwelling model** suggests that immediate ancestors of hominids used a bipedal posture even as they still inhabited trees, and could then expand on this behavior when they became more ground-living.

Illustration of Kevin Hunt's idea for the origin of hominid bipedalism.

(Kevin Hunt/Original by Jeanne Sept)

Standing Before Lucy?

Since the discovery of Lucy in 1974 and many other specimens assigned to the roughly 3.5 M.Y.A. *Australopithecus afarensis*, additional tantalizing fossils have been found that might well extend the origin of hominids farther back into time. One such discovery was reported in 1995. Its name is *Australopithecus anamensis*, and it is dated between 3.9 M.Y.A. and 4.2 M.Y.A. The "anam" part means "lake" in the Turkana language spoken by the people living near the site just to the east of Lake Turkana in Kenya. Quite a few teeth were found, but most significantly was a portion of the lower leg bone that seemed to signify bipedalism. Other bones of the skeleton and skull, as well as the teeth, were considered rather apelike. This tends to match the situation seen in Lucy, but now the time range for the origin of hominids was extended backward another half million years or so.

A walk through evolutionary time. Notice that the chimp on the far left is knuckle-walking.

(Buntschu. Photo Researchers, Inc.)

As happens so many times in prehistoric and paleoanthropological research, when it seems that enough evidence is collected, major changes are not expected. The previous models of when, how, and why bipedalism evolved appeared to cover the ground quite well. No great surprises were in store. Then, surprise! A new discovery made in November 2000 has the potential to hake the family tree of hominids right down to its roots. A combined team of researchers from the Collège de France and Community Museum of Kenya discovered fossils from a site in the Tugen Hills of Kenya. A confirmed K-Ar date of around 6 M.Y.A. has been derived from two volcanic beds that sandwiched or "sealed in" the fossils. That situation doesn't allow much chance for error in assigning a date.

The researchers claim that these fossils are hominids. Recall that bipedalism is the defining trait here. Well, the evidence rests on details seen in the thighbone or femur that happens to be less conclusive than the knee-to-hip angle that we talked about earlier. But there is another clue seen in the teeth, which the researchers consider to be hominidlike. The next chapter discusses how teeth provide clues to prehistory. It should also be noted that evidence for bipedalism, and thereby, the origins of hominids, is expected to be less conclusive the closer it gets to the common ancestor of hominids and the apes.

The scientific name given to the new discovery is *Orrorin tugenensis*. (Try to say that with a French rolled *r* three times.) Juxtaposed with its time of discovery, it acquired the common name of Millennium Man. Several implications must be considered to

see if this is, in fact, a hominid. First, the split between our family line and those that led to modern apes would have taken place much earlier than now thought. But then that splitting event has shifted around a good deal in the past decades. Some 20 years ago, it was believed that the division took place around 15 M.Y.A. Then, with the use of newly applied genetic analysis, it was moved all the way to around 5 M.Y.A. Millennium Man would move that back in time somewhat.

> **Paleofacts**
>
> Genetic analysis can't be done directly on these fossils, since no genetic material can be recovered from them. The genetic analysis that is done compares modern primates and estimates how long ago divisions between them took place.

Then there is the matter of trees—real trees, not dendrograms. Millennium Man lived at a time before the change in climate and reduction of forests in East Africa, so the creature was possibly tree-dwelling. That's no problem for the researchers to resolve, for they consider tree limbs to have been a nursery for walking.

Remember that Kevin Hunt's "postural feeding hypothesis" proposed something quite similar. In fact, the major difference is that a scenario based on the new discovery has prehominids walking on the tree limbs, much like that seen in the "red ape" or orangutan rather than the chimp. Primate analogy comes into play once more.

The upshot is that the savannah model for bipedalism joins the tool-use model in not being well supported right now in comparison with the tree-dwelling model. But wait: Two other models have been proposed. Admittedly, the aerial model was offered only in jest by a publication devoted to jesting, *The Journal of Irreproducible Results*. That leaves the aquatic model, which most, if not all, paleoanthropologists would also classify in the less than serious category.

> **Paleofacts**
>
> Donald Johanson believes that Lucy actually lived in a more forested environment than had been previously proposed. In general, it appears quite likely that hominids continued to live and travel near dependable water sources offered by lake shores and river banks.

Aquatic Ape Theory—All Wet?

The Aquatic Ape Theory (AAT) has been around in some form for more than 75 years. Its most recent advocate is Elaine Morgan. She has found fault with the savanna model of human evolution primarily for what she claims is its inability to fully account for much of what is considered human. Notable are traits such as our relative hairlessness, a layer of fat just below the skin, and that hallmark of hominids, bipedalism. The first two of these three are found in aquatic mammals, like the famous TV star, Flipper the dolphin.

At least the first trait, our so-called naked skin, is included in the savanna model and is linked to our ability to effectively lose body heat through sweating in a hot, sun-drenched environment of open grassland. The possibility also exists for rather quickly switching back on those genes that control hair growth stemming from our abundant hair follicles, thereby reversing the turnoff of those genes back in the days of hominid origins.

The AAT proposes that flooding of habitat, or perhaps scarcity of food, forced pre-hominids into the water along the East African coast. Hair would have been lost to streamline the body for swimming, and fat would be stored for insulating the body against the colder water temperature. And what about bipedalism? Walking upright in water does keep the head higher. That would be advantageous—and a distinct improvement over drowning. Imagine if human evolution had taken a different twist under this scenario. We might have joined Flipper as creatures beneath the sea.

Making light of the AAT is easy; it just hasn't gathered enough scientific support to warrant serious consideration. It may become even less credible because of the shift away from the savanna model toward the tree-dwelling model. This would remove the foil that AAT sets up to oppose.

No model of the origin of bipedalism is now and perhaps ever will be fully documented. We know that it happened, and we are walking for better or for worse.

From the evidence, Lucy probably did climb trees, but she is also judged to be well adapted to bipedalism—but not to the degree that we are. This does not mean that we are fully adapted or that we don't pay a certain price for assuming our erect posture. A good lesson seems to be that no adaptation is ever perfect.

> ## Paleofacts
>
> It is important to note that humans are relatively hairy and not much different than apes from the standpoint of the number of hair follicles or sites of hair growth. What differs is the length of hair. It is a mistake to consider ourselves as naked of hair, or entirely lacking the potential for growing longer hair over our bodies.

> ### Fieldnotes
>
> Many ailments seem to accompany our incomplete adaptation to bipedalism, including lower back pain, varicose veins, hernias, and foot problems. Pity the poor person who ends up with all of these.

In a sense, this chapter starts us down the long road to becoming human. Our first step, literally, was in acquiring our unique primate locomotor pattern, bipedalism. We now move from our feet and go on to the next chapter, which deals with our mouth. Hopefully, there will be no placing of the former into the latter.

The Least You Need to Know

- ◆ Lucy provides conclusive evidence of hominid origins some 3.5 million years ago.

- ◆ Several models are currently proposed to account for adaptation to bipedalism in hominids.

- ◆ No solid evidence supports the Aquatic Ape Theory.

- ◆ Human evolution occurred in steps as a mosaic pattern.

- ◆ New fossil discoveries may push back hominid origins another half million years or even much longer.

Chapter 6

Toothy Tales

In This Chapter

- ◆ The truth about teeth
- ◆ Canines are more than fangs
- ◆ The teeth of Pliocene hominids
- ◆ Diet and teeth

It's an ironic twist of evolutionary fate that we tend to have so much difficulty maintaining a healthy set of teeth while we are alive. This was even more true before fluoridation. Yet, after death teeth preserve so well that they make up a disproportionately large percentage of recovered fossil materials. That's because they are so heavily mineralized. The bright side is that teeth have high diagnostic value when it comes to making decisions about evolutionary significance. So they are valuable and there are a lot of them in the fossil record. This chapter covers ways in which teeth have been helpful in understanding evolutionary change, particularly related to dietary habits in early hominids. We compare our teeth with those of apes and focus on Pliocene hominids that are contenders as our direct ancestors.

The Dental Formula

If you looked into the mouth of an alligator—from a safe distance, of course—you would see a series of teeth all fairly similar in shape but different in size. They are said to be *homodont* teeth ("same teeth"). But look into your own mouth, and you will see teeth that vary in both size and shape. This is called *heterodonty* ("other" or "different teeth"). Heterodonty is characteristic of all primates and thus would have been present in all earlier hominids. But the number of the different kinds or shapes of teeth is not the same for all primates, nor do primates all have the same total number of teeth.

Anthrolingo _____

Homodont refers to teeth that are closely similar in shape but that differ in size. These are typically found in reptiles. **Heterodont** teeth vary in size and in shape and generally are found in mammals and in all primates, including humans.

Anthrolingo _____

Dental formula is shorthand notation that specifies the number of incisors, canines, premolars, and molars for one quadrant of the total teeth found in both the upper and lower jaws.

Paleoanthropologists have found it convenient to summarize this information into a *dental formula*. Let's use the human dentition, or set of teeth, to illustrate this. Normally, humans have a total of 32 teeth, 16 in the upper jaw and another 16 in the lower jaw.

Each jaw then can be divided into halves of eight teeth each, if we start right at the front and middle of the mouth. Considering both upper and lower jaws, there are four sections, or quadrants. Working with just these eight teeth, we can classify them into four different kinds: incisors (I), canines (c), premolars (P), and molars (M). Now, to arrive at the dental formula, we simply count the number of each kind. For humans, that is 2I:1C:2P:3M, or 2:1:2:3 = 8. In sum, for the 4 quadrants, there is a total of 32 teeth. We share this dental formula with all of the apes and monkeys native to Asia and Africa.

Mapping the human dentition.

(Scott Brish)

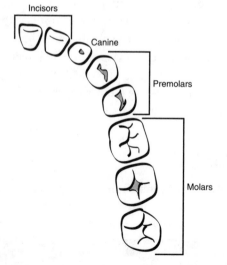

Incisors

Canine

Premolars

Molars

Baby Formula

Of course, children start off with a deciduous, or milk, set of teeth, that gets replaced by permanent teeth as they erupt from below. The term *permanent teeth* should perhaps be placed in quotation marks. The dental formula for a child's first set is 2I:1C:2M, or 2:1:2 = 5, and this times 4 quadrants = 20 teeth total. The deciduous set is normally complete at about two years of age, give or take some months. Afterward, the child's jaws need to develop and grow to accommodate the second set of teeth, or there can be crowding problems. And that might mean orthodontic treatment and braces.

Tooth Gain

We have already used dental eruption information on two fossils discussed earlier. First, the Taung Child was assigned an approximate age based on the timing of eruption for the first permanent molar. That would be about six years of age for children today, but it probably was much earlier for early hominid children like the Taung Child. Then Lucy was determined to be an adult because her third permanent molar had erupted. In present-day humans, this tooth erupts around 18 years but may be delayed into the 20s. Or it may not occur at all if the wisdom tooth is impacted against the second molar. Ouch—you probably know what that means.

Patterns of tooth eruption are useful for estimating age throughout a child's growing years—and, in the case of the third molar, even into early adulthood. But tooth eruption must be used with caution when applied to early hominids because their timing of tooth development was not exactly the same as ours. It was advanced because they grew up faster and died earlier than we do today.

> **Paleofacts**
>
> Why is the third molar called the wisdom tooth? The origin of this use goes back at least to the early nineteenth century. It refers to the fact that since this tooth erupts during the late teen years, it was presumed to coincide with the attainment of wisdom. I think I hear dissenting opinion from several directions.

Tooth Loss

Combining the quadrants means that adults have $4 \times 8 = 32$ teeth, as did all of our hominid ancestors. But much earlier in our evolution, back into the beginning stages of primate evolution, the dental formula was probably 2:1:3:3. The difference is an extra premolar. Going back even farther seems to indicate that our mammalian ancestors had more teeth. So there has been a long-term evolutionary trend toward the reduction in the number of teeth in mammals and in primates. But no tooth loss has occurred for the past tens of millions of years. That means that as we trace our hominid origins and later development, we will be looking at only tooth size and shape changes.

There has been conjecture that modern humans are in the process of losing their third molars, or wisdom teeth. This tooth is the most variable in terms of its size and shape and the time when it erupts. Perhaps this variability is brought on by our extensive consumption of soft and processed foods, along with increasing exposure to growth-influencing substances. So it might be that tooth crowding results from our jaws not growing properly.

> ### Paleoquest
>
> In about 20 percent of people in the United States, the third molar doesn't erupt at all. Impaction of the molar may be the result of a lack of jaw growth. Could this be an evolutionary trend in the making? Certainly, there is no answer at this time.

> ### Paleofacts
>
> Early hominids had a thicker enamel covering than found in fossil or modern apes. This is due to different chewing movements or mechanics. Without interlocking canines, hominids can swivel or rotate their jaws, sliding upper and lower crown surfaces against each other. Thickened enamel is adaptive in slowing the wearing of the crown.

Parts of a Tooth

The basic parts of a tooth are the crown, neck, and roots. Teeth differ both in their crown surfaces and in the number of roots. This is a hint that differently shaped teeth have different functions, which we discuss shortly.

The outer covering, or enamel, of a tooth makes it so hard. Enamel is entirely mineralized. But inside the tooth, in the pulp cavity, are vessels and nerves (you might have felt these) that keep the tooth healthy. In the fossil record, teeth are found still embedded in the jaws, or very often they occur by themselves. Fossilized teeth have portions of the enamel still intact, and sometimes even the entire outer covering is preserved.

Chew on This

Eat an apple. Or think about eating an apple. First you bite into it, and then you transfer that morsel backward and continue chewing. Biting and chewing are different functions aided by differently shaped teeth. Up front are the incisors and canines for biting off or cutting up a piece of food. Behind are the premolars and molars that grind up that food. These two steps obviously prepare our consumed foods for swallowing and aid in their digestion.

Canine Points

Discounting Count Dracula, real people have rather puny canine teeth in comparison with other primates. Paleoanthropologists can maximally exploit this fact when they find just a single tooth in a fossil site. Small canines signify hominid status. Recall that the Taung Child was classified as a hominid based on its relatively small canine. Lucy showed a mixture of apelike and humanlike traits in her teeth. Her canine, for example, was smaller than what is expected for an ape, but larger than those of later hominids. The mosaic picture of humans was still being developed at the time of Lucy.

Why do the Great Apes have such big canines? Fanglike canines could obviously be useful as weapons of defense or offense against threatening enemies. But African apes don't have any major predators, aside from poaching human hunters. Chimpanzees, but not gorillas, do engage in hunting monkeys on occasion, so their canines come into play in these hunting episodes.

> **Paleofacts**
>
> Finding a highly diagnostic single tooth, such as a canine, allows for some broader inferences about other linked traits making up a complex. For example, a large cone-shape canine would imply that this individual also had a canine gap and other related features that make up a canine complex.

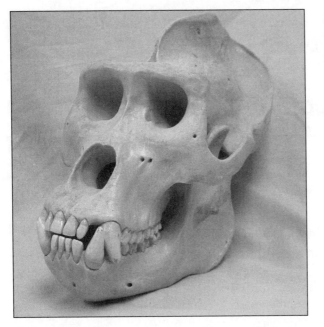

Big gorillas have big canine teeth.

(Leslie Harlacker/Scott Brish)

Then, too, apes are highly sexually dimorphic, and males have larger canines. It is conjectured that large canines might assist in determining which male would be most suitable as a mate. In these circumstances, generally the canines of the competing males are displayed, and actual attacks and fights don't always occur. Bearing canines has real meaning as a deterrent in this context. These situations have also been interpreted as females making the choice among competing males.

A third line of reasoning is that canines are useful in feeding behaviors. Gorillas are able to split open bamboo stalks and extract soft pulp with the stripping ability of their canines. Other primates use their canines for piercing fruits. These observations are important because they establish multiple adaptive bases for having large canines. In this instance, they equip the primate with built-in tools for eating.

> **Paleoquest**
>
> The explanation for why early hominids show some reduction in canine size requires further study. It doesn't look like primate analogy will be much help in this regard, since all nonhuman primates have large canine teeth.

Earlier we discussed the savanna model for bipedalism that proposed a reduction in canine size as hominids took up tool making. It was argued that tools would replace the need for large canines.

Yet, early hominids like Lucy, who was a biped, had intermediate-size canines but no stone tools. Lucy, a member of the species *Australopithecus afarensis*, is generally regarded as a hominid directly in our line of evolution. What additional fossil evidence is there of Pliocene hominids?

Let's return to the human paleontological record and consider some hominid fossils in terms of their dental traits. Their teeth may provide a basis for answering questions about our direct ancestors.

Robust and Gracile Australopithecines

Some years ago there was an attempt to explain why some australopithecines (called robust) had very large molars and small canines, while another group (called gracile) had large teeth overall. This became known at the "dietary hypothesis," as offered by John T. Robinson. We present this shortly—but first, some background.

> **Anthropos**
>
> John T. Robinson was born and educated in South Africa. Along with his colleague Robert Broom, he was instrumental in discovering hundreds of hominid fossils in the Transvaal Region from the 1940s onward. Upon leaving the University of Witwatersrand in 1963, he joined the faculty at the University of Wisconsin-Madison and pursued his seminal work in paleoanthropololgy. He died at the age of 78 in 2001.

Finding Taung Child Relatives?

In the 1930s, soon after the discovery of the Taung Child, more hominid fossils were found in South Africa. These fossil discoveries were very important for building the authenticity of the Taung fossil.

Once again, these fossils came from South Africa, from stone quarry caves clustered in the Transvaal Valley. Recovery of hominid fossils from these sites continues to this day. Hundreds of fossil specimens are now available, consisting of skulls, jaws with teeth, and many bones of the *post-cranial* skeleton.

Anthrolingo

Post-cranial refers to all of the skeleton below the head.

It's important to note that hip and leg bones clearly indicate that all of these hominids were bipedal. Again, continuing debate circulates over whether they walked exactly as we do today. The important thing is that they were adapted to walking, and that makes them our possible ancestors. Likewise, at least some of them could have descended from the Lucy group, *A. afarensis*.

In the 1950s, John T. Robinson, who was then at the University of Witwatersrand, began publishing his interpretations of the newly discovered fossils from the Transvaal caves. Robinson determined that the hominids could be separated into two groupings. One group was placed in the same taxonomic category set up for the Taung Child. These would be adults of *Australopithecus africanus*. The second group was seen as quite different; after some initial classification changes, it is now usually known as *Australopithecus robustus*. I guess that name of robustus gives a clue as to what it looked like. "Robust" here means muscular and strongly built. Its counterpoint, *A. africanus*, became known as the gracile form of australopithicine. "Gracile" refers to a slighter and less muscular body build.

Casts of gracile (left) and robust australopithecines.

(Leslie Harlacker/Scott Brish)

Body Double

Both gracile and robustus forms were between 4 and 5 feet tall. Compare this with Lucy, whom we said was around 3 feet tall. Thus, the hominid trend toward increasing body size took a pretty big jump. But there is also quite a big difference in their dates. They all lived during the Pliocene, but during different periods. Lucy existed around 3.5 M.Y.A., while the gracile dates fall between 3.0 M.Y.A. and 2.0 M.Y.A.

Paleoquest
Paleoanthropogists continue to work out ways for estimating body size and weight of early hominids. Bones and the muscle markings found on them can be very useful for doing this.

Robustus came somewhat later, between 2.5 M.Y.A. and 1.0 M.Y.A. So this jump in body size was really in slow motion.

How did the two forms differ? Well, robustus was probably a good deal heavier and more stocky in body build. Adult males might have weighed in at 100 pounds, and females might have been 70 pounds. Gracile likely weighed a little more than half this much.

Taking a Bite Out of Time

But the real difference between them was seen in their teeth. Robustus possessed huge molars and premolars, combined with absolutely small incisors and canines. In one specimen, the tiny canines are nearly crowded out of normal position. And the molars are the size of nickel coins. On the other hand, gracile's teeth were shaped much like ours but were quite a bit larger—sort of in the range of dime-size.

Lower jaws and teeth of gracile (left) and robust australopithecines.

(Leslie Harlacker/Scott Brish)

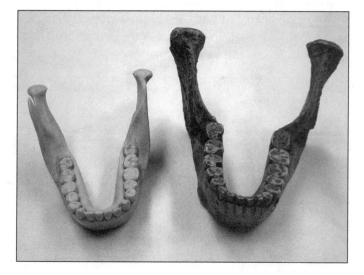

Of course, big teeth require space in big jaws. And big jaws must have big muscles to operate them. Apply this logic to robustus, and that's is what you see: large jaws and flaring cheeks, more so than in gracile. Also, robustus skulls developed a ridge of bone down the center called a *sagittal crest*. This crest is very noticeable in all animals possessing large lower jaws.

Anthrolingo

A **sagittal crest** provided additional bony surface area for the muscles that operate the lower jaw to attach to. It is massive in adult male gorillas and is fairly well developed in the robust australopithecines.

You Are What You Eat

These differences in teeth led Robinson to a dietary hypothesis that proposed that robustus and gracile were adapted to eating different diets. He employed inferences in his argument. In this case, the morphology of teeth was used to infer behavior—that is, eating habits.

With its large molars and premolars for crushing and grinding, robustus probably ate hard objects like nuts, seeds, and tough-shelled fruits. This sounds much like a vegetarian diet, and Robinson claimed that robustus was indeed a vegetarian. More recent evidence suggests that meat was also a part of the diet of robustus.

Robinson concluded from his studies of teeth that the gracile form was an omnivore in its eating habits. This means that it would have consumed a variety of edible plant foods along with meat in its diet. How was that meat obtained?

Fieldnotes

Detailed microwear studies of tooth crown surfaces can indicate diet. For example, minute scratches and pits seen through an electron microscope suggest that hard, gritty foods were regularly eaten. These dental "footprints" are found in the robust form. Softer foods, such as those eaten by the gracile form, left long, shallow grooves or striations, but no pitting.

Scavenging for a Living

The savanna model for bipedalism, which we discussed earlier, postulated that hominids moving out to the open plains began an active hunting way of life. Read that to mean that the men did the hunting. This interpretation receives little support today. In its place is the notion that meat in the diets of robustus or gracile probably came from scavenging large game animal kills of carnivores. Of course, there might

Paleoquest

Was there any connection between dietary adaptation and the evolution of bipedalism? That is currently an active research question.

have been some minor hunting of small animals, such as turtles and porcupines, when the opportunity arose. Chapter 9 has a more complete discussion of how hominids gained their livelihood.

We might find scavenging to be rather disgusting. Certainly, not many of us include road kill in our diets. But there might also be a rational side to scavenging, when considering the situation of the australopithecines. Hunting big game is a dangerous, risky endeavor—especially because there is little evidence that the australopithecines possessed suitable hunting tools. And remember, they didn't have large canines, either. But if they were somehow successful in chasing off a big cat that just made the kill, then dinner was on the table. *Ethnographic analogy* provides a basis for making this scenario a possibility.

Anthrolingo

Ethnographic analogy refers to behavioral observations made at the present time using living peoples as a model or guideline for interpreting the behavior of ancient peoples. This is comparable to primate analogy and bears the same caution: An analogy uses simple logic and doesn't provide actual proof.

East African tribal hunters has been filmed while chasing away cheetahs from a kill of a gazelle, a deer-like animal. Their weapon was nothing more that willow branches. Obviously, the hunters knew this scheme worked well with cheetahs. But it wouldn't likely be so successful with lionesses, which competitively guard their fresh kills.

It can't be said that australopithecines actually possessed this level of intelligence. If they did, then their scavenging efforts look a lot more noble. But their brains were only about one third the size of ours. Wouldn't that have been a limitation? We explore more of the connection between brain size and behavior in the next chapter.

Hominid Contenders

The robust form of australopithecine existed outside of Africa. You already know about Mary Leakey's 1959 discovery of Zinjanthropus, in Olduvai Gorge, Tanzania. "Zinj" was nicknamed "Nutcracker Man", and its molar crowns were even bigger than the South African robustus. Then in 1968, Richard Leakey (son of Louis and Mary) made another find that was considered to be hyperrobust. It has a massive pair of cheeks and a dominating sagittal crest. This fossil came from the important site Koobi Fora, which is located on the east side of Lake Turkana, Kenya. Finally, more recently, another hyperrobust form was found on the west side of Lake Turkana and was dated at 2.5 M.Y.A. (I shouldn't say "finally," I suppose, since there are likely to be more such fossil finds in the near future.) This one is popularly known as the Black Skull because of dark mineral stains.

The robust line is generally regarded as an extinct side branch in human evolution. These hominids probably were highly specialized in their diet of foods that required a lot of crushing. Whether they died out for lack of food or competition, or some other reason is not known. But they were not our ancestors. That doesn't mean that they were not successful. In fact, with the Black Skull dated at 2.5 M.Y.A. and the South African robust form dated at 1 M.Y.A., our modern species would be thought very successful if we stick around for a million and half years. So far, we have been here less than 10 percent of that time.

> **Paleofacts**
>
> There has been speculation, of the wild variety, that robust australopithecines were the ancestors of some allegedly sighted large hairy creatures going by several names around the world. They are popularly known as Bigfoot in this country. But until some solid scientific evidence is found, they may also be called Big Doubt.

As for the gracile form of australopithecine—that is, *A. africanus*—it's still in contention as our direct ancestor. But there is a rising competitor. In 1999, there was a report of a new fossil. Parts of a skull and limb bones were found in Ethiopia. These all confirm that it is a hominid and place it in the right time frame between *A. afarensis* and the subsequent Pleistocene hominids, which we will be referring to based on the genus, Homo. This form has been classified as *Australopithecus garhi* and is dated at 2.5 m.y.a. In the native Afar language, garhi means "surprise," and that may turn out to be its role. With further study, *A. garhi* may, in fact, replace *A. africanus* as our direct ancestor. In this sense, prehistory is still being written—and, of course, subject to continual revision.

We are now ready to consider hominids of the Pleistocene. In the next chapter, we introduce fossils that are classified as Homo, which is the same genus that we belong to. So we might expect that the Early Pleistocene hominids are more like us than the australopithecines of the Pliocene were. A hint of what this involves is a "no brainer."

The Least You Need to Know

- ◆ Teeth are highly informative with regard to inferring diet and in assigning evolutionary relationships.

- ◆ At least two kinds of hominids were alive in the later Pliocene, a robust form and a gracile form.

- ◆ The robust form probably became highly specialized in its diet and became extinct.

- ◆ At this time, the gracile form is considered more likely to be our direct ancestor.

7

Sizing Up the Hominid Brain

In This Chapter

- ◆ How to measure a brain
- ◆ *Homo habilis* enters the brain game
- ◆ Bigger brains mean what?
- ◆ Two other contenders in our hominid ancestry

Primates are brainy mammals. Humans are brainy primates. If there is anything we take great pride in, it is our large brain. It has literally gone to our heads that bigger brains are better. But better for what? Neuroscientists, who specialize in the study of brains, are actively seeking a clearer understanding of how our brain works. In this review of human prehistory, we attempt to describe the major changes that have taken place in brain evolution over the past millions of years. Some of these changes are quite obvious: The hominid brain did get bigger. In fact, our brains today are about three times larger than brains of our hominid ancestors of the Pliocene. We look at this major trend in the fossil record and then offer some suggestions as to why brain increase occurred.

We also bring out other changes in the brain that are probably just as important. This chapter introduces three species of hominids, all considered our possible ancestors. But we start by looking at methods for measuring brain size.

Measuring Gray Matter

Several ways of estimating brain size have been devised, some rather simple and others high-tech. The simple methods have been used for more than a couple of centuries. One of the earliest was employed in the context of forensic medicine. During autopsies, brains are removed and weighed. A lot of historical records of brain weights have been used and misused in making claims about intelligence and race.

Stoned Brains

As you realize, the prehistoric record doesn't preserve brain tissue. But rare and fortunate situations have resulted in endocranial casts—stoned brains, if you will. Such was the discovery of the Taung Child fossil. This cast, of course, has been measured, and its volume was easily determined by that good old Archimedes principle of water displacement. These measurements indicated that the Taung Child (*Australopithecus africanus*) did not have a much bigger brain than that a young ape of a comparable age. Would the brain of *A. africanus* have grown much faster so that adults would have larger brains than apes? Let's look at another widely used method for estimating brain size of fossils.

Grains for Brains

Fossil skulls are often fragmented, with portions of the *braincase* and the face separated. This is good and bad. It is bad in that any reconstruction of the pieces depends on how much of the skull is intact. But it is good if most of the brain case is intact and can be reassembled to form a bowl-like container. Ideally, all of the cranium is there and all of the holes are plugged except for the foramen magnum, that large opening at the bottom.

This handy container then can be filled through the foramen magnum with small hard objects, measuring volume by displacement, thanks again to Archimedes. Choice of objects have included sand grains, mustard seed, and lead shot. Lead shot is obviously the least affected by compression, but its heavy weight is a minus. Some researchers have tried placing a balloon inside the cranium and filling it with water, but this has the risk of breaking and making a bit of a mess.

Anthrolingo

The **braincase** is literally bones of the cranium that cover the brain. Four major bones and some smaller ones make up the braincase.

Paleofacts

Actual brain size is about 80 percent of endocranial volume. The other 20 percent includes brain vessels, membranes, and cerebral/spinal fluid.

Whatever the choice of filler material, this is the method of measuring endocranial volume, also called cranial capacity.

You probably realized that the methods described so far are rather invasive. Taking the brain out or not having the brain in the cranium pretty well rules out applying these methods in living people. Yet, there are good reasons for estimating brain size in people, and, of course, measuring brain activity is a very exciting branch of current neural research. One obvious and simple solution is to measure the outside of the cranium.

Calipered Cranium

Physical anthropologists have included measurements with calipers as an instrumental part of their research. This has been given the descriptive label of *anthropometry*.

Head measurements are taken from standardized points on a person's head. For research purpose only, if we consider the braincase to be shaped like a cube, then its height, length, and breadth dimensions can be multiplied to yield its volume.

Anthrolingo

Anthropometry ("measure of man") refers to taking measurements of the body with the aid of calipers of different designs. Commonly used instruments in fitness and weight control clinics are skin-fold calipers, which estimate amounts of body fat.

Paleoquest

Higher-tech medical instruments, such as x-rays, MRI, and PET scans, can peer inside the head and produce images that are helpful in measuring brain size. In the case of PET, brain activity can also be observed. Use of these machines in studies connecting brain evolution with prehistory is increasing.

Anthropometric calipers in use.

(Scott Brish/Leslie Harlacker)

Of course, this also yields a crude estimate. There have been mathematical improvements of this basic method of estimating brain size from outside the head.

Bigger Brains, Bigger Bodies

Measuring and comparing brain size is usually accompanied by a need to correct for body size. Whales have the largest brains in absolute terms. But they are also the largest of mammals. So, in the evolutionary brain game, the brain-to-body-size ratio counts—but not entirely.

> **Paleofacts**
>
> The ratio of brain weight to body weight in humans is 1:49. This means that our body is 49 times heavier than our brain, which is a couple of pounds.

Humans do have a high ratio of brain weight to body weight in comparison with some, but not all, primates. For example, our ratio is around 1:49, but the ratio of the squirrel monkey, a rather tiny South American form, is 1:31. This means that the squirrel monkey has a bigger brain for its body size than we do. Given that fact, we probably don't want to stake a claim on this ratio as a measure of our intelligence.

The Brainy Handyman

As we noted earlier, the Leakeys spent decades trudging up and down the rocky slopes of Olduvai Gorge in search of evidence of ancient humans, which they initially found in the form of stone tools. We discuss these tools, appropriately called Oldowan tools, in detail in the next chapter. But now the prime question was, who made these tools? Who was the toolmaker? Well, you also know that Mary found Zinj in 1959, but there was serious doubt that this robust guy was the toolmaker. So the search continued, but not for long. The next year, they discovered skull fragments indicating a larger brain, and some teeth that were smaller than those of australopithecines.

They seemed to be on the track of more advanced hominids. By 1964, they announced a new species and the first of our very own genus, *Homo habilis*. This scientific name is translated as "able man" or "handy man." Here was the toolmaker. Remarkably, K-Ar testing dated *H. habiis* to around 2 M.Y.A., which made this form the earliest hominid proven to have culture by virtue of its tool-making abilities. How did these abilities arise? Possibly brain size increase was involved. Here are some facts, or data, as researchers would say:

◆ The average cranial capacity of the gracile australopithecines was around 450 cubic centimeters (cc).

- The average cranial capacity of *H. habilis* was more than 600 cc.

- This difference would amount to a one-third increase in brain size over a time span of maybe half a million years.

Cast of Homo habilis, *the "handy man."*

(Scott Brish/Leslie Harlacker)

Those are the facts—now how are they to be understood? You might say that circumstantial evidence indicates that, with larger brains, *H. habilis* was able to think in more complex ways and to solve basic problems more efficiently than australopithecine ancestors. Making stone tools to assist in getting and preparing food are implicated as more complex behavior. Of course, as with all such interpretations, this one remains tentative and subject to modification as new evidence is discovered.

Paleofacts

Since there will never be direct observation of prehistoric behavior, indirect and circumstantial evidence must be the foundation for interpreting and reconstructing the past. Our judicial system is substantially based on the same foundation, in spite of what appears to be a lot of videotaping of criminal acts.

Paleoneurology

If a bigger brain did make *H. habilis* more capable of producing stone tools, then what more can be learned about brain evolution from the fossil record? Not very much, according to Ralph Holloway, a professor of anthropology at Columbia University. Holloway has spent his career making and studying endocasts of the major fossil hominids.

Holloway makes his endocasts by building thin layers of latex on the inside of the cranium. When it is thick enough, it is pulled out through the foramen magnum and quickly resumes its shape.

He points out that endocasts are pretty much featureless. They are quite smooth and don't record all of the grooves (sulci) and folds that make up the outer layer of the brain, called the *cerebral cortex*.

Anthrolingo

The **cerebral cortex,** also known as gray matter, is a layer or sheet of brain tissue that is highly folded in humans. Because of this folding, we have three to four times more brain surface area than that found in chimpanzees. Our intelligence is attributed to the great expansion of the cerebral cortex during evolution.

This is because the cerebral cortex is covered by membranes, vessels, and fluid that obscure brain surface features. So endocasts do reflect the overall size of the brain. And to some extent, they could show shape changes, if some areas of the brain got larger than others. These changes may accompany reorganization of the brain functions.

As you might recall from Chapter 1, Raymond Dart argued that the Taung Child was humanlike because it had a larger forebrain, or prefrontal cortex, than the chimpanzee. The forebrain in humans is integral to our ability to plan and make decisions. It also controls our ability to make moral judgments and to express empathy toward others. No wonder it has been called the "headquarters of humanity."

The forebrain needed to be reconstructed in the Taung Child fossil. This may or may not be a concern. But Ralph Holloway has asserted that the prefrontal cortex does not differ in size between humans and chimpanzees. If so, then changes that are not readily observable have taken place in the forebrain during human evolution.

Paleoquest

An intriguing area of brain evolution research involves the study of brain asymmetry, in which the left and right halves or hemispheres differ in size. A notable difference involves a larger left hemisphere and its relationship with the production of language and handedness. More on these topics comes in a later chapter.

It should be noted that not all researchers working in the area of paleoneurology agree with Holloway about his observations on the Taung Child and other endocasts. Nor do they all accept his interpretations. Alternative explanations have been offered by Professor Dean Falk, from the Anthropology Department at SUNY-Stony Brook. She has also proposed an intriguing theory that human brain size could have undergone a major size increase when an important vessel drainage system of the brain was established. This allowed the brain to cool properly; hence, her idea became known as the "radiator theory."

The question still remains as to what hominid brain size increase means, especially if it occurred in selected regions. Did it add memory, improve problem solving, and lead to spoken language? Sticking to broad generalizations, bigger brains likely did enhance early hominids in their thinking and learning capacities. Automated behaviors driven by instincts were in the distant past.

Hominids were becoming increasingly dependent on cultural behavior for making decisions and taking actions. This meant that learned behavior shared among members of the community took on increased significance. And for better or worse, this was the path that all of our later ancestors faithfully followed. Learning and sharing knowledge became our means of advancement and survival.

I am purposely avoiding using phrases suggesting that hominids were becoming more "intelligent" or were getting "smarter." One obvious reason is that I am not sure how to measure intelligence in the prehistoric context. There is quite enough controversy in measuring intelligence today.

> ### Paleofacts
>
> It used to be thought that behavior could be simply divided into instinct and learned categories, sort of a false dichotomy between nature (heredity) and nurture (environment). This is no longer the case. Instinctual actions have a learned component, and genes interact with the environment in producing some behaviors. Other behaviors, which we call cultural, are not directly influenced by genes.

> ### Paleofacts
>
> Studies have shown a weak relationship between human brain size and intelligence, as measured by IQ tests. Thus, differences in IQ are better explained by factors other than brain size.

More specific answers are forthcoming from functional neurology and studies using PET that can observe brain activity as a person performs different tasks. These studies likely will shed some light on specific behavioral aspects of hominid brain evolution, including those aspects that we include in our definitions of intelligence.

But for now, paleoanthropologists have to work with mostly brain size increase. We will continue to map the progress of this evolutionary trend in succeeding hominid fossils. We will also continue to offer some conjecture on what brain size increase might have meant regarding an increase in complexity and evidence of cultural activity seen in the archaeological record.

Habiline Contempories

It appears that *H. habilis* was not the only species of the genus Homo present in East and South Africa some 2 M.Y.A. If we consider body build, then *H. habilis* was probably in the size range of *A. africanus*. But it had rather long arms, which suggests to some that it regularly climbed trees, along the lines of apes. This obviously is a primitive trait and raises questions concerning its ancestral status to later hominids.

Other hominids were living at the same time, which complicates the matter somewhat. One contemporary is called *Homo rudolfensis*. Its name is taken from Lake Rudolf, which was the former name of Lake Turkana.

What makes *H. rudolfensis* so interesting to paleoanthropolgists is that its brain size is close to 750 cc. That's 25 percent larger than in *H. habilis*. Just to add a little perspective here, our modern brain size averages about 1,350–1,400 cc. So *H. rudolfensis* is about halfway toward the completion of the brain size increase trend. (No, I did not say half-brained.)

H. rudolfensis showed brain asymmetry with the left hemisphere larger than the right. Start the conjecture ball rolling. Was it really *H. rudolfensis*, not *H. habilis*, who was our ancestor? Which form made the Oldowan tools? Maybe both of them did. Very important, did *H. rudolfensis* have speech capability? There aren't clear-cut answers to these questions. But another question can be posed.

How about adding one more contender to the mix? Almost 2 M.Y.A., a third hominid inhabited East Africa. It has been classified as *Homo erectus*. This name may be familiar territory to you because it is the same species that we said the Java Man would be assigned to. The story for *H. erectus* is filled out in Chapter 9. Here, in our discussion of brain size increase, *H. erectus* bumps up cranial capacity once again, to an average of about 1,000 cc. This places it within the lower end of the range for modern *Homo sapiens*.

So now, nearing the end of the Pliocene and beginning of the Pleistocene, we find three hominid species, *H. habilis*, *H. rudolfensis*, and *H. erectus*, in contention as our direct ancestor.

For some researchers, this represents a rather crowded picture. It could be simplified if it turns out that one or possibly even two of these species are not so different after all. They could then be reclassified into just one, quite variable, species.

It usually is said at this point that perhaps with the discovery of additional fossils, the picture will become clearer. These are the kinds of challenges that spur on research in prehistory. Tentative

> **Paleofacts**
>
> Average numbers hide information on variation. For example, the range of cranial capacity for *H. erectus* is approximately 800–1,200 cc, and for modern humans the normal range is from less than 1,000 to more than 2,000 cc.

> **Paleoquest**
>
> Active debate in paleoanthropology surrounds what constitutes separate species. This determination is based on morphological traits and perhaps on information about the paleoenvironment. Different interpretations from the same material can result.

answers are followed by new questions or *hypotheses* that require more fossils to resolve. In sum, the science of prehistory cycles on itself.

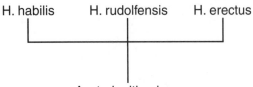

H. habilis   H. rudolfensis   H. erectus

Australopithecines

Hominid contenders of the Plio/Pleistocine around 2 M.Y.A.

(Scott Brish)

We end this chapter of human prehistory with hominids that are well on the way to becoming modern humans. In biology, they have slightly smaller teeth but greatly expanded brains. As evidence of their cultural behavior, they have stone tools. The next chapter is devoted to stone tool manufacturing. It's pretty hard to overemphasize what tool making means to our development. Just look around us today, and you will see our nearly complete dependence on tools and technology for our very survival. How this all began some 2.5 M.Y.A. is the topic coming up next.

Anthrolingo

Hypotheses in prehistory refer to formally constructed questions that are to be researched and that are either supported or not supported by discovered evidence. Theories are broad explanations based on already tested hypotheses.

The Least You Need to Know

- Several methods exist for measuring and estimating brain size.

- An increase in brain size in early hominids very likely meant an improved ability to think and learn.

- *Homo habilis* is the first recognized hominid toolmaker.

- Three hominid species in the Late Pliocene vie as our possible ancestors.

Earliest Tool Kits

In This Chapter

- ◆ The first stone tools
- ◆ Tools made from other materials?
- ◆ Experimental toolmaking in a chimp
- ◆ How were stone tools used?
- ◆ Living in Oldowan style

Tools maketh the man. Man, the toolmaker. These claims from the past ring true today, in a qualified context. The "man" part is mostly qualified away. Tools and technology do define us as a unique primate species. Our tool-making signature first appeared more than 2.5 M.Y.A. in the form of stone artifacts. But we also know that becoming and being a human goes well beyond our technological prowess. Acknowledging that, this chapter recounts the remarkable development that began with such humble beginnings on battered boulders. What did the earliest stone tools look like, and how were they used?

We offer some answers, with the assistance of experimental toolmaking and tool use. Stone was not the only raw material of early toolmakers. There have been claims that animal horns, bones, and teeth were also utilized, and we examine these claims in this chapter. Finally, we look at research on chimpanzees to see whether they could master the rudiments of stone toolmaking. Successful chimp efforts might force some revision of our proud notion of "Man, the toolmaker."

Oldowan Tools

"Oldowan" is the term applied to the discovery made by the Leakeys of stone tools at the Olduvai Gorge site. The term now refers to all other stone tools of the same type found at other sites. Some of the artifacts were small, roundish cores of stone from which chips had been removed. Other recognized artifacts are the chips or flakes themselves. As we will see, both categories make useful kinds of tools.

Oldowan core and flake tools.

(Nick Toth/Kathy Schick)

The Oldowan tool discovery formally ushered in the Lower Paleolithic, which is also called the Early Stone Age in Africa. The Lower Paleolithic extends forward in time to around 200,000 years ago. Based on this original Oldowan stone or *lithic* tools, it harkened back in time to 2 M.Y.A.

Anthrolingo

Lithic ("stone") is often used to describe artifacts fashioned from various kinds of stone materials.

As we noted in the last chapter, Oldowan stone tools were found in the 1960s in close association with *Homo habilis*. It was logically inferred that the tools were, in fact, made and used by *H. habilis*. But then we also introduced two other hominid species, *H. rudolfensis* and *H. erectus*. Could they have been the toolmakers? For now, we must accept a large dose of uncertainty and allow that any and all of these ancient Homo species were toolmakers.

Since the 1960s, time has marched on—or, really, marched backward to the origin of toolmaking. With recent discoveries and dating of older stone artifacts, even earlier toolmakers emerge.

At a site in Gona, Ethiopia, Oldowan tools were dated between 2.5 M.Y.A. and 2.6 M.Y.A. This takes us back to the period of earlier hominids known as the australopithicines. You should remember the gracile and robust forms discussed in the last chapter. So repeat the previous question: Who were the toolmakers? Then repeat the previous answer, except that there is some leaning toward the gracile form as the more likely candidate.

There is no reason to expect that this will end the quest for origins. Tools made earlier likely will be found—perhaps even more crudely made than those attributed to the *Oldowan Industry*.

And then there is every reason to expect that tools were also made from materials other than stone. They just haven't withstood the ravages of time and are not preserved as often.

> **Paleoquest**
>
> Some research on fossil hand bones indicates that the robust form of australopithicine could have performed well in tool-making activities, but the question remains open.

> **Anthrolingo**
>
> **Oldowan Industry** refers to the collective assemblage of the earliest made core and flake tools. The Oldowan Industry represents the initial documented manufacture of stone tools in various sites in East and South Africa, the earliest of which is dated between 2.5 M.Y.A. and 2.6 M.Y.A.

Osteodontokeratic Tools?

Did Oldowan toolmakers use raw materials other than stone? Some evidence supports this. Animal bones found at two South African cave sites had rounded and smooth tips, as if they had been used to repeatedly dig into the ground.

These "digging sticks" have an ethnographic counterpoint. Cultures in various parts of the world have used sticks made of wood, bone, or horn to dig out edible roots and tubers of plants.

If the bone sticks found in South Africa are actually tools, this would confirm what prehistorians generally believe happened. Again, we have said that early hominids were probably not big animal hunters, but instead scavenged big game carcasses. Most often this would have meant that they ended up with parts of the skeleton that didn't have much meat left on them. That is, after chomping and chewing of big cat carnivores, what's left is mostly defleshed leg bones, heads, and jaws. And, quite obviously, these parts would have been scattered about, readily available for immediate use.

Paleoquest

Ongoing research is being done to determine how animal bone accumulations occurred at sites, particularly in cave deposits. Earlier, it was thought that hominids carried them into the caves, but the thinking more lately is that carnivores deposited them.

Anthrolingo

Osteodontokeratic Culture was named by Raymond Dart in his interpretation of accumulated animals bones, jaws with teeth, and horns at a cave site in South Africa. This interpretation is no longer accepted by prehistorians.

The bony parts wouldn't even have needed to be modified very much. Their anatomic structure could have served as clubs, hammers, probes, and sticks—sort of a workshop of skeletal proportion. But thinking that unmodified bones were employed as tools is one thing. Speculating that they were part of an australopithecine arsenal is quite another. That is where Raymond Dart comes back into the picture.

Dart found thousands of broken bones, jaws, and heads in one of the cave sites of South Africa known as Makapansgat. This cave also yielded fossil hominids of the gracile form. Dart built a connection between animal parts and hominids, and he referred to it as the *Osteodontokeratic Culture*, which translates to "bone-teeth-horn." Dart claimed that the hominids did modify leg bones by cracking them to produce sharpened points. Since long bones had knobby ends, they were already clublike. Lower jaw bones with teeth embedded and skull foreheads with horns attached were also natural weapons, according to Dart.

Bones, teeth, and horns from the Zooarchaeology Collection, Indiana University. These kinds of raw materials are proposed for the Osteodontokeratic Culture.

(Dick Adams/Scott Brish)

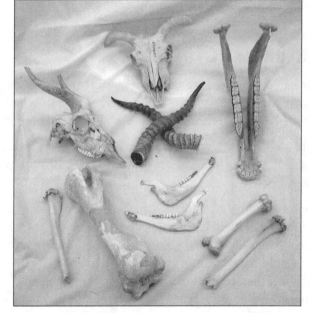

This accumulation of animal body parts led Dart to propose that the australopithicines were engaged in some kind of confrontation involving hand-to-hand to bone-teeth-horn combat.

The Osteodontokeratic Culture did not survive the close scrutiny of a paleoanthropologist in 1980. He found that the bone breakage, as well as the accumulation of body parts in the Makapansgat cave, was most likely the result of carnivore activity.

A Bonobo Tries His Hand

Tool use has been observed in a number of animal species. For example, California sea otters crack open shellfish by banging them against a stone. Shifting closer to our evolutionary past, chimpanzees use hammer stones to crack open nuts, and they crumple leaves to use as sponges to sop up water to drink. In a more complex behavior, chimps make probes of small branches, which they insert into termite mounds.

Chimpanzee "fishing" for termites.

(Kevin Hunt)

Termites attach to the probe, and the chimp removes it and eats his catch. This has been called "termite fishing," and it represents a learned behavior that is transmitted from one chimp to the next. These examples are cited to show that animals, particularly our close primate relatives, regularly modify natural objects for an intended use. It's sort of a rudimentary definition of cultural or *protocultural* toolmaking and use. Let's raise the stakes here. Could the chimpanzee be taught to make stone tools?

Anthrolingo

Protoculture is the term that some researchers find more appropriate to define chimpanzee learned behavior. They restrict the term **culture** for hominids who employed language in transmitting learned behavior.

You probably guessed the answer. Just a little twist to start out with before filling out the details. The experiments on chimp toolmaking were done on a species classified as *Pan paniscus*. Also called the "bonobo" or "pygmy" chimp, it differs from the "common" chimp (*Pan troglodytes*) because it is somewhat smaller. But of great interest to primatologists (who study primates) and paleoanthropolgists is that the bonobo tends to be more humanlike in certain aspects than the common chimp.

Now let's get up close and personal. Kanzi is a 20-something bonobo who was born at the Yerkes primate facility near Atlanta, Georgia. He had already learned elementary aspects of human language by typing commands on a keyboard. Then he was entered into a toolmaking/tool use experiment. Initially, he was shown what the experimenters wanted him to do: basically attempt to make Oldowan-like flake tools. After the demonstrations, he was set to work on his own in more or less trial-and-error fashion, but also with some motivating goal to achieve.

Kanzi chipping stone tool.

(Nick Toth/Kathy Schick)

Kanzi was to chip a flake from a core blank, and then use the flake to cut through a string that released a trap door and gave him access to candies. He apparently desired this strong enough to set him working. Over 10 years, he has progressed to producing tools in the general Oldowan style, but he's still short of actually replicating the Oldowan technique.

These experiments are enlightening in showing both the Kanzi's capabilities and limitations. He is also known, in a play on words used by the experimenters, as "Pan, the toolmaker." The experimental results perhaps generalize that chimpanzees—at least, the bonobo—have mental and hand-eye coordination abilities that might have been present back some five to seven million years ago. This is the time frame when they shared a common ancestry with emerging hominids. Of course, these abilities could also have developed after the time of the hominid-chimp split.

Now that we have formally introduced Oldowan tools, dismissed Osteodontokeratic Culture, and portrayed Kanzi as a moderately proficient toolmaker, let's turn to the nitty gritty of how Oldowan tools were made.

Making a Stone Tool

A reasonable place to start is to inquire about what kinds of thinking goes on before the actual toolmaking. Call it planning ahead. Likewise, the earliest toolmakers must have possessed a head suitable for planning.

Core Concepts

You saw the examples of Oldowan tools. Pretty crude, right? But imagine what kinds of mental processing is required to make these objects, both the cores and the flakes? They are fashioned with a definite idea or model in mind. Once made, they are used for an anticipated purposes. All of this thinking would have put a lot of brain cells to work.

Sure, there was probably a lot of trial and error, and some serendipitous accidents that helped to mold the learning process. We can presume that teaching by the early hominids was primarily done through imitative learning of the young apprentices. You know, a "watch and do what I do" method. We aren't quite ready to make claims about spoken language. But then, nonverbal communication, like gesturing with hands and eyes, could well have been practiced.

The toolmakers were looking for rocks that chipped with some expected outcome, although flaking may have been sort of haphazard as well. You might say that either early hominids had fuzzy *mental templates* or their hand-eye coordination may have been poorly developed, or both.

Anthrolingo

Mental template is a more formal term designating what forms in the mind as it plans to carry out actions, such as making a tool. The mind "sees" what it is going to make before making it.

The rocks they chose do give up chips when struck with another rock. Later, in the Paleolithic, antlers were also used for chipping off stone. That produced a fairly sharpened edge that could be used for a number of activities described shortly.

Anthrolingo

Percussion toolmaking involves striking a "blank" core with a **hammerstone,** which removes flakes that also can be used as cutting tools. Percussion toolmaking is distinguished from pressure-flaking, which removes smaller flakes in a more controlled manner by applying pressure and pushing off flakes. The result is retouched tools.

The Percussion Section

Making a core tool required the toolmaker to steady a pebble or cobble in one hand and then strike it with another cobble, called a *hammerstone.* This is called *percussion* toolmaking.

The product of this effort, the core tool, can be used repeatedly. It can be rather quickly made and perhaps wouldn't have to be saved and carried with early hominids as they moved about. Perhaps the discovery of so many of these core tools was enhanced by their abundance due to cheap labor and disposability.

Cutting-Edge Technology

When Oldowan core tools were first found, it was thought that these were, in fact, the only ones that the ancient toolmakers had. But later careful study of the flakes removed from the cores indicated that flakes could have been the intended purpose of toolmaking, not necessarily the cores. These unmodified flakes have sharp edges that are very useful for cutting activities. Later, flakes were modified by removing small chips using *pressure-flaking* or *careful percussion.* This is called *retouching.*

When we discuss later developments in tool manufacture, retouching becomes increasingly prominent. It culminates in the exquisite stone blades made during the Upper Paleolithic.

Is This a Hammer?

How do prehistorians know how stone tools were made or how they were used? How do they assign function and purpose to the tools? Interpretations can be based on several lines of evidence, along with a healthy measure of reasonable inference. Here is a list of the kinds of evidence that have been used:

◆ Observations of the properties of the artifact—its shape, sharpness, size, and so on

◆ Magnified observations of microwear patterns

◆ Identification of hair, feathers, plant parts, and genetic material left on the tool

◆ Experimental studies of making and then using the tools

◆ Ethnographic analogy, observing people of today who continue to employ a stone tool technology

Glimpses of the Past in the Present

Let's consider the last of these first. In very few places on Earth, stone tools are still being made on a regular basis.

One such place is West Papua, New Guinea. Here, men are still engaged in the production of stone ax heads that they attach to handles and use in woodworking. Their tool-making activities provide an ethnographic analogy for prehistorians to study and perhaps gain some insight into how early hominid toolmakers behaved.

Paleofacts
More that 90 percent of our history and prehistory was spent as hunters and gatherers, using stone implements.

Anthropos
Dietrich Stout, from the Anthropology Department of Indiana University, has been doing fieldwork among the New Guinea ax makers. He is also carrying out PET brain studies of people while they make tools to see what areas of the brain are most active.

Experimenting with Rock

Professors Nick Toth and Kathy Schick, from the Anthropology Department of Indiana University, have carried out extensive and illuminating experimental work on Oldowan-type tools.

They have made and then used their duplicated products on projected tasks likely to have been done by early hominids. From their studies, core tools, whether modified or not, likely were used for these purposes:

◆ For breaking bones, to extract marrow for eating

◆ For woodworking, possibly in shaping wooden sticklike tools

◆ For cracking nuts

Anthropos
Professors Nick Toth and Kathy Schick are codirectors of the Center for Research into the Anthropological Foundations of Technology (CRAFT). They have conducted major research into experimental toolmaking and then into using those tools for tasks that they have proposed they were designed for.

- As hammerstones for chipping other cores in producing flake tools

- As missiles thrown in defense or in hunting activities

Talk about all-purpose tools. Cores were probably the very first Swiss Army Knives.

Nick Toth making tools.

(Nick Toth/Kathy Schick)

What about flake tools? Using the experimental approach, Toth and Schick have shown that stone flakes are fully functional for slicing through hides and muscles of large African mammals, such as the wildebeest and elephant.

Experimental use of flake tools for butchering.*

(Nick Toth/Kathy Schick)

*Note: The animal used in this experiment died of natural causes.

Now, it is interesting to point out that early hominids were not successful big game hunters, but they scavenged their meat feasts from already killed animals. The flake tools were probably another version of the all-purpose knife. Cutting and slicing needs were part of many prehistoric tasks.

The list of purposes or functions of tools should be considered as possibilities. Since they were successfully used in experimental situations, it is logical to infer that they could have been used in a like manner in the past. Of course, if they didn't work out so well in the hands of the experimenters, doubt might be raised.

Ancient Scars

Cut marks are another important line of evidence seen on mammal bones found at Oldowan sites. These are likely incised scars left by the use of flake tools during butchering activities. Animal bones that show evidence of cutting are called *ecofacts*.

Tools of the Trade

Core and flake tools make up the meager Oldowan tool kit. But, as we have pointed out, these multipurpose tools did many things. They probably made life easier. They may even have reduced a dependence on teeth and jaws that led to their reduction in size over many succeeding generations. And we know, however crude and simple we regard them, they were adequate enough to successfully adapt our hominid ancestors for more than a million years without very much change. Compare that with our modern technology, in which a "new and improved" this or that comes out about every year. Is there a lesson from the past to be learned here?

> ### Paleoquest
>
> It has been proposed that the reduction in the size of hominid teeth came about as tools took their place for some functions, such as cutting food into smaller bites. Research continues in this area.

> ### Paleofacts
>
> Nick Toth has experimental evidence showing hominid toolmakers between 1.5 M.Y.A. and 2 M.Y.A. were possibly right-handed. This means that strong hand preference for the right side, which we see today (only about 10 percent of people are left-handed) may have been well established very deep into the past.

Anthrolingo

Ecofacts are natural items, such as bones, found at an archaeological site that indicate human activities, or they are animal and plant remains that provide information regarding past environmental and climatic conditions.

Lifestyle of the Oldowan Hominids

Life must have been at the most basic level during the time of these earliest toolmakers. Think prolonged primitive camping experience, probably without much shelter and certainly without fire. The scattered distribution of the stone tools and associated bones might indicate that Oldowan hominids stayed in an area for some period of time. But did they set up "base camps" or more permanent places of residence? That notion is contested, and in its place is the idea that these hominids were mostly opportunistic. That means that they stayed and moved about as conditions, perhaps availability of food and water, dictated. We have noted that their basic food acquisition in terms of meat was through scavenging rather than active hunting of big animals. And it is very likely that a large portion of their diet came from gathering edible plants, fruits, and nuts.

> **Paleofacts**
>
> Don Johanson made a highly significant discovery at the Hadar site in Ethiopia that consisted of a collection of skeletons of several individuals in proximity. Were these individuals related to one another, and did they all meet a calamitous ending together? Possibly. They are popularly known as the First Family.

> **Anthrolingo**
>
> Taphonomy ("study of graves") is the reconstructed history of archaeological site formation. It traces how bones and tools got to where they are when eventually recovered by the prehistorian. It also studies what processes accounted for their disposition at that site.

Family Matters

Increased brain size was probably accompanied by increased levels of social complexity in the hominid groups. But what groups? The fossil record doesn't have many solid clues as to how large social groups were, who were in the groups, and how they conducted their affairs. That is, we don't know much about their social structure and social organization.

Very rarely, groups of fossilized individuals are found at the same site. Such was the case for the First Family at the Hadar site in Ethiopia. Then the widely scattered but abundant tools and bones indicate that some sort of group of individuals was actually living together.

Virtual Prehistory

Prehistoric archaeologists conduct research, called actualistic studies, in which they try to duplicate the kinds of conditions that would explain how prehistoric sites came to look the way they do. For example, they might record the history of animal carcasses as they are exposed to predator activity, and natural processes like wind and water as bones are moved about and get buried. Tracing the history of site formation is called *taphonomy*.

Both ethnographic analogy and primate analogy offer possible insight to the paleoanthropologist on the size, nature, and composition of early hominid social grouping. Some rather isolated cultures of today may represent models of how early hominid groups might have lived. Then, too, the social behavior of nonhuman primates might be roughly comparable to that of the earliest hominids. But this kind of model building-

ing must be done with caution. As we said earlier, analogies might present logical arguments, but no proof of what actually happened in the past.

In succeeding chapters, we continue to explore the nature of social grouping in hominids. The level of social organization of Oldowan toolmakers must have been high enough for them to take the next major step—or, actually many, many steps—in human prehistory. Whether by design or not, hominids began to move out of Africa for the first time during the Early Pleistocene. This is the topic of the next chapter.

> **Paleofacts**
>
> The notion previously existed that so-called primitive isolated cultures were "living museums" of Stone Age life. This idea has been abandoned, and in its place is an understanding that while these cultures may be lacking in technological development and perhaps even in written language, they nevertheless possess and express high levels of social and linguistic complexity.

The Least You Need to Know

- Stone toolmaking began at least 2.5 M.Y.A.

- Materials other than stone were probably used, but not in the manner proposed by Dart and his Osteodontokeratic Culture.

- A bonobo chimp was trained to make Oldowan-style tools.

- Functions of Paleolithic tools can be inferred from different kinds of experimental studies.

- Oldowan toolmakers were probably scavengers and gatherers of food, not hunters of big animals.

Part 3

Out of Africa

We now move ahead in time to follow the dual developments of our biological and cultural evolution. Tool-making technology has improved and brains have increased in size. Is this a coincidence? Probably not. And we look at another hallmark of hominids, the movement out of Africa and into Eurasia.

We also take up a continuing and vexing issue in human prehistory, the fate of the Neandertals. They certainly weren't the brutish cavemen and cavewomen depicted in some films, cartoons, and pieces of fiction, so we examine the Neandertal and their cultural and extinction.

Fashioning New Tools and New Hominids

In This Chapter

◆ Acheulean tools, their structure and function

◆ *Homo erectus* in Africa

◆ Evidence for controlled use of fire

◆ Hominids spread from Africa to Java, China, and Russia

◆ Why did they leave home?

We referred to Oldowan tools as "all purpose" and stone versions of the Swiss Army Knife. They seemed to do all that is required of them at that time. The basic Oldowan style persisted for a million years or more. Then there was change. First, there was some technical improvement in the Oldowan tools themselves. But then a new technique emerged. This chapter describes these new tools. As if to go along with the new tools, there are also some continuing changes, probably improvements, in the hominids. Thus, we will keep up with the evolutionary trends, as we get ever closer to modern humans.

This chapter also documents one of the greatest events in prehistory. I rank it fourth up to this point. First, there was the origin of hominids, revealed through erect bipedalism. Then there was the invention of stone toolmaking, followed by a doubling in brain size. And now for the first time, there were hominids outside of Africa. When and why did they migrate from Africa into Eurasia? A series of major cold spells occurred in Eurasia during the time period. How did the migrants face and conquer these challenges? Could they have invented fire to keep them warm? Possibly—we look at this evidence. You might want to think ahead about how many possible uses fire could have had for the migrant hominids. (Hint: four or more.) Let's start with the new tools.

Biface Tools Make Handy Axes

Oldowan tools did show some technical advancement from the earliest to the latest examples found. The later versions are called Developed Oldowan. It's worth repeating that the Oldowan industry lasted for a million or more years in Africa. Then this tool technology was carried out of Africa by the earliest of migrants. Doesn't that say something about how successful Oldowan tools were? Surely they must have performed all the tasks required of them.

Paleoquest

It has been argued that the basic design of Oldowan tools remained unchanged for so long because this style was as good as the toolmakers could make. Their brains were not sufficiently developed to go beyond this level. Continuing research may help to decide this issue.

Paleofacts

The name Acheulean comes from the nineteenth-century discovery of hand-axes at sites along the Somme River near the French town of St. Acheul.

Whatever the reason, about 1.5 M.Y.A., there appeared a major shift in stone toolmaking. A set of new techniques produced a highly recognizable stone tool commonly known as the hand-ax or biface. These hand-axes were called Acheulean tools, which may or may not sound like a sneeze, depending on your pronunciation.

Acheulean hand-axes are readily distinguished from Oldowan core tools by the following traits:

- They have many more stone chips removed.

- They tend to be oval and somewhat flattened with a narrow point rather than a spherical shape.

- Both sides of the tool have flakes removed, hence they are often called biface tools.

- They show symmetry in overall shape.

- By inference, they seem to be made with a clearer mental template of what kind of tool was desired.

Acheulean hand-axes, the Paleolithic Swiss Army Knife.

(Nick Toth/Kathy Schick)

These differences generally indicate a higher level of skill and more time required during tool manufacture. But the earliest examples tended to be thick and crudely chipped. Perhaps the more skilled Oldowan toolmakers began to experiment with naturally oval cores. This would set up a transition. They may also have been testing new ways for removing flakes.

Hammerstones were likely used to make Oldowan tools. But it is proposed that Acheulean bifaces, at least the latest ones, were struck with a "soft" hammer made of bone or antler. The soft hammer allowed for more control in removing flakes. How were Acheulean tools used?

> ### Paleoquest
> Flake tools were also in the Acheulean tool kit. They were probably used for woodworking, bone, and hide. One proposal under investigation is that bifaces were actually the cores for producing flakes.

All-Purpose Revisited

Acheulean tools might well have continued to serve many tasks, perhaps in the range of butchering and smashing bones (which contain edible marrow) or splitting wood. Variant tools also are found in association with the bifaces. These are large cleavers (with broader cutting edges) and picklike implements (with longer, narrow points). They, too, conjure up industrial-size jobs, possibly along the lines of wood splitting and digging. No evidence indicates their use as missiles or handheld weapons, but it doesn't seem too far fetched to suggest that they could have been used in this fashion. Remember that many of the projected uses for Paleolithic tools come from experimentation. Well, experimenting with tools as weapons is out of bounds—for good reason, don't you think?

It is significant that Acheulean bifaces are similar from Africa to Europe and Asia.

But to complicate this picture, stone tools more along the lines of Oldowan and called chopper-chopping tools were recovered in Hungary and China. How were these related to Acheulean? Was there no connection, or did they represent different kinds of activity?

Erectus Profile

Can we put a face on the makers of the bifaces? This requires a few steps. First, Acheulean bifaces were made in Africa some 1.5 M.Y.A., probably by *Homo erectus*. But they were also made by a group that we will come to know as Archaic *Homo sapiens* around 200 K.Y.A. (remember that K.Y.A. = thousand years ago). Then, while Acheulean bifaces were found in some sites in Asia and Europe, other sites during this time period carried on the tradition of the Oldowan industry. So what's going on here? It's an unsettled picture showing a mixing of developments in tool technology and evolution of hominid morphology. Add to this the complication of migrations within and outside Africa. Can we straighten this out a little? Let's start with homeland Africa and *Homo erectus*.

At the end of the last chapter, we mentioned the presence of *Homo erectus* in East Africa at 1.5 M.Y.A.. Very likely, this species made the Acheulean bifaces found in several East African sites. Then about 1 M.Y.A., there is evidence of *H. erectus* and its Acheulean tool kit in North Africa. In Algeria, there is a very early date of about 1.6 M.Y.A. Now we are getting someplace. Actually, before and after this time period, *H. erectus* was getting much farther; it showed up in East Asia and Southeast Asia, but probably not yet in Europe. Here is a little twist. At the lowest levels of stratified sites, Oldowan-like tools rather than Acheulean bifaces have been found with many of these *H. erectus* sites outside Africa. The likely interpretation here is that *H. erectus* left Africa before the development of the Acheulean. But then later strata have Acheulean bifaces. Clearly, while hominids are migrating out of Africa, new tool technologies are spreading, just not at the same time.

> **Paleoquest**
>
> A hominid species from East Africa is classified as *Homo ergaster*, which some believe should be classified as *Homo erectus* and others consider to be a separate species. Its dating is around 1.9 M.Y.A., which would mean that it predates *H. erectus*. More studies might sort out this matter.

Erectus on the Runway

We have described the biface tools. Let's have a look at *Homo erectus*. The basic traits listed here might be familiar to all of us—we have them, but to a very different degree. This means that if we saw *H. erectus* dressed in modern attire (that would give a lot a leeway) and walking down the street, we might well take second and third glances.

Homo erectus *from Africa.*

(Scott Brish/Leslie Harlacker)

Some defining physical features of *Homo erectus* are these:

♦ A long, low skull

♦ Thick skull bones

♦ Face area with large *browridges* that form a *supraorbital torus*

♦ Big jaws with fairly large teeth, especially the molars

♦ A sloping chin area, with no prominent chin

♦ Average cranial capacity of 1,000 cc

♦ Height near to ours, but a heavier build and muscular body

Anthrolingo

Browridge refers to the raised area just under the eyebrows. It is also referred to as supraorbital ridge. In *Homo erectus*, the ridge is continuous across the forehead, so it is referred to as **supraorbital torus**. This is considered a primitive trait.

We are keeping track of evolutionary trends, and at the time of *H. erectus*, body size was likely to be not much different than ours. The range of modern human height and weight is quite broad; *H. erectus* was at the stouter muscular build end.

Fieldnotes

One of the most spectacular of fossils finds was a nearly complete skeleton of an *H. erectus* (some say *H. ergaster*) boy, about 12 years old. The find is unusual because of the preservation and completeness of so much of his skeleton. But even more of a surprise is that, given his size at around adolescence, had he survived, he would have been around 6 feet tall.

It is thought that the larger size and muscular build of *H. erectus* meant that this species was biologically adapted to living in cold climates. Certainly, that would have been helpful; we will soon note that they lived in Asia, possibly also Europe, during times of glacial advances and cold temperatures.

Paleofacts

Human and other animal bodies adapt to cold temperatures by decreasing the amount of skin surface from which body heat can be lost. Larger, stouter bodies have less skin surface area than tall, thin bodies.

You have perhaps seen reconstructions of hairy hominids, with hairy heads and hairy faces in males. But we really don't know what hair styles were preferred by *H. erectus*. We can presume that the hair was kept long. If so, that would mean that the scalp would not have been directly exposed to losing heat, but was kept somewhat insulated with hair. Since the head area is the place from which much of our body heat is lost, even without headgear of some sort, *H. erectus* was better protected. I don't really have anything to say about balding here.

Brain size in *H. erectus* was within the lower range of modern brain size. Of course, the question still exists whether further brain reorganization was taking place or whether selected regions of the brain were increasing in size. Finally, *H. erectus* had teeth that were larger in the molar region than ours, but overall they were much smaller than the earlier ancestral hominids, such as *A. africanus* and *A. garhi*.

Summing up at this point, the mosaic picture of modern *H. sapiens* is beginning to fill out. What's left? Well, there will be a continuing increase in brain size and a continuing decrease in tooth size. Otherwise, physical appearance will not change much from here.

Now let's shift to a hot spot in prehistory—at least, potentially a hot topic.

Got a Light?

Remember that list of important events in human prehistory that opened this chapter? Well, let's add the invention of using fire to it. I suppose it sounds strange to refer to the use of fire as an invention. But it does have the basic element that we usually attribute to inventions: a discovery, perhaps even a Eureka discovery of how fire can do something new and innovative.

There is no doubt that all early hominids had seen and possibly felt the effects of fire. Fire started from natural causes like lightening strikes, volcanic eruptions, and rare occurrences of spontaneous combustion. No, I don't mean human bodies suddenly and without explanation bursting into flames. (Does that really happen?)

At one time, several Lower Paleolithic sites seemed to indicate that intentional fires had been maintained by the hominids. Here are the lines of evidence used:

- Ground or soil that had been discolored due to high heat

- Burnt bones

- Ash and charcoal remains

- Circular stone structures that resembled hearths

Were these due to natural causes or caused by hominids? Under closer scrutiny, at this stage in the research the case for hominids' controlled use of fire is not strong, but it also is not a closed case. There have been experiments to try to duplicate the presumed conditions of the past, and more of this work might help to clarify the matter. For now, it is safe to assume that *H. erectus* possibly did have controlled use of fire. Furthermore, this capability was instrumental in its survival after migrating out of Africa and into the colder climes of Eurasia.

As long as we are allowing *H. erectus* the possibility of using fire, we should lay out its likely uses. Here's the benefits package:

> **Paleofacts**
>
> It should be clarified that "controlled use of fire" refers to the capability of maintaining and perhaps carrying already burning fires for relatively long periods. This completely rules out being able to start a fire, as through the rapid spinning of a wooden stick in shavings or dry moss, or by striking a flint to spark a fire. These inventions came much later in prehistory.

> **Paleofacts**
>
> Unexplained circles of stones regularly appear way back into prehistory. One rough assemblage was found in an australopithecine site in South Africa. Because the stones had come from a river bed much lower than where they were found, they must have been brought there by the hominids.

- ◆ Gives off heat and provides warmth

- ◆ Cooks foods and destroys germs

- ◆ Provides light to see into the night

- ◆ Protects against predators, perhaps of the big cat variety

This list could be greatly expanded, for both prehistoric uses of fire and some that appeared later in our cultural and technological development. We cover additional prehistoric uses in succeeding chapters.

Now it is time to take a trip. We are ready to recount that great event in prehistory mentioned in the introduction to this chapter. *Homo erectus* is on the move, and where in the world did this species end up?

Travel Plans

If you look over a map of Africa, you will see that exits from the continent are pretty much limited to the northeast section. The deep sea at the Strait of Gibraltar would not have allowed a hominid crossing there. But in the northeast, there might have been a number of possible routes somewhere along the Arabian Peninsula up to the region now known as Israel. So researchers looking for evidence of the migrants might do well by concentrating on the Arabian Peninsula itself. Research up to now has revealed limited confirmation that the hominids passed through that area. But there isn't much, and it isn't the earliest dated material of hominids outside Africa.

Migration routes out of Africa.

(Scott Brish)

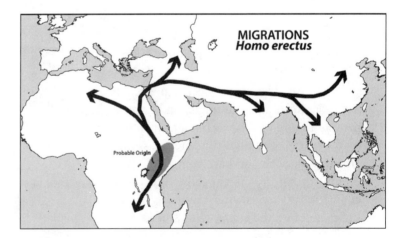

Farther north, in the Jordan Valley of Israel, are early dates, more than 1 M.Y.A., in a stratified site. The lower levels contain Oldowan-style tools, while the upper levels have Acheulean implements. Does this mean that the strip along the eastern Mediterranean was a veritable hominid highway? This has been proposed, and we return to this idea in the next chapter.

Although there are bits and pieces of hominid presence along the way, let's concentrate on a few easterly destinations of hominids. These probably were not actually planned destinations, and I correct that notion shortly. We discuss the appearance of hominids in Europe in the next chapter. Current evidence indicates that Europe lagged behind Asia, but it could have been populated by hominids in the range of 500–750 K.Y.A..

These hominids will link us to later European groups. Here we consider three locations, two known for a long time and one that just came into the news.

Java Bound

The first of these places was Java in Southeast Asia. The island chains extending from Southeast Asia at the time of hominid movements would have been connected with land bridges. Sea levels were lower due to glacial buildup.

So hominids at this time likely did not need boats or some other means to cross large, open areas of water. They probably walked it.

As you recall from earlier mention, the fossils on Java were discovered by Eugene Dubois toward the end of the nineteenth century. We already noted that the fossils were originally called *Pithecanthropus erectus* but are now classified as *Homo erectus* from Java.

The sites containing this fossil and related forms have not been securely dated yet. But there is one such date indicating *H. erectus* on Java about 1.8 M.Y.A. This is really astounding because it puts the departure from Africa much earlier than now thought.

Few stone tools have been found on Java in association with *H. erectus*. And these are not Acheulean bifaces; they may relate to the

> **Paleofacts**
>
> When global temperatures drop, ice sheets or glaciers grow and lock up more of the total water present on Earth. This means that ocean and sea levels are lowered, which exposes more of Earth's surface. The opposite takes place when global temperatures rise. A series of these glacial and interglacial episodes occurred during the Paleolithic period.

> **Paleoquest**
>
> An intriguing proposal is being made that *H. erectus* in Java actually evolved from an earlier australopithicine ancestor. This ancestor would have left Africa around the 2 M.Y.A. mark. Obviously, further study needs to be done on this idea.

chopper-chopping tools found in China during the same time period. We cover the China situation next. This story is full of drama, involving a world war and missing fossils.

The Bone Cave in China

China entered the fossil hominid news early, about the same time of the discovery of the Taung Child in Africa in the 1920s. At a very well-known cave site called Zhoukoudian (you will see variant spellings of this), partial skeletons of some 40 individuals were recovered from within cave deposits. Animal bones were also recovered, including those of saber-tooth tigers. Their discoverer, an anatomist named Franz Weidenreich, made an extensive study of the hominid fossils and reported on them in a major publication.

Franz Weidenreich's book on the missing Homo erectus *skulls from China.*

(Scott Brish/Leslie Harlacker)

THE NATIONAL GEOLOGICAL SURVEY OF CHINA

IN COOPERATION WITH

THE NATIONAL RESEARCH INSTITUTE OF GEOLOGY OF THE ACADEMIA SINICA,
INSTITUTE OF GEOLOGY OF THE NATIONAL ACADEMY OF PEIPING,
THE GEOLOGICAL DEPARTMENT OF THE NATIONAL UNIVERSITY OF PEKING,
THE GEOLOGICAL SURVEY OF KWANGTUNG AND KWANGSI,
AND
THE GEOLOGICAL SURVEY OF HUNAN

Palaeontologia Sinica

BOARD OF EDITORS:

T. H. YIN (CHAIRMAN), T. ᵔ CHOW (SECRETARY)
A. W. GRABAU, J. S. LEE, Y. C. SUN, C. C. YOUNG, T. K. HUANG

NEW SERIES D. No. 10   WHOLE SERIES No. 127

THE SKULL OF SINANTHROPUS PEKINENSIS;

A COMPARATIVE STUDY ON A PRIMITIVE HOMINID SKULL

BY

FRANZ WEIDENREICH

WITH TABLES I-XXXVIII AND PLATES I-XCIII

PUBLISHED BY THE GEOLOGICAL SURVEY OF CHINA
PEIPEI, CHUNGKING, DECEMBER, 1943

古生物誌
地質調查所

For Sale at the Office of
G. E. Stechert & Company, 31–33 East 10th Street, New York, N. Y.

PRINTED IN U. S. A.
LANCASTER PRESS, INC., LANCASTER, PA.

How very fortunate this was for the budding science of paleoanthropology. It turns out that just before the breakout of World War II, the *H. erectus* fossils (which at the time were called *Sinanthropus pekinensis*) were packed up in trunks and readied to be shipped out of China. The fossil-laden trunks apparently got to a port on the Sea of

China and then disappeared. To this day, there is no clear explanation of what happened to the fossils.

The value of Weidenreich's report with its detailed drawings of all of the missing Zhoukoudian fossils peaked in paleoanthropological stock. Subsequently, more hominid fossils have been recovered from the deep cave site.

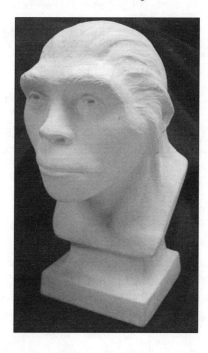

What Homo erectus *from China might have looked like.*

(Leslie Harlacker/Scott Brish)

The physical appearance of *H. erectus* from China does not differ to a great degree from the features listed earlier. The skulls do tend to have a raised area that runs down the center of the top of the head, called *sagittal keeling*.

What about the tools found with *H. erectus* from China? They have been called chopper-chopping tools, but there is no clear evidence for whether they were used as core tools or perhaps were sources of flake tools. In any case, they are not considered to be of the Acheulean hand-ax style; they are more in the mode of Oldowan-type tools.

Anthrolingo

Sagittal keeling refers to a raised area along the center of the skullcap. It should not be confused with a sagittal crest found in apes and robust australopithecines. The crest has jaw muscles attached to it, but the keel doesn't.

How long ago were hominids in China? The estimated date for Zhoukoudian is only about 500 K.Y.A. Now there is one of those relative statements that hardly sinks into consciousness. How could 500 K.Y.A. be "only"? Well, other sites in China are fairly securely dated to more than 750 K.Y.A. Some are perhaps substantially much older, but their dates have not yet been confirmed.

Let's look at one more location that extends the distribution of *H. erectus* into a rather unanticipated area of the world: Russia?

Paleofacts

Previously, it was thought that Acheulean hand-axes were geographically distributed to the East up to a Movius Line, which separated off the Far East. Hand-axes were believed missing from the eastern side of the line. But more recent discoveries and restudy indicates that hand-axes do appear in China. This means that the Movius Line (named for a prominent Harvard archaeologist) is blurring.

North to Russia

In a site called Dmanisi, in the country of Georgia, Russia, major discoveries of both hominid fossils and stone tools were found in the 1990s. The most recent was in 1999, so this is sort of hot off the presses here. Researchers actively working with the fossils propose that the hominids most closely resemble the African species called *Homo ergaster*. Recall that we have lumped this species in with *Homo erectus*, until better evidence requires that it be separated. Its brain capacity is estimated at about 800 cc, at the lower end of *H. erectus*. The associated tools are made of a form of volcanic rock called basalt and consist of chopperlike implements along with flakes and scrapers. We discuss the scraper tool type more fully in the next chapter. These are the most significant facts about the Dmanisi finds:

◆ They indicate that the early migrants out of Africa left before Acheulean hand-axes were developed.

◆ Given the assigned K-Ar date of 1.7 M.Y.A., the hominid migrants must have left Africa earlier than previously thought.

The Dmanisi story is hot off the presses and into the fray. That's what keeps human prehistory so vital. This is the field of study for those who like the uncertainty of what is going on, for those who enjoy the excitement of new discoveries, of broken bones and chipped stones, and for those who don't mind being confounded and confused. Speaking of uncertainty, it's time to deal with the perplexing questions of why did hominids left Africa at all.

> **Paleoquest**
>
> The very early dates for both Dmanisi and Java raise the question that possibly even later australopithicines spread from Africa. This proposal needs further study.

Push from Homeland or Pull to New Land?

Remember way back in Chapter 2 when I said that prehistory was studied because it was there? Well, let me play off that comment here. Leaving Africa for the early hominids may have been mostly unintentional and unplanned. They did move about as gatherers and hunters, although their hunting was mostly limited to small animals and scavenging. So it was quite natural for their sojourns to carry them on and beyond a confined region. Generations of movements could have led the groups into the new lands of the Old World of Eurasia.

Travel of this sort is in the category of going nowhere in particular, but going somewhere because it was there.

If the spread from Africa was not planned, migration would not be a suitable term to apply to the expansion of hominids out of Africa. Migration usually implies some intention to go from one place to another.

> **Paleofacts**
>
> Estimating the sizes of hominid populations falls within a study called paleodemography. Knowing this information is highly valuable for constructing theories of population growth and movements. Unfortunately, there were no census takers back then.

To be sure, these groups must have had the wherewithal to carry out their territorial expansions, unintended as they might have been. I am speaking of their cultural preparedness, as in tool kits, and also unknown social factors such as leadership. We can add in some possibility of their ability to use fire for desired purposes. And there is the presumption that *H. erectus* was biologically adapted to the colder temperatures they encountered as they moved northward.

> **Paleoquest**
>
> An important matter to investigate is the extent to which there was also movement back into Africa from Eurasia—sort of a reverse migration. This must have occurred and deserves continued research effort.

Two other possible reasons for the movement out of Africa are more along the lines of intended migration:

♦ A sense of adventure and opportunity that might stretch out ahead. This would be a pull force.

♦ A necessity to move due to increasing population growth and greater pressure on limited resources. This would be a push force.

Anthrolingo

Diffusion refers to the spread of cultural ideas and goods from one group to the next, with or without the accompaniment of persons.

The fact that some sites show Oldowan-type tools followed later by Acheulean hand-axes gives a hint that probably successive movements of groups took place. As an alternative, there might also have been a dispersion and *diffusion* of new tool-making technologies without the actual transfer of groups.

The next chapter covers the action and changes that took place throughout Eurasia and Africa in the time period of about 0.5 M.Y.A. The next big event? The origin of our very own species, *Homo sapiens*.

The Least You Need to Know

♦ Acheulean bifaces begin to replace Oldowan core tools.

♦ *Homo erectus* was found in all of the Old World.

♦ Europe seems to have been settled last.

♦ Limited evidence suggests the controlled use of fire.

♦ Spreading out from Africa may not have been through planned migrations.

10

Branches of Our Family Tree

In This Chapter

♦ The face of Archaic *Homo sapiens*

♦ Europeans at the dawn

♦ Middle Pleistocene Asians and Africans

♦ The classic Neandertal

♦ Neandertal genetics

The pace of human evolution quickens as we enter into the last half-million years of prehistory. As documented in the last chapter, hominids began to inhabit the other two parts of the Old World: Asia and then Europe. The other half of the world, the Western Hemisphere, has its day, but not for some time into the future. The central theme of this chapter is to present the major hominid fossil finds from the Far East to the British Isles. We look at their defining physical and morphological features, and we pretty well finish off our tracing of major trends in human evolution. We consider just how different these human groups are and whether they should be recognized as separate species.

The time period covered in this chapter is from roughly 0.8 M.Y.A. to 125 K.Y.A., although we jump a little more forward to present the Neandertals in physical form. This span of time is called the Middle Pleistocene, but it still remains completely contained within the Lower Paleolithic. Recall that the Lower Paleolithic makes up around 90 percent of human prehistory. In the next chapter, we continue with Neandertals, but this time with their culture. Following that, we take up the veritable explosion that takes place in cultural evolution. There are some spectacular new developments to announce and a far richer prehistoric record to describe. But for now, the Archaic *Homo sapiens* are grabbing our attention.

Archaic *Homo sapiens*

Archaic means ancient, but when coupled with *Homo sapiens*, it means trouble in River City. Some paleoanthropologists don't recognize the taxonomic qualification. Either they are *H. sapiens* or they are not. And if they are not, then they are *H. erectus*. A third position is that those fossils assigned to Archaic *H. sapiens* are actually separate ancient species that existed before the appearance of modern *Homo sapiens*. So what's a person to do?

First, some of this dispute centers on a basic problem of taxonomic classification, mentioned in Chapter 4. A classification is a static naming system that is imposed on a dynamic evolutionary process. So while a classification attempts to reflect what we think we currently know about evolutionary relationships, it cannot be made to reveal evolution in motion. And the Middle Pleistocene happens to be a rather animated time period, in the sense of multiple hominid groups. But culture tended to keep these groups from diverging biologically.

Culture in this time period became important—maybe the major means for adapting to the environment. So while human groups may go off in different map directions and encounter new and differing conditions, they share basic cultural means, such as their common tool kits. This helps maintain their similarity. Culture is a cohesive force here as ideas and goods *diffuse* across groups.

> **Paleofacts**
>
> Culture is sometimes defined as a buffer between people and their environment. It provides the means to quickly accommodate environmental changes without having to undergo a long-term and extensive biological adaptation.

> **Anthrolingo**
>
> **Diffusion** is the culture process of transmitting ideas, language, and material items from one group to the next. It can help to explain similarities among cultures.

That Archaic Look

At this point, it is time to put a face on the Archaic *Homo sapiens*. Here's a list of their most recognizable features:

- Large heads, with average cranial capacity larger than that of *H. erectus* but smaller than that of modern *H. sapiens*

- Skulls that are low and that have backward-sloping foreheads, as contrasted with modern skulls that are higher and that have bulging or rounded foreheads

- Large, rugged-looking browridges

- Large jaws and teeth

- Absence of a projecting chin, with a chin area that slopes inward

- Body size that is pretty much within the modern range, but tending toward greater muscularity and ruggedness

You will see some photographs of Archaic *H. sapiens* coming up. For now, we want to point out that in terms of hominid trends, the Archaic *H. sapiens* are just a little shy of average modern brain size and have larger teeth and a much more rugged facial appearance, due largely to the massive browridges.

Paleofacts

The function of large browridges has been studied, and they appear to relate to strengthening the forehead especially during heavy chewing. The browridges are pronounced in *H. erectus*, Archaic *H. sapiens*, and Neandertals, all of whom have big jaws and teeth. They do not, as was once claimed, serve as built-in sunshades or bony protectors for eyes from club-wielding enemies.

Let's now have a look at the map of Middle Pleistocene hominids, starting with Europeans. They were left out of the last chapter, so we will catch up with their prehistory here.

The First Europeans

A number of fossil and tool finds have been used to claim great antiquity for hominid occupation of Europe. Most of these just haven't been confirmed. The problem is a lack of chronometric dating for much of Europe. Is this good or bad? Well, there haven't been any volcanoes in Europe, at least not in the time period we are interested in. But then for prehistorians, this means not having very precise dating methods. One method that has been very useful is *magnetic reversal.*

Anthrolingo

Magnetic reversal, or **archeomagnetism,** is a dating method based on Earth's magnetic poles that reverse at random intervals about every 200,000 years. Iron particles in rocks record the position of the North and South poles both when they are normal and when they are reversed. This variation builds a sequence that can be compared with a "master sequence" to arrive at a date.

Magnetic reversal dating has been applied to a site called Atapuerca in Spain that contained hominid fossils and associated stone tools. This testing yielded a date of 780 K.Y.A. So here we have hominids in Europe in the vicinity of a million years ago. For now, this places Europe later than Asia on the scale of hominid occupation.

Paleoquest

Atapuerca sets up the kind of question that is common in prehistoric research. When there is a change in artifacts, such as the progression from Oldowan to Acheulean tool kits, does this mean that a new human group replaced the older group? Or did the original group itself develop the new technology with no intrusion from outside?

Paleofacts

Cranial capacity of normal modern humans ranges from less than 1,000 cc to more than 2,000 cc. At the lower end of brain size, Anatole France (1844–1924), an eminent French writer, had a brain that weighed only 1,017 grams.

Yet, basically the same tool kit is found at Atapuerca as in Asia. This is in the Oldowan style, with chipped cores and flakes. Acheulean hand-axes are still far into the future; some were discovered at more recent levels at Atapuerca.

Now, what about the hominid fossils? If you said they were *Homo erectus,* you would probably be partially correct. Given the early date of 780 K.Y.A., that would be very early for *Homo sapiens,* even of the Archaic variety. That's what the discovers who named the form *Homo antecessor* thought. There was no ambiguity as to what they had in mind with that name: To them, this was the species that gave rise to *H. sapiens.* Still unanswered is the question of where *H. antecessor* originated and whether there are even earlier *H. erectus* hominids yet to be found in Europe.

Unfortunately, there aren't enough diagnostic *H. antecessor* fossils to make adequate comparisons with either *H. erectus* or *H. sapiens.* For example, there is no estimate of cranial capacity, which might help to clarify its evolutionary position. The average cranial capacity of the Archaic *H. sapiens* is 1,350 cc, which is virtually the same as ours. But remember that averages hide underlying variation, so some Archaic *H. sapiens* fall close to the 1,100 cc mark.

Other reported fossil or tool sites were found in Europe between Atapuerco at 780 K.Y.A. and 500 K.Y.A., although we won't deal with them here. We do want to rejoin European prehistory when a flurry of fossils show up around 400 K.Y.A.

Later, but Still Very Early Europeans

If *Homo antecessor* from Spain turns out to be the ancestor of later Archaic *Homo sapiens*, this would be one of the finest examples of reproductive success known in prehistory. Of course, that statement plays a little loose with the rules of reproductive biology. Remember we said earlier that we really don't know whether any of the hominid fossils even had children. But they do represent groups some of whose members were parents, or we wouldn't be here, right?

Here is a partial list of putative descendents of *H. antecessor*:

- Swanscombe, from Britain, dated at 400 K.Y.A.

- Arago, from France, dated at 400 K.Y.A.

- Steinheim, from Germany, dated at 300 K.Y.A.

- Atapuerca, from Spain, dated at 300 K.Y.A.

- Petralona, from Greece, dated at 200 K.Y.A.

European Archaics from Steinheim, Germany, and Swanscombe, England.

(Scott Brish/Leslie Harlacker)

None of these dates is set in stone, so to speak. That's why they appear so nicely rounded off. But they are probably in the right chronological ballpark.

For making comparisons, and for their high diagnostic value, the Archaic European fossils are all skulls, or skull bones, except for those at Atapuerca. This is one of the rare and highly fortunate discoveries of multiple individuals. By multiple, I mean that 30 individuals have been found so far, and more are likely to be recovered. By prehistory standards, that number could be considered astronomical.

> **Fieldnotes**
>
> Another of the Archaic European discoveries offers a lesson in just how unpredictable finding fossils is and how luck plays a big part. The Swanscombe find consists of three bones of the braincase of a single individual. In 1935, the occipital bone (the very back part of the skull) was found; the very next year, the left parietal bone (the side of the braincase) turned up. That's pretty fortunate. But wait: In 1955, the right parietal bone was found in the same gravel pit. This might be called luck, but persistence, along with smart hunches, may also have been key to this extraordinary discovery.

Middle Pleistocene Asians

From Europe, we now head eastward and mention some of the more prominent fossils that established the Asian branch of Archaic *Homo sapiens*.

Here's the list:

♦ Dali, from China, dated at 300 K.Y.A.

♦ Yingkou, from China, dated at 280 K.Y.A.

♦ Narmada, from India, dated at 300 K.Y.A.

♦ Ngandong, from Java, dated from 200 K.Y.A. to 50 K.Y.A.

We noted that the Far East (China) and Southeast Asia (Java) had earlier hominids in residence, of the *H. erectus* species. So it is logical at this point to assume that Dali and Yingkou (China) and Ngandong (Java) are continuing the *H. erectus* line as later descendents.

> **Paleoquest**
>
> The Ngandong skull series (there are 11 of them) have been more recently considered to be possible late-term survivors of *Homo erectus*. That case would be even stronger if the date of 50 K.Y.A. is correct, instead of the earlier assigned date of 200 K.Y.A. Straightening out the date is needed now.

What's new is that India has entered the prehistory books for the first time. Many very important fossils of early primates have been found in India and surrounding regions. But the fairly recent find at Narmada sends out a Paleolithic signal that this area, too, has participated in hominid evolution.

Now let's return to Africa to complete our survey of Archaic *H. sapiens*.

Middle Pleistocene Africans

There's no difficulty establishing continuity here. Africa has had hominids for at least the past 3.5 M.Y.A., and probably for a couple more million years before that. Here's a shortened group of forms assigned to the Archaic *Homo sapiens* category in Africa:

◆ Bodo, from Ethiopia, dated Middle Pleistocene

◆ Lake Nduto, from Tanzania, dated at 400 K.Y.A.

◆ Kabwe, from Zambia, dated at 300 K.Y.A.

The Bodo skull deserves special mention. Upon close study, it was revealed to have striations, or fine grooves, in several places. These have been interpreted as cut marks made by someone who intentionally removed flesh from the skull with a stone implement. Other speculation can be held in abeyance. It is also of note that there appear to be traces of fire at the Bodo site. More withheld speculation is probably in order.

The Kabwe skull from Zambia (formerly known as the Broken Hill Skull from Rhodesia) has received considerable attention from paleoanthropologists. At one time, Kabwe was called a neandertaloid, as sort of reference to being like a Neandertal but outside Western Europe. That's before its date of 300 K.Y.A. removed it from the time period of Neandertals, which runs from about 150–35 K.Y.A. Even though it is not connected to Neandertals, Kabwe serves as a segue to that discussion, which comes up next.

Classical Neandertals

If any of the earlier hominids made the general public aware of our ancestors, both in fact and in fiction, it was the Neandertals. They are the "cave men" of cartoons and film. They usually are portrayed as hairy, brutish, stoop-shouldered, bent-kneed clouts with a big club in one hand and dragging a female of its kind by the hair in the other hand. Some of this unjustified portrayal may have stemmed from descriptions of one of the first nearly complete skeletons of Neandertals. A *paleopathologic* study showed that the skeleton was of an elderly male, who during his life had broken some bones, was afflicted in his later years with osteoarthritis, and as a child suffered from rickets. These conditions probably would

Anthrolingo

Paleopathology is the science that studies skeletal and dental material for signs of birth defects, disease, injury, and other such health problems afflicting ancient humans and prehumans. One of these conditions is osteoarthritis.

have left him bent in body. But this was his medical history, not traits of Neandertals in general.

We will try to correct erroneous notions regarding Neandertals. First, we present a list of some of the major Neandertal fossils and then describe their main physical features. That will do for the biology part. The next chapter is devoted to Neandertal behavior. So much has been written and surmised about Neandertals that it seemed only right to give them a lot of space here—even if, as some have proposed, they were a side branch in human evolution and did not contribute to our later modern *Homo sapiens* development.

First, here is the list:

- Neandertal, from Germany, dated at 50 K.Y.A. The first Neandertal fossil was found in 1859.

- La Ferrasie, La Chapelle, La Quina, and Le Moustier, all from France, dated 70–40 K.Y.A.

- Saccopastore (100 K.Y.A.) and Mt. Circeo (55 K.Y.A.), both from Italy.

- Forbe's Quarry, from Gibraltor, dated at 50 K.Y.A.

- Krapina, from Croatia, dated at 130 K.Y.A.

We can add to the list these forms from the Middle East:

- Shanidar, from Iraq, dated at 50 K.Y.A.

- Tabun (150 K.Y.A.), Kebara (60 K.Y.A.), and Amud (45 K.Y.A.), all from Israel

The first group, from Western Europe, has been referred to as the Classic Neandertals. The second group is recognized as Neandertals from the Middle East. There is general agreement that Neandertals, especially the Classic Neandertals, are descendents from an earlier *Homo erectus* or from the recent find of *Homo antecessor* in Spain. It perhaps is a curious twist of fossil discovery that, so far, no Neandertals have been found in Spain.

What did the Neandertals look like? Certainly, there was variation. You couldn't say, "If I've seen one Neandertal, I have seen them all."

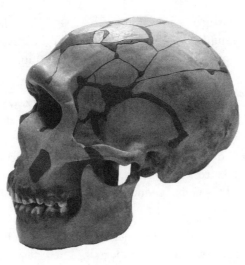

Classic Neandertal from Western Europe.

(Leslie Harlacker/Scott Brish)

Here's a list of the most prominent physical traits of Classic Neandertals:

♦ Long, low skulls with sloping foreheads

♦ Large browridges

♦ Development of the back of the skull, called an *occipital bun*

♦ Prognathic (projecting) faces, with a large nasal (nose) region

♦ Large set of teeth

♦ Lack of a projecting bony chin

♦ Large cranial capacity—average about 1,500 cc.

♦ Muscular, with a short and stout body build

It should be emphasized that not all of these features are present to the same degree in all Neandertals. There is variation, and it is not appropriate to relegate all Neandertals to an unfounded stereotype.

First things first. Neandertals were not stoop-shouldered, nor were they bent-kneed. And I rather doubt that they dragged women about by their hair. They were fully erect bipeds and did not likely differ in any significant way from us

Anthrolingo

Occipital bun refers to the pronounced rounded region of the back of the skull. The bun is seen in Neandertals and may be related to other rugged features of the skull that developed in response to heavy use of the jaws and large teeth. The bun is the area for attachment of neck muscles that might be needed to hold up a large prognathic skull.

with in their standing posture or in walking. To be sure, muscle markings on their bones indicate great strength. This comes into play in the next chapter when we discuss the kinds of behavior they might have been engaged in.

But we can mention another line of reasoning here. We brought up this argument earlier when we considered the possibility that *Homo erectus* was biologically adapted to cold stress because of a large, heavy body build. Neandertals also were exposed to cold temperatures, as glacial advances extended southward and right into the habitats of Neandertal groups. Thus, by the same argument, Neandertal body build may be explained in part by cold stress adaptation. They had short stocky bodies with especially short lower legs. This would reduce skin surface area from which heat would be lost.

This argument has even been given broader support in reference to the projecting face and large nose area observed in Neandertals. These features may have also developed in response to cold stress.

Paleofacts

The projecting face of Neandertals could have housed expanded sinus cavities along the nasal area. This might have insulated the underlying blood vessels, some of which travel to the brain, against cold. Also, the large nose could have provided increased surface area for inhaled air to be warmed and humidified before reaching the lungs.

Fieldnotes

Ethnographic field studies show the use of teeth in chipping stone tools. By analogy, is this what Neandertals were doing with their teeth as well?

All of this discussion of biological adaptation must be tempered with that culture "buffer" that we mentioned earlier. Without doubt, Archaic *H. sapiens* had some material means to protect them from cold temperatures. These would have included some kind of shelter and clothing, none of which has been preserved, unfortunately.

As you might suspect, there are also other explanations in the mix for Archaic *H. sapiens'* dental features. These have to do with the way in which Neandertals might have used the jaws and teeth. We noted that Neandertals had big teeth overall, including their front teeth. Could they have been doing some heavy-duty chewing, or, as some researchers have suggested, did they use their teeth in making tools? If so, this would be a cultural explanation for a biological condition.

From a biological point of view, Neandertals do differ from us. Here's a little game sometimes posed by paleoanthropologists. If a Neandertal man were dressed in a business suit, would you be able to pick him out from other men walking on Wall Street? Recall that I had said that *H. erectus* would probably get at least a second glance due to its highly distinctive features. On the glance meter, Neandertals would then get at least one very long side glance.

The look of a Classic Neandertal.

(Tom McHugh/Field Museum, Chicago. Photo Researchers, Inc.)

One of evolutionary trends that we have been following got sort of stalled in Neandertals. It's the large size of their teeth. These made the face prognathic, or projecting. Large teeth resulted in the lack of a pointed chin and may also account for the extended bun on the back of the skull, as large neck muscles supported the ruggedly built skull.

One trend that did not stall was brain size increase. The average size of the Classic Neandertal brain was even larger than that of modern humans. But then, if brain size is measured relative to body size (remember the brain-to-body-size ratio from a while back), the difference is lost. There is also some basis for arguing that the larger brain of Neandertals did not necessarily result in better functioning. Internal reorganization and improved connections between regions of the brain could have led to further development of modern *H. sapiens*.

Paleofacts

The physical appearance of a "live" Neandertal is obviously the work of an artist who makes use of the underlying bony skeleton. These flesh reconstructions are meant to be treated cautiously, since we really don't know details about "soft-part" anatomy of, say, the nose and ears, or about the amount and distribution of hair. It's sort of like an very ancient forensic case.

Another Species or Not?

Much of this discussion of the differences between Neandertals and modern humans is leading to the inevitable question facing paleoanthropologists of whether they were separate species. If they were, then they should be classified as *Homo neanderthalensis*. But a debate would still arise over whether there was really so much genetic difference that successful mating resulting in children would not have occurred. Remarkably, some genetic evidence is now available to begin to tackle that question.

Analysis of the genetic evidence so far indicates that Neandertals were quite different than modern humans. Does this settle the matter? Not at all. More complete genetic material from the past, called *ancient DNA*, needs to be studied.

We cover this topic of ancient DNA in greater detail in Chapter 13 as we review the highly charged issue of origins of Anatomically Modern Humans (AMH). But a certain fossil find seems to play a part in answering the question of whether Neandertals were a separate species.

In 1998, the fossil of a young child, probably a four-year-old boy, was discovered at a site in Portugal. The find immediately created a stir in the scientific world because the researchers connected with the discovery claimed the boy to be a hybrid between Neandertals and modern humans.

Dates are important here. The estimated date for the fossil, based on the *Carbon-14 dating* method, is 25 K.Y.A. This is several thousand years after it has been assumed that Neandertals were no longer around in person.

Anthrolingo

Ancient DNA consists of genetic material that has been extracted from either bones or teeth of individuals that lived from hundreds to tens of thousands of years ago. Specifically, this DNA is not from the nucleus of the cell, but from the extracellular mitochondria.

Carbon-14 dating is a method that measures the level of radioactivity in a bone or other organic materials. It is useful for dating specimens up to about 75,000 years old.

But now with the hybrid, they would be present in genes. And that would mean that Neandertals could successfully mate with moderns and produce children. Therefore, technically, they could not be a separate species.

Hybrids tend to show a mixture of traits from both sides of the family, and the boy fits that expectation. But it is not clear why these particular traits were involved the way they were. In general, his face and teeth were more like modern boys', but his legs, especially his lower leg, was very short to be of modern proportion.

Opponents of the hybrid proposal state that this was just a stout but modern boy. Looks like this question remains open for now. But before leaving the boy, we should mention that he was probably intentionally buried. That and other humanlike behaviors form the stuff of the next chapter.

We can end this segment on Neandertals with no final answer on their separate species status. That perhaps is the right thing to do because we have yet to describe their cultural behavior. And that might provide additional evidence for making informed decisions.

> **Paleoquest**
>
> It will be necessary to construct new lines of research and thinking to better understand what a cross between a Neandertal and a modern human would look like. The traits mentioned here are not very clear in explaining why the hybrid process worked this way for the boy.

> **Paleofacts**
>
> The leg has two main supporting bones, upper (femur) and lower (tibia). These bones are measured to provide an index of how long the tibia is relative to the length of the femur. A lower index means that the tibia is shorter in comparison with the femur. This is called the Crural Index.

The Least You Need to Know

- Archaic *Homo sapiens* is a transitional form between *Homo erectus* and modern *Homo sapiens*.
- All of the Old World was populated by hominids during the Middle Pleistocene.
- Classic Neandertals are in a class by themselves.
- The debate continues over whether Neandertals were a separate species—and, if they were, whether they were also an evolutionary dead end.

Chapter 11

Neandertal Ways and Means

In This Chapter

- ◆ Neandertal lifestyle
- ◆ Mousterian tool kit
- ◆ Neandertals beyond Europe
- ◆ Intangibles of Neandertal culture
- ◆ What happened to the Neandertals?

Some Neandertals were cave dwellers. But not much more of the popular portrayal of Neandertals holds up to scientific scrutiny. They lived in a time of extreme cold and sparse resources. Naturally, caves would offer some protection, and they also had fire. This chapter describes Neandertals, where and how they lived. Their tool kit, which is expanded beyond the Acheulean, offers some discussion regarding new tool functions. And then there is intriguing evidence for presenting Neandertals in light of uniquely human behaviors, such as the use of symbols, care-taking and compassion, burial of their dead, and a capability of speaking. But were the Neandertals humans? We complete the chapter with another look at their fate in human prehistory. Did they go extinct, or were they us?

Cave Dwellers and Plains Hunters

Neandertals lived during the Middle Paleolithic. Notice that we have finally moved out of the Lower Paleolithic, which accounted for 90 percent of human prehistory. Alternative names of this time period are Middle Stone Age (commonly used for African sites) and the Mousterian. The last name derives from a famous tool-bearing site in France, Le Moustier. For approximate dates of the Neandertals, 150–35 K.Y.A. is often used, although you will also see a cut-off date of 28 K.Y.A. It is good to realize that dates of this sort are meant to be rather flexible.

There is ample evidence that Neandertal groups occupied caves and *rock shelters*. Their cultural and fossil remains have been found in several cave sites in Western Europe, the Middle East, and Central Asia. There are also remains of wooden huts and hearths at a Ukraine site.

Anthrolingo

Rock shelters are shallow caves or cliff overhangs that offer some protection against wind and weather, and perhaps could be successfully occupied and defended against unwelcome intruders.

Usually there is evidence of continued cave occupation over extended time periods. This indicates that they were successful in their way of life. And their way of life was that of hunter-gatherers. Again, in some areas, the cold temperatures and seasons of snow and ice meant that gathering of edible plants, fruits, and nuts would have been highly limited.

Cave dweller home of the Neandertals.

(Volker Steger/Nordstar. Photo Researchers, Inc.)

The Neandertals may have been able to store up some foods for the winter, but there isn't a lot of documentation of this.

A fair abundance of cold-adapted animals to hunt, such as the woolly mammoth and the woolly rhinoceros, would have been available. Their bones have been found at Neandertal sites. But, then, there were also carnivores, such as the saber-tooth tiger and the cave bear, who may have been the ones to accumulate the bones—perhaps even some of the Neandertal bones.

Our picture of Neandertals, fuzzy as it is, is that they lived in small groups, probably around 25–50 individuals, composed of men, women, and children. They gathered food during warm seasons, hunted small and large animals year-round, and moved about as food and other resources dictated.

Neandertal movements would have been somewhat restricted by glaciers and mountains in Western Europe and Central Asia. But they could have crossed open plains and traveled through river valleys. This scenario has played out in more recent hunter-gatherer groups of northern latitudes. We return to the topic in Chapter 17, which covers peopling of the New World across the Bering land bridge.

What did the Neandertals have in their Mousterian tool kit? We have already said that it expanded upon Acheulean tools. But there was also technological continuity, as in still making and using hand-axes. Let's have a look.

> **Paleofacts**
>
> Neanderthals show the first clear evidence of hominid exploitation of seafood in the form of shellfish remains at one site. But this does not confirm the Aquatic Ape Theory discussed in Chapter 5.

> **Paleoquest**
>
> There is an ongoing discussion as to how much Neandertals were active hunters or were even more successful in obtaining animal food from scavenging efforts.

Mousterian Manners

Here's another aspect of continuity. During the making of Acheulean tools, it was discovered that there was less chance of breaking a flake tool if chips were removed before the flake itself was removed from the core. This is called the *Levallois* technique.

The Levallois technique carried over to the Mousterian, and perhaps became even more important. There are more tool types, and presumably more specialized functions of Mousterian tools. Here is a list of many of them:

> **Anthrolingo**
>
> **Levallois** is a tool-making technique that involves preparing the core by taking off chips from a flake tool that eventually is removed intact. The Levallois technique began with Archaic *Homo sapiens* and the Acheulean tool industry.

- ◆ Hand-axes
- ◆ Scrapers of several shapes and sizes
- ◆ Knives
- ◆ Burins
- ◆ Awls
- ◆ Denticulates
- ◆ Spear points

Tools in the Mousterian kit.

(Leslie Harlacker/Scott Brish)

How were they used? By descriptive name, there were tools for cutting, incising, and puncturing (knives, burins, awls); for scraping animal hides and wood (the various kinds of scrapers); and for performing more heavy-duty activities (hand-axes). Finally, there were tools for hunting (spear points). Spear points were attached to wooden shafts, which made them effective in thrusting, but they probably were not thrown with great accuracy.

Mainly, these tools were used to kill and prepare animals. But it might be that the denticulate tools were involved with producing plant fibers, for making mats and containers. Denticulate means that the stone tool has a wavy, toothlike working edge. And there is some thinking that certain tools, like the burin (which has a very sharp angular point), could have been used to make other tools, such as bone needles. The use of the burin reaches a high point in the Upper Paleolithic, which is coming up next.

Hardy has also found evidence that some Mousterian tools were attached to wooden hafts, and may have been used in exploiting birds and plants.

Experiments have been done in making and using these tools in their predicted fashion. More recent ethnographic accounts of the use of some of them have been formulated as well. Both of these offer clearer insight into Paleolithic tool functions.

An ongoing debate rages regarding Mousterian tools. This debate has two sides; some debates in prehistory are polyhedronlike.

Different Tools, Different Groups

On one side of the Mousterian tool argument is Francois Bordes, a prominent French prehistorian, who proposed that different sets of tools actually represent different ethnic groups or populations that replaced earlier ones without much intermixing of the groups. In short, different tool sets means different groups.

Different Tools, Different Functions

Opposing this reconstruction are the American archaeologists Lewis and Sally Binford. They argue that the different tool sets really reflect different activities carried out by the same group but at different times and different locations. In short, different tool sets mean different functional sites— sites where the animals were killed, other sites where their hides were worked on, and still others where tools were made.

Three Times and Out

A more recent interpretation proposes that some of the tool types changed their function as they were reworked and resharpened. If so, here's a good example of some ancient recycling. As we will see later, good raw materials

Fieldnotes

In following the argument posed by the Binfords, what if a house of today were left to ruin and decay for thousands of years, and then was excavated and studied by archaeologists of the future? Well, there would be tools that reflected different activities. There could be kitchen tools, exercise equipment, and garage and gardening tools.

were valuable. And new technologies were developed along the way to reduce waste. This trend culminates in the Upper Paleolithic production of blade tools. More on that shortly.

For now, there continues to be discussion on how much movement of groups explains the different sets of Mousterian tools. Or perhaps they were all made by basically the same group.

Speaking of different groups, let's mention some more Neandertals that were found outside Western Europe, expanding the geographic locations where Neandertals or their Mousterian tools were found. We listed several Neandertal fossils in the preceding chapter.

Neandertals Outside Western Europe

Moving eastward, Middle Paleolithic remains have been found in the Near East at such sites as Tabun, Haua Fteah, and Shanidar. We say more about Shanidar shortly. Going south into North Africa is the important cave site of Jebel Irhoud, in Morocco. It is important because Neandertal sites in North Africa are very rare. Finally, turn north and head all the way to Central Asia, to a Neandertal burial site of Teshik-Tash, in Uzbekistan.

These sites are important for establishing the wide range of successful occupation of the Neandertals. Some of this can be attributed to their well-equipped tool kit. But there is more—much more.

Neandertals Did Not Live by Bread Alone

Neandertals were known to live beyond mere existence. They possessed some of those intangible traits of humans that could be argued to be just as important in gaining a living. And they could have played into the successful presence of Neandertals in the prehistoric record. It's time to review the intangibles.

Symbols and Arts

Our world is filled with symbols, so many that we probably don't even recognize them as such. In a word, we are symbolizers. We have religious symbols, military and patriotic symbols, and symbols peculiar to each of the sciences. Now, of all of the symbols that we have about us, how many would be preserved over the long haul of time? I don't mean in maintaining their present meaning, but actually physically preserved. And if they are, how will meaning be assigned to them by future archaeologists?

The challenge of recognizing prehistoric art is even greater. That's anticipated, given that today there is considerable division and dispute over what constitutes art. How successful can we expect to be for the distant past? These are the kinds of questions now posed in the context of Neandertals some 50,000 or so years ago.

Let's start with a list of objects or artifacts:

- Finely made stone tools

- Perforated teeth and bones

- Incised bones

- Strings of shells

- A bone flute

- Red ocher, associated with Neandertal burials

- Flowers, associated with one Neandertal burial

All of these have been interpreted as evidence of Neandertal creativity and expression of abstract thinking. You might ask how stone tools could be so interpreted. Well, there is the reasoning that tools are made for certain functions. But some of the Mousterian tools *appear* to go beyond necessary function. They have aesthetic qualities presumed intended by the toolmaker.

What about the use of red ocher in burials? We discuss human burials shortly. Red ocher is clay that contains iron, which gives it a reddish-brown color. Is it used as a symbol? Of course, blood comes to mind. Even more precisely, blood outside the body does not retain its brighter red color, but it turns a reddish-brown. But then, the reddish color is decorative, especially in a drab world.

Paleofacts
The "What is art?" question has been extended to our primate relatives. For example, Koko, a gorilla from the San Francisco Zoo, has "painted" nine paintings that are on display at a Florida gallery.

Paleoquest
Some question surrounds whether Neandertals had fine motor skills needed to manufacture some of these objects that require a high level of manual dexterity.

Paleofacts
Sometimes, in a not so charitable vein, it is said that prehistorians who are stumped in trying to determine the function of an artifact assign it to a religious or ceremonial category. Well, that doesn't happen—and if it does, they might be right.

And the flowers, which were found in a Shanidar Cave burial in Iraq? First, the flowers—that is, the pollen that was recovered—indicate that the burial probably took place in the spring. But did they signify something from Neandertal beliefs?

Beliefs of an afterlife, of beauty? Maybe so. But in reality, the pollen could have been carried by burrowing animals after the burial. Or, and please take this for the sake of completeness, flowers might have helped to mask the odor of a deceased body. It's that kind of thinking that grounds researchers in reality.

Finally, let's consider the bone flute. The object is a portion of a bear's thigh bone found in Slovenia in the 1990s. It is dated between 67 K.Y.A. and 43 K.Y.A. This places it squarely within the Middle Paleolithic and the time of the Neandertals. The natu-

---

Paleoquest

The debate continues over whether the holes on the bone actually represent a musical scale or perhaps were chewed by some animal.

---

rally hollow bone had several fashioned holes at fairly precise distances apart; they seem to match up with a musical scale. And there you have a bone flute. Well, you do have a controversy of just what this object is. And the discussion goes on.

From one controversy to the next. That seems to be the underlying theme of this chapter.

Acts of Compassion

Health problems of many kinds afflicted Neandertals just as they afflict us today. Of course, there are certainly differences in the kinds of diseases present now. For example, currently there is a much higher prevalence of infectious diseases that require dense populations for continued transmission. In the day of Neandertals, who lived in small, widely scattered populations, infectious disease was probably not a great cause of sickness or death. But, in general, there might have been higher risks in Neandertals of injury and death due to accidents. And then a highly strenuous lifestyle likely took a heavy toll on Neandertal bodies.

As mentioned in the last chapter, paleopathologists examine skeletal and dental remains for possible injuries and disease. Here's a partial list of medical conditions seen in Neandertals that have been identified through paleopathological research:

Anthrolingo

Osteoarthritis is inflammation of bone that leaves several telltale signs on skeletons, especially in the joint areas. It can severely hinder normal activities.

- Highly worn teeth, with one jaw missing most teeth

- Man with a withered arm and blind in one eye

- Skeletons with severe *osteoarthritis*

- Skulls with multiple fractures

It doesn't take a board-certified physician to conclude that the first three of these are not necessarily life threatening—at least, not to us today. Of course, all of these Neandertals did die at some point. And they all got buried. We take up that topic next. But there are reasons to think that the individuals suffering these conditions did live in spite of them. Now, the question here is, would the Neandertals have been as fortunate to survive without assistance and care?

Once again, there are at least two sides to the controversy of interpretation. Of course, some claim that those individuals listed received support from other members of the group. Therefore, this would be evidence of compassion on the part of Neandertals.

But there is an undercurrent of displeasure from the side of those who oppose interpreting the evidence for compassion in Neandertals. It has to do with who is capable of caring for himself or herself, in spite of old age or disability. They point out that elderly and disabled persons often continue to be productive and contributing members.

Other studies show how important elders are in both assisting in the care of their grandchildren and in serving as repositories of important historical information. They may have already experienced some crises that reoccur and may have had knowledge of how to resolve them.

Once more, we leave a matter unsettled. I am not so sure that there is strong resistance to the notion that Neandertals actually possessed compassion for each other. The opposition is mainly against the evidence that has been used to support it. More firm evidence may or may not be forthcoming. Are you ready to dig into another Neandertal controversy?

Fieldnotes

Continuing research on the "grandmother hypothesis" proposes that families who involve grandmothers in the care of children have greater reproductive success than families that don't.

Grave Decisions

Up to the time of Neandertals, all of the recovered hominid fossils came from sites of some unknown ending for the deceased. There was the *Australopithecus afarensis* "First Family" from the Hadar site in Ethiopia that might have all drowned. Likely many of the other hominids met similar fates due to accidents, mishaps, or "death by carnivore." But Neandertals are the first to show solid evidence of intentional burial of deceased individuals.

I want to cover one burial site in more detail because it has so many insightful elements to Neandertal life and death. This is the Shanidar cave site in Iraq. The site actually contains bones of nine individuals. They were covered with pollen, which could mean they were originally buried with fresh flowers. Then there was this man, the one with severe arthritis, a missing part of one arm, and a damaged eye socket that left him blind. None of these conditions was recent, and the injuries showed signs of healing. But he eventually died and was buried. Why?

Here, we could invoke our own understanding of human burials, with all of its religious and sentimental attachments. How much of this can be imparted to Neandertals? Did they think so highly of the once-living persons that they gave them respectful burials. Did they have a concept of afterlife? Of a spirit or soul? Was there a supernaturally based belief system? You probably are becoming impatient with my inability to make clear-cut decisions on these grave questions. But I don't see it possible to go very far beyond the facts. And the fact is that Neandertals buried their dead. Talk about jumping from the frying pan and into the fire, we now go to one more issue surrounding Neandertals: talking.

> **Paleofacts**
>
> Intentional burials by the Neandertals enhanced the possibility of preservation and also increased the completeness of the skeleton recovered.

Talk the Talk

Much of what we have been saying about Neandertals possibly using symbols and making art objects, demonstrating compassion, and having extra corporeal reasons for burying their dead cries out in support for their ability to think big thoughts and communicate them via articulate speech. In short, did Neandertals talk? Let's consider this question by first looking at the anatomical evidence.

This Vocal Apparatus Is Made for Talking

Over numerous years, many studies, and claims and counterclaims, the evidence is coming down on the side that Neandertals had a vocal anatomy that would not have restricted its speech capability. That is the ability to make vowel and consonant sounds. Perhaps a clinching piece of evidence was the discovery of a Neandertal *hyoid bone* that was just like ours.

> **Anthrolingo**
>
> The **hyoid bone** sits at the base of the tongue. It's U-shaped and is important for supporting the tongue while producing recognizable speech sounds.

We mentioned earlier that brain endocasts are not reliable indicators of brain function. But the limited evidence showing left side enlargement, where the language areas are located, supports the contention that the brain was developed to a level that would make spoken language possible. Of course, many other aspects of brain organization and neural functioning might not have been fully developed in Neandertals.

The upshot is that while Neandertals may not have had the exact anatomical structures or brain function that is found in modern humans, they likely would have been able to carry out a relatively efficient form of spoken language. If that is true, the next section is mainly useful for confirming how spoken language entered into Neandertal activities.

> **Paleofacts**
>
> One study contends that a vocal tract capable of carrying out spoken language could have been present in hominids at least by 400 K.Y.A. If that's the case, the argument shifts from Neandertals and back to earlier Archaic *Homo sapiens*.

Speaking Up

Stone toolmaking is one activity that researchers believe might have required some fairly precise communication skills. A second area of Neandertal life in which spoken language could have found fertile ground for development was in hunting and gathering activities. If you think about it, much of our language is full of words for naming objects. We literally label our total environment with nouns, some proper and some not-so-proper.

When giving out directions, our hand/arm and eye gestures are accompanied by verbal details. Transfer these activities back to the Neandertals, and there again is good reason to suppose they, too, had begun to build a vocabulary of object names and crucial information for imparting directions and planning daily and future activities.

> **Paleofacts**
>
> Another use for fire during the Middle Paleolithic might have emerged when groups gathered to share the day's events and plan for the next day's activities.

These claims for Neandertal language are obviously tied to logical reasoning, but they are not outlandish. Here's another part of the argument: The origin of human language was not an event, but a process. Without going into the specifics, suffice it to say that elements of spoken language could have been and probably were accumulated over a very long time period. Some of the most basic of these are found in our chimpanzee relatives. And this might mean that they were present before our split from a common ancestor.

> **Paleofacts**
>
> Experiments to teach chimpanzees to speak have been moderately successful in showing how human children learn language and also in shedding light on the origin of human language.

So following this evolutionary argument, language development progressed over the long haul. By the time of the Neandertals in the Middle Paleolithic, many of the elements that we find in our language ability were in place. What's left are some further refinements, at least in the brain, but apparently not much in the vocal tract.

Given the background of this discussion, the time has come to once again face the big question of what happened to the Neandertals. Actually, even a bigger question might be, "Were the Neandertals human?"

End or Beginning?

To recap, Neandertals lived during glacial conditions in small, scattered groups. They probably represented a large extended family. Their subsistence was based on gathering and hunting. While small groups likely interacted on a regular basis, sometimes they were also quite isolated from one another. This happened as groups more or less settled in certain areas that were separated by rivers, hills, and mountains. In brief terms, this scenario sets up the possibility for some small groups to go extinct, to not leave enough descendents to carry the family into the future.

Could this have happened to all of the groups that made up Neandertals living in Europe and the Middle East? I don't think so—at least, not in the manner sometimes portrayed for Neandertal extinction. This would have them quickly and completely disappearing from the hominid scene. Let me expand on the matter of extinction. Here's a list of previously offered reasons that I don't think explain Neandertal prehistory:

 ◆ They lacked the ability, cultural or biological, for adapting to the glacial conditions.

 ◆ They did not have enough brain power to make intelligent decisions.

 ◆ They were all exterminated by modern humans because they lacked the technology (that is, adequate weapons) for winning hand-to-hand combats.

I don't believe that these explanations are logical, and they also are not demonstrated in the prehistoric record. But then, I will now replace them with yet other explanations without hard evidence. However, I think they do make sense.

What I propose is that some portion of Neandertals died out because of their small, scattered, rather isolated groups. I don't know how to accurately estimate the size of this portion, so I will simply say that the remaining portion became "extinct through interbreeding" with other groups moving into the area.

That these incoming groups were entirely modern in physical appearance and were also migrants from well outside the local area, I rather doubt. I do think that some changeover in the physical traits of Neandertals to that of modern humans took place within the evolving groups.

The upshot is that Neandertals were us. That is to say, I think they were a branch on our ancestral tree and that they did contribute to our gene pool. Place that statement in broader evolutionary terms, and I believe that our gene pool also retains contributions from *Homo erectus,* the australopithecines and common ancestors of us and apes. You get the idea. Compelling genetic evidence states that even the most diverse living forms share some of their genetic material as retentions from the very distant past. Even so, I am not quite ready to say that fruit flies are also us.

So, in formal taxonomy, I place the Neandertals in a subspecies category, *Homo sapiens neanderthalensis.* Well, the "h" is back in its proper place, for classification purposes only. This allows some recognition of their physical differences. But now, what about that really big question of their "human" status?

This chapter has reviewed admittedly shaky evidence of Neandertal cultural expression in symbols, art, music, compassion, respect for the deceased, and language. We can add that their subsistence activities would have required a degree of cooperation during gathering and hunting episodes. And then there is the matter of parenting and raising children. In the next chapter, we more fully discuss social groups and bonding. But here, we would have to assume that Neandertal mothers played the major role in the early educational development of their children. One of the consequences of having a large brain, such as found in the Neandertals, is that childhood dependency requires active and long-term parental care and investment, as studied within *sociobiology.*

Putting all of this together indicates to me that Neandertals were "human." I suppose there is ample room to qualify this and say that they were still "becoming human." I am not sure how it will ever be possible to unequivocally demonstrate empathy, altruism, free will, and morality in human prehistory. We carry on this discussion of social behavior, along with some speculations, in the next chapter, which highlights Paleolithic cultural development.

Anthrolingo

Sociobiology is the study of the biological/evolutionary basis of social behavior. Parental investment is one of those behaviors.

The Least You Need to Know

- ◆ Neandertals lived in small, widely scattered, and highly mobile groups mainly in Europe and the Middle East.

- ◆ The Mousterian tool kit and other cultural means of the Neandertals equipped them very well for survival in a cold environment.

- ◆ Neandertals apparently possessed the beginnings of artistic and symbolic expression, which was aided by spoken language.

- ◆ Some of the Neandertals did contribute to our modern gene pool.

- ◆ Neandertals were not a separate species from us.

Part 4

Out of Africa, Again?

The crux of this section is to review two quite different models to explain the origins of Anatomically Modern Humans. Did they evolve from the earlier settlers in Eurasia, or were these settlers displaced and replaced by a second major wave that once again came out of Africa? We will look at the lines of evidence seen in fossils, artifacts, and recently developed genetic analysis.

WELL, DID YOU FIND A WALLET OR A PURSE? PERHAPS THERE'S A BUSINESS CARD THAT MIGHT INDICATE WHERE HE OR SHE CAME FROM.

Chapter 12

Highlights of the Paleolithic

In This Chapter

- Divisions of the Upper Paleolithic
- Blades and burins: making and using them
- Life in the Upper Paleolithic
- Upper Paleolithic art as a many-splendored thing
- Language spoken in the Upper Paleolithic

It's time to celebrate the Paleolithic—the Upper Paleolithic. Some refer to the Upper Paleolithic as a "revolution"; others see it as a "creative explosion." The second refers to the high level of artistic development. The first covers all of the advancements seen, especially in stone tool manufacture. Given the exquisite, delicate stone blades that appear toward the end of the Upper Paleolithic, it is hard to imagine how they could be improved today—short of laser cutting, that is. I am speaking about that basic chipping technique that had its beginning at least 2.5 M.Y.A. The technique reaches it highest level of expression in the final 20,000 years of the Paleolithic.

In this chapter, we describe the tools of the trade for Upper Paleolithic peoples. (Notice that I have stuck "people" in the discussion for the first time.) We then look at their lifestyle, their social behavior, and their considerable talents as artists, and we finish with some final thoughts on the origin of language. Many of the issues and questions that we left with the Neandertals in the last chapter are now resolved in the Upper Paleolithic.

Let's start by framing the Upper Paleolithic within some conventional divisions or timelines.

Dividing Upper Paleolithic Time

The time period of the Upper Paleolithic is variously recorded as 40 K.Y.A. or 30 K.Y.A. to about 10 K.Y.A. While most prehistorians would view it as a continuation of the preceding Mousterian, any connections with Neandertals remain in dispute. One side of the argument has marshaled evidence to show continuity in both tool technology and hominid physical evolution. The opposite side claims that Neandertals abruptly disappeared around 30 K.Y.A. The first view is being followed here. Along this theme of continuity, the Upper Paleolithic then progresses through a series of developments. Here are the divisions for the Upper Paleolithic as seen in Western Europe, most of which are named for sites in France:

- **Perigordian**—Had curved, pointed blades and carved human figurines.

- **Aurignacian**—Had a highly varied tool kit of stone and bone, stone blades made from a new technique, shell and tooth necklaces, and the first evidence of cave art.

- **Solutrean**—Were noted for finely made laurel and willow-leaf spear points that were hafted to wooden or antler shafts, needles as evidence of clothing, and abundant art of many kinds. They're especially noted for the cave paintings in France and Spain.

- **Magdalenian**—Shift to using more bone and antler for tools and art objects. Microliths (small triangular stone blades) were inserted in bone handles. Cave art was highly expressive.

> **Paleoquest**
>
> The Upper Paleolithic divisions are sometimes labeled as "cultures." Continuing research is helping to determine whether the successive changes are due to local development or the result of newly introduced ideas and people.

Let's now take a closer look at some of the tools that typify Upper Paleolithic skill in working stone.

Finer Points

Increasing use of raw materials other than stone occurred in the Upper Paleolithic. Bone and antler were extensively used. Wood also probably was used, but it doesn't preserve as well. So there is a perplexing question of why stone continued to be so important to the Upper Paleolithic toolmakers? There may be the obvious quality of durability and sharpness, which we discuss shortly. But there is also beauty in the material. The Upper Paleolithic folk (now I have introduced "folk" into the mix of humanly labels) chose colorful specimens of jasper, quartz, and beautifully grained flint. And speaking of flint, let's zero in on a couple of the high points in Upper Paleolithic stone tools.

A Sharp Idea

Standing out is an implement called a *blade*. For the first step, blades were made in a fashion similar to that for making flakes, by percussion. But the similarity ends there.

In making a blade, it was first important to get the right kind of raw materials, those that would yield the desired long, thin product. Flint and obsidian worked best. Then blank cores had to be prepared so that when one end was struck, using a "soft" bone or antler hammer, the thin blades flaked off. Now, if efficiency in toolmaking is measured by inches of cutting edge, then these blades set all sorts of Paleolithic records.

Anthrolingo

A **blade** is a thin, very sharp implement that is at least twice as long as it is wide. They were also modified to make other tools such as scrapers, awls, and burins.

A spread of Upper Paleolithic tools.

(Scott Brish/Leslie Harlacker)

Recall that flakes were hammered off cores in rather crude fashion in Oldowan technology. Then flake manufacture greatly improved when the Levallois prepared-core method was developed in the Acheulean and continued into the Mousterian. But even with those improvements, a rather small number of flake implements could be made from a single core.

Now introduce the blade-making technology of the Upper Paleolithic. It has been stated that when measured by the amount of cutting edge derived from a given core, blades production was a hundred times more efficient than that of the earlier technologies. Another kind of advancement also lights up the Upper Paleolithic charts.

Tools That Make Tools

Somewhere in the Upper Paleolithic, it became a custom for people to put on clothes. Of course, it was not a Garden of Eden in northern Europe for the *Homo erectus* and Neandertal groups. So what did they wear? The most reasonable conclusion is that they donned the hides of the animals they ate—well, the bigger skinned forms anyway. These hides were prepared by initial skinning and then scraping to make them somewhat flexible as they dried out.

Anthrolingo

A **burin** is a modified blade that has a very sharp angular point used for gouging and engraving on bone and antler.

Fieldnotes

Thus far, we have described the major tool-making activity as that of chipping stone. Methods of working on stone and other materials that became popular in the Upper Paleolithic were drilling and grinding. These aided in the production of more refined and specially designed tools. They probably also enhanced their beauty at times.

Hides made suitable cloaks, robes, and covers. We know that they assisted survival in the cold environments. But somewhere, someone's mental wheels were turning—turning toward altering robelike covers into body-conforming clothing. I know, I could claim this would have been the first evidence of a tailoring and alteration business.

But one essential tool of the Upper Paleolithic clothing business is the needle. And a second necessary item is thread. The solution to making these was nothing short of ingenious. First, the needle. One of the prominent stone tools in the Upper Paleolithic tool kit was a *burin*, made from a blade.

With a burin, a piece of antler or bone could be gouged with long, closely parallel groves that eventually would produce a thin sliver roughly in the shape of a needle.

Now we have a needle, and we just need the thread. Without actual preservation of any garments or pieces of clothing from the Upper Paleolithic, it requires a reasonable assumption that thread and ties also came from animals. Most likely, this was stringy sinew and ligaments, although some plant fibers may also have been used.

Do you see a pattern here? Needles and thread. Spear points attached to spear shafts. Microliths inserted into bone handles. All of these are examples of composite tools, or tools with two or more parts. Composite tools also reach a high point of development during the Upper Paleolithic. Clearly, we are looking at a brain that is able to generate new ideas and transfer basic innovations across a number of applications.

These simple developments in toolmaking yielded profound advancements in cultural expression. That is, with the appearance of fitted clothing in the Upper Paleolithic, two major goals are achieved. First, there was protection from cold. But then there was an opportunity to express style and individuality. I can't resist the urge to say that the Upper Paleolithic could have seen the first style show. Who knows? These are humans we are dealing with. What do we know or think we know about the lifestyle of Upper Paleolithic people?

> **Paleofacts**
>
> With the manufacture of burins, which had occurred earlier but reached a high point in the Upper Paleolithic, we can recognize that this was a tool for making other tools. So, if we are looking for a distinction, since humans are not the only toolmakers, maybe we are the only animals who make tools for making other tools.

Home Is Where the Hut and Hearth Are

The Upper Paleolithic continues in a gatherer-hunter subsistence mold, but with some changes. First, it appears that dependence on fishing increases. This is seen in the presence of specialized fishing implements. One is the barbed harpoon, which allowed for spearing of fish. And then there were stone weights that might have been attached to fishing nets. There is even the possibility that fish hooks were used.

Fishing then joined hunting and gathering as a three-pronged approach to making a living. In fact, hunting took on bigger challenges in the form of *megafauna*.

Hunting these very large animals required close cooperation and keen communication. An apparent advantage was gained by the Upper Paleolithic hunters when they invented the spear-thrower, also called the atlatl. The spear

> **Anthrolingo**
>
> **Megafauna** ("large animals") refers to the huge herbivores (plant-eating) that went extinct at the end of the Ice Age. An example is the woolly mammoth.

was placed in the atlatl device, which acted like an extended arm. When released, the spear was thrown with tremendous thrust and, with practice, rather precise accuracy.

Cooperation and communication were the very same attributes that would have played into successful gathering activities. And there is solid evidence to suggest that the Upper Paleolithic peoples were actively filling out their food pyramid with collectible plant items, nuts, and berries. A rather interesting source of information about ancient diet is examination of *coprolites*, or fossilized feces of hominids.

Unfortunately, coprolites haven't yet been found in Upper Paleolithic sites. But intensified efforts are being made to find the residue of plant, berry, and nut remains in the Upper Paleolithic, and these efforts are meeting with success. Root residue and berries have been found in hearths at several European Upper Paleolithic sites.

With a broader and possibly more secure food base, Upper Paleolithic groups could have gotten larger and would not have been so mobile, in comparison with the Mousterian. There is evidence of the use of well-built huts, some made of wood and bone, and some dug out of the earth (that is, "pit houses"). During the winter, warmer, dry caves likely still would have been used as residences. And there is abundant evidence for the controlled use of fire, with stone hearths associated with living areas. We can be quite sure that these "fireplaces" provided all of the benefits we listed earlier, most decidedly for cooking and warming. Without intending to romanticize life in the Upper Paleolithic, it does look like home was where the hearth was. And what about the social makeup and organization of Upper Paleolithic groups?

Banding and Bonding

Earlier, I promised that there would be some wide-open speculation. Here it is. Upper Paleolithic social life must have centered on relatively small groups, probably the well-extended family model that we mentioned earlier.

Family life was likely strongly committed to raising children to achieve successful ways of living. To be sure, this would have been a rigorous, at times very risky life to endure. So it would have been important for children to learn their survival skills early and well. And it seems quite reasonable to propose that strong bonds within the family and strong banding among neighboring groups would have promoted the learning process.

We have already noted that children go through a long period of dependency. They do have a large brain that is evolutionarily primed to take in and process a lot of new information. This means that parents need to make a heavy investment in their children's welfare in order to carry them into a time when they can fend for themselves.

Humans generally operate on the reproductive strategy of having relative few offspring but devoting a lot of energy to their survival. And continued survival of our species according to this strategy carried us very well throughout the Paleolithic.

Perhaps in more recent history of our species, reproductive success has gone well beyond an earlier controlled population growth by natural checks of limited food supply, rigors of life, and accidents.

On the other hand, life in the Upper Paleolithic must not have been so terribly bleak or precarious. Otherwise, how do we explain the "creative explosion" of the many forms of Upper Paleolithic art? Well, perhaps some artistic expression is born out of suffering and deprivation.

> **Paleofacts**
>
> Brain growth in children is so rapid that by the time a child is about 12 years old, brain growth is approaching completion. Yet, the body will still go through some major development. So while this adolescent may be able to wear his father's hat, he's not quite ready to fill his father's shoes.

Artistic Expressions

Cave art was first discovered by modern Europeans in France in 1835. Befitting the thinking at the time, it was thought that it had been produced by the Celts or some recent humans. Certainly, there was no idea of ancient humans from tens of thousands of years earlier. But by the 1860s, as we noted back in Chapter 2, the association of extinct animals with stone tools and fossils shifted the opinion toward accepting the antiquity of humankind. Cave art experienced the same shift. And once more credit is due to extinct animals, like the woolly mammoth. These often were the subjects painted on cave walls, and art objects were found with extinct animal bones. Fairly straightforward reasoning won out. Ancient humans once lived with ancient animals.

Types and Techniques

Upper Paleolithic art comes in many forms or types, is produced by varied techniques, and is found in a number of locations. Oh yes, there is a long list of reasons why it might have been produced. Let's have a look at art from these aspects, starting with artistic forms and the techniques used to produce them.

Mobile Art

These objects are easily carried and include figurines and other small sculptures; bones, teeth, and shells that were modified and perhaps strung; musical instruments; and includes tools or implements that have been intentionally enhanced with artistic renditions. Examples might be the finely made Solutrean spear points, some so small and delicate that they probably couldn't be used. Then there are spear-throwers that have intricately carved figures on one end where the butt of the spear point rested.

Rock Art

Examples of rock art could be engravings or *petroglyphs* done on outside rock faces—or, the opposite, it could be bas-relief or raised areas. You can imagine how much work went into carving on rock. It would have required using a stone implement that was harder than the rock being carved. Then, it would have taken countless hours of tedious scraping and pecking before the image finally appeared. And, of course, we can assume that the stone carver had an image or mental template in mind before beginning the project. But then, there might have been a little doodling on stone for practice.

Cave Wall Art

This art also is called parietal art—for good reason, since the term means "wall." This form appears on the inside walls of caves or rock overhangs and includes paintings, bas-relief, and engraved images.

> **Paleoquest**
>
> The delicate, highly fragile Solutrean spear points don't have a clear function, since they would likely have broken if used. Could they have served as models of some sort, or even carried symbolic meaning? Further research might have an answer.

> **Anthrolingo**
>
> **Petroglyphs** ("stone writing") are made by etching or engraving on rock surfaces. This removes the darker outer layer and exposes the lighter underlying surface. The design then stands out. These are distinguished from pictographs, which are paintings done on rocks or cave walls.

Paintings were often done with two main colors: red (from the reddish-brown ochre clay containing iron oxide) and black (from charcoal), or manganese.

Cave art was often done in the deep recesses of limestone caves. These places were devoid of sunlight and maintained a constant, cool temperature. Three of the best known cave art sites are listed here:

- Chauvet, in France. Discovered in 1995. Date: 31 K.Y.A.

- Altamira, in Spain. Discovered in 1868. Dates: 16–14 K.Y.A.

- Lascaux, in France. Discovered in 1940. Dates: 15–10 K.Y.A.

> **Paleofacts**
>
> The use of carbon in cave wall paintings allows dating to be done with the radio-carbon or Carbon-14 dating methods.

Fieldnotes _____

There is also a "faux" Lascaux cave, called Lascaux II. Some years ago, it was noticed that with all of its visitors of tourists and researchers, the cave interior let in light and warm moisture that began to destroy the magnificent paintings with algae growth. So a fake virtual cave was constructed nearby to handle the throngs. Entry to the real cave is sharply restricted, and has allowed only five visitors a day since 1969.

Much older examples of cave art have been found in France, going back to 30 K.Y.A. or so. Art forms have been found throughout Europe, Africa, and Australia in about this same time period. This indicates a cultural tradition that is of extraordinary geographic spread and persistence. Why was it done?

Art for Art's Sake, and More

Here's a list of reasons given for the production of Upper Paleolithic art:

- Instruction and learning

- A record of events (possibly a prehistoric form of writing)

- Enjoyment

- Decoration

- Religious and ceremonial occasions

- Magical "kills" and success in hunting

- Fertility enhancement

(I think this sets the record for highest number of items on a list in this book.) These reasons are not mutually exclusive. That is, they all might apply, not necessarily in a single art form, but across the different forms and at different times.

Ancient Jewelry

Mobile art objects of shells, teeth, and bone fragments were used as body and clothing adornments. These fall into the category of jewelry. Surely, we modern humans are familiar with this kind of artistic expression, although our choices of objects to hang from assorted body parts might differ. And we might well expect that Upper Paleolithic peoples adorned their bodies for many of the same reasons that we moderns do.

Venus Figurines

Human figures or sculptures from the Upper Paleolithic have generated a lot of interest. Some of these, known as Venus figurines, portray women who are likely pregnant, and have enlarged breasts and buttocks. The most famous of these is the Venus of Willendorf, on dramatic display (with lights and music) at the Vienna Museum of Natural History.

A Venus figurine.

(Scott Brish/Leslie Harlacker)

Interpretation of the Venus figurines has run along the lines of fertility enhancement, and recognition and appreciation that all human life springs forth from women.

While this may be true but not directly confirmable, the full range of Upper Paleolithic sculptures of women depicts them in all sizes, from young to elderly, and not always pregnant. There are even a few of men. Some researchers see the bigger picture that figurines were meant to more or less portray the makeup and distribution of the whole social group. Nevertheless, pregnant women did receive greater attention.

Painting the Walls

Then there are the cave wall paintings. Rightfully so, they have attracted much of the attention of serious researchers and the public alike. They are as intriguing as they are aesthetically pleasing. Tapping into some of the reasons listed previously, the wall paintings may have been done to instruct hunting novices, to show pictures of great hunts, or to induct them into a ritual. In general, cave paintings may have served to perform some ritual or ceremonial rites that might have enhanced the hunters' chances of successful outcomes and reduced the risks that they faced during dangerous hunts.

The interpretation that cave paintings had symbolic and ritual meaning stems from their location deep in the dark caves. They were not readily accessible areas. Sometimes there were very narrow passages, and torches were required to dimly light the way and to bath the walls with what must have been an eerily lighted "canvas" for the artists to paint upon.

> **Paleofacts**
>
> For painting tools, the artist's probably used twigs, animal hair, and tufts of animal fur. And they also "blew" pigment onto the walls in outlining objects such as their hands.

But let's not picture a modern art gallery here, with all of its neatly framed pieces. The painted walls of the Upper Paleolithic had incomplete images, animals that overlapped, and strange positioning of other animals. These paintings quite obviously were not for public viewing in the sense that we know.

Subjects ranged from all sorts of animals to humans, to geometric designs and dots and dashes. Was this some ancient counting system? Animals included those that were hunted and likely on the Upper Paleolithic menu, such as deer, bison, and horses. One cave had a record 50 woolly rhinoceros images. But there were also many carnivores, such as cave lions, bears, panthers, and hyenas. The animal figures are realistic and anatomically correct, and sometimes in action poses. Some paintings show bison impaled with spears; these are interpreted as magical kills, in what is known as *sympathetic magic*.

Example of Upper Paleolithic cave art.

(De Sazo. Photo Researchers, Inc.)

Anthrolingo

Sympathetic magic is based on the principle of "like produces like." So "spearing" a painting would bring about an actual spearing during the hunt. This form of magic has a long history of application. For example, it can involve burning in effigy—there is documentation of this going back to the Greeks and Romans, and the practice even occurs today. Success rates are unknown.

An analysis of the human images has led to a proposal that men and women perhaps performed different roles in the group. Of the roughly 100 images studied, men make up three fourths of the subjects and are usually seen individually in action poses. Women are not often pictured in active behaviors and are usually shown within a group.

Paleoquest

Continuing research is needed to completely resolve the question of who made the art—men or women, or perhaps both?

Could these provide a glimpse of how the Upper Paleolithic artists viewed the respective roles of men and women? Perhaps. Given the incomplete and sketchy nature of the evidence, questions interpretations of this sort could be forever destined to remain unresolved. The issue that we end with in this chapter, that seems to have reached a final resolution, is that of human language.

Last Word on Language Origins

Can anyone doubt that Upper Paleolithic peoples possessed a fully competent level of spoken language? Some questions are asked for effect, not answers. Given the range of topics covered in this chapter, from making tools to making art, there is the strongest evidence yet that these kinds of activities would not have been possible without the ability to effectively communicate by word of mouth. No manner of gesturing or "ughing" would have worked very well.

The kind of symboling and abstract thinking that must have gone on in the minds of Upper Paleolithic people in making tools and crafting art had to be on our level. With some sense of finality, we can claim that Upper Paleolithic people had a language. No one that I know is quite ready to tackle the next question of what that language actually looked or sounded like. Perhaps the paleolinguists of the future will do so.

Of course, accepting this conclusion means that we have to go back into the prehistoric record to find language origins. Language just didn't appear full-blown in the Upper Paleolithic. Just as we have tracked trends in hominid physical evolution, language proceeded through a sequence of developmental stages. It was probably tied to that of brain development.

Did Neanderthals speak? What about the Archaic *Homo sapiens*, *Homo erectus*, and the australopithecines? For now, all of these can be covered by the same answer: to a degree. But then, Neandertals had a greater degree of language ability, while the australopithecines had a lesser degree.

That's pretty much the words of an evolutionist who subscribes to the notion that complex development of something—say, language—takes time and change. In the next chapter, we look at the physical evolution that led to Upper Paleolithic peoples. In Chapter 14, we grapple with the hotly debated matter of when and where these people or peoples came from.

Fieldnotes

Exciting new research is proposing that language did not develop in specialized areas of the brain, as has been previously claimed. Instead, it was connected with broader aspects of brain development and may even be tied to such early events in hominid prehistory as the origin of bipedalism. Walking and talking may actually have evolved together.

The Least You Need to Know

◆ Stone toolmaking reached its highest levels of quality and efficiency during the Upper Paleolithic.

◆ Upper Paleolithic peoples seemed to live a more settled and secure life, and in larger groups, than the Neandertals before them.

◆ Partly because of these better living arrangements, the Upper Paleolithic saw an explosive development of several kinds of art forms, most notably cave wall paintings.

◆ Upper Paleolithic art was produced for many reasons, most that we can only speculate about.

◆ Upper Paleolithic peoples had a spoken language.

13

AMH Stands for Something

In This Chapter

- ◆ The face of Anatomically Modern Humans (AMH)
- ◆ The origin of AMH in Africa
- ◆ AMH in Eurasia
- ◆ Biology and behavior interact during evolution

In the last chapter, we celebrated the arrival of the Upper Paleolithic. That seemed fitting, given the great advancements in stone toolmaking, most notably in blades and spear points, and in the creative explosion of art, highlighted by cave paintings and Venus figurines. Now it is fitting to celebrate the appearance of modern humans from the standpoint of physical features. We have been tracking a number of evolutionary trends, and in this chapter they all come to completion. At least there have been no major changes in our bodies for at least the past 30,000 years. According to some, the appearance of modern humans could go back very much earlier.

We begin the chapter by describing typical traits of modern humans, in comparison with Neandertals. But a number of hominid fossils within and beyond Africa must be introduced in order to better understand who the Anatomically Modern Humans (AMH) were and where they came from.

We consider those issues in the next chapter. Here, we also look at some connections between our bodies and our behavior. To an extent, the evolutionary trends in our physical form relate to behavorial changes that took place in our cultural adaptation. In a way, most of this book has dealt with the topic of change and variation, in bones and in stones. Let's begin with a view of modern, but still quite ancient, humans.

Anatomically Modern Humans

First, what's in a label? Well, the label that comes into play here is Anatomically Modern Humans, also known as Anatomically Modern *Homo sapiens*. A third is our scientific name of *Homo sapiens sapiens*. This distinguishes us from the Neandertals, *Homo sapiens neanderthalensis* (or, for those who insist on a distinct species recognition, *Homo neanderthalensis*). Okay enough of the name game. We can reduce much of this terminology to simply using AMH, except when we need to be a little more precise.

The anatomy part of AMH obviously refers to the morphology, which is the size and shape of physical traits. The list of traits characterizing AMH are as follows:

- High, rounded skull

- No bun or extension of the back of the skull

- A forehead that is pretty straight up and down—that is, vertical

- Relatively small browridges

- A flatter, less prognathic face

- A projecting bony chin

- A taller, less robust body build

The look of modern humans. Cro-Magnon from France, dated at 30–25 K.Y.A.

(Scott Brish/Leslie Harlacker)

This trait list is based on the traits that are seen in the poster hominid of AMH, the Cro-Magnon skull from France.

The Cro-Magnon site is dated in the range of 30–25 K.Y.A.

From a somewhat earlier site, another AMH fossil has received a lot of attention. This is the very nicely preserved skull found at Combe Capelle, France, dated at 35–30 K.Y.A. Combe Capelle has a modern-looking skull in general, but it also has somewhat larger browridges and more facial prognathism than seen in modern humans.

From an even earlier site yet comes a skull (actually, a skeleton) from Saint-Césaire, France, dated at 36 K.Y.A. It is a Neandertal, with features such as a sloping forehead, large browridges, a prognathic face, and a sloping chin area. It would be very tempting to conclude that these three fossils from France actually represent an evolutionary sequence, going from Neandertal to modern human. I will resist the temptation for now but succumb to it in the next chapter.

Fieldnotes

Beyond studying traits indicating evolutionary status, paleoanthropologists need to determine the sex, age, medical status, and individual traits of fossils. All of these are not always possible to observe on fossils.

Cro-Magnon, both as an individual and as a representative of AMH, differed from the Classic Neandertal. Cro-Magnon's group was the earliest AMH to appear in Europe, again about 30–25 K.Y.A. But there has been a concerted effort to demonstrate that AMH actually evolved much earlier in Africa and, after appearing in Africa, left the continent to spread across Eurasia and replace those hominid groups already living there. But that gets us a little ahead of the story. We take up this matter of how and when AMH got to Eurasia in the next chapter.

The African Origin of AMH

Here we want to cite the fossil evidence of AMH in Africa. This is a list of the fossils to consider:

- Border Cave, Southeast Africa, dated at 80–70 K.Y.A.

- Klasies River Mouth, South Africa, dated at 90 K.Y.A.

- Omo, Ethiopia, dated at 130 K.Y.A.

- Laetoli, Tanzania, dated at 120 K.Y.A.

Paleofacts

The dates given are estimated by various dating methods, including electron spin resonance (ESR), thermoluminescence, and uranium series dating. We do not take up the details here, but none of these is as accurate as the K-Ar or carbon-14 methods already described. Of course, they are certainly better than having no dates.

So, from about 30 K.Y.A. in Europe, we now go back four or more times that age to reach the AMH in Africa. Even if these are very approximate dates, they still establish that AMH were in Africa well ahead of when they appeared in Europe. Recall that this means that AMH and Neandertals in Europe would have lived over pretty much the same time period. The dates that we gave for Neandertals were about 125–35 K.Y.A.

Fieldnotes

At the Klasies River Mouth site, footprints of AMH were preserved in once soft sand. The site is dated about 115 K.Y.A. Not surprisingly, the footprints were virtually identical with those of modern humans in size and shape.

But, then, the African AMH are not as fully modern-looking as Cro-Magnon or later AMH, either. Of course, there would be quite enough time for these changes to take place.

How do these early AMH from Africa compare to Neandertals and modern humans? The answer to this depends on the twin questions of whether AMH and Neandertals were separate groups but still could and did interbreed. Or did some Neandertals evolve into AMH? We take up these questions in the next chapter. But there are still fossils outside of Africa that we need to introduce to the picture, as if it wasn't kind of messy already.

Paleoquest

An ongoing question is how much genetic change is needed to bring about morphological change. Specifically, how many genes were changed to alter Archaic *Homo sapiens* to Modern *Homo sapiens*?

Paleoquest

Continuing research hopes to find out whether AMH originated in Africa and then spread out to Eurasia, or whether AMH also evolved independently and separately in parts of Europe or Asia.

Looking for AMH Beyond Africa

These sites come into consideration: one in China, one in Eastern Europe, and several from the Middle East.

The Chinese site is known as Liujiang and is dated at 100 K.Y.A. The hominid fossil there is said to be absolutely modern. That makes it an AMH outside Africa, about the same time they were present in Africa. Did they move in from Africa or evolve from pre-existing Chinese hominids? There's no answer for this yet.

Transitions in Croatia

The second site is Vindija, in Croatia. This is a cave site that has yielded many hominid fossils; unfortunately, they are rather fragmentary. The site also had stone tools, some Mousterian and later some Upper Paleolithic. The principal researcher at this site, Professor Fred Smith, concluded that the Vindija fossils were, in fact, intermediate between Neandertals and AMH. Their skulls were less rugged, with smaller browridges, and their faces were less prognathic than seen in the Classic Neandertal. The logical interpretation is that Neandertals did evolve into modern humans in Eastern Europe.

Neandertals and Modern Humans Coexist

And then there are the fossils from the Middle East. They have been categorized as either Neandertals or AMH. First, here are the Neandertals:

- Kebara, Israel, dated at 60 K.Y.A.

- Amud, Israel, dated at 70 K.Y.A.

- Tabun, Israel, dated at 100 K.Y.A.

For physical traits, these all are skulls that appear rather heavy, but they do not have bunlike extensions of the back of the skull; they have rather large browridges, sloping foreheads, and prognathic (projecting) faces. The absence of the bun and some differences around the nose make them different than the Classic Neandertals from Western Europe, but otherwise, they approximate that Neandertal "look."

These are the candidates for AMH status:

- Skhul, Israel, dated at 80–100 K.Y.A.

- Qafzeh, Israel, dated at 92 K.Y.A.

Skhul and Qafzeh are described as "near" AMH, with rounded skulls, nearly vertical foreheads, flatter faces, and developed chins. But their browridges are still rather large, possibly outside the modern range. Now it is time to put together a few points.

First, we must be cautious about the estimated dates for the Israel fossils: They are not as firmly established as would be preferred. But geographic placement is a plus. All of the fossil specimens come from closely clumped nearby caves. So, if the dates are even reasonably accurate, interpretations will have to deal with the fact that they seemed to have lived about the same time period in the same general neighborhood.

The next chapter reviews the significance of the Israel and other Neandertal and AMH fossils. But it should be emphasized here that there clearly was variation in the physical appearance between fossils from different sites and, in the case of Israel, a lot of variation of fossils from closely located sites. Variation may be a key to understanding what was going on as we get closer to modern humans. Speaking of variation, here we want to review the major changes that took place over the long haul of hominid evolution.

We first look at evolutionary trends and then consider how the environment might have shaped our physical appearance, even up to this day. Overall, this is a review of how biology and behavior have interacted during our evolution.

Evolutionary Trends and Biobehavorial Interactions

As you now realize, the fossil record consists of just that: hard, inanimate objects of once living organisms. Yes, they did behave in their ancient lives. And it is a part of the paleoanthropologist's job to infer and reconstruct what kinds of behavior they had engaged in. This can be called a biobehavorial approach.

We can apply the biobehavioral approach in summarizing the main points that occurred in the evolutionary trends leading up to modern humans.

Trend Toward Bipedalism

We know for sure that hominids around 3.5 M.Y.A. had adapted to upright walking. This was the evidence of "Lucy," or *Australopithecus afarensis*. There is some fossil evidence that bipedalism had actually occurred several million years before that. But going back that far places the question right at the doorstep of the time when our hominid ancestors split off from the ancestors that led to the chimpanzee. It will be a fascinating question to observe unfold over the years ahead.

Paleofacts
Genetic information indicates that chimpanzees and humans last shared a common ancestor somewhere between 5 M.Y.A. and 7 M.Y.A. ago. Then their respective evolutionary lines split apart. This estimation continues to be studied.

For now, we should deal with the solid evidence provided by Lucy. Her biology or morphology is clearly adapted to upright walking. Why did she and her direct ancestors assume bipedalism over the locomotor pattern of the shared human-chimp ancestor? Most likely, this would have been a combination of four-legged knuckle-walking on the ground and some arm-hanging and arm-swinging brachiation while in trees. We offer these considerations for the origins of bipedalism, all of which are based on behavioral activities.

From Trees to Savannas

Either the trees left the early hominids or the hominids left the trees, in response to environmental change that reduced a forested habitat. Upright walking may have been a more efficient way for them to move about, find food and mates, and avoid enemies.

Reaching for New Heights

Change occurred in their feeding behavior. This argues that the prehominids were actually standing up on tree limbs and then moved this behavior to the ground as they continued to rely on food in trees. Standing on the ground while reaching into trees led to walking on ground between trees.

> **Paleoquest**
>
> Ongoing research is trying to reconstruct the ancient environments and ecology of early hominids of the Pliocene and Pleistocene. This information is vital in interpreting the evolutionary and behavioral status of hominids.

It's Not Heavy—Carrying Is My New Life

Freeing the forelimbs and hands from locomotion could have promoted their enhanced use for holding, carrying, and performing related activities. Obvious objects to hold and carry are food and babies. Better handling of either of these could have increased the reproductive and survival outcomes for early hominids.

Small Brains and No Tools

We also know with certainty that these earliest hominids, the australopithecines, had small brains, about one third our average brain size. We infer that a small brain did have a bearing on how they behaved, probably in limiting their abilities to engage in very complicated behaviors. So far, there has been no discovery of stone tools with them. That discovery wouldn't come for another million years into the future.

The upshot is that hominid biology shows convincing evidence for erect bipedalism by around 3.5 M.Y.A. and some relatively minor further developments after that time. Then it must be concluded that bipedalism was driven by some kind of behavioral impetus. What this might have been will continue to be on the agenda of research of paleoanthropologists.

> **Paleofacts**
>
> Using primate analogy, we could argue that australopithecines were probably at least making and using tools on the level we noted for chimpanzees in the wild, such as in fishing for termites with sticks.

Bigger Brains Are Better

A. afarensis was small-brained. But then, brain size dramatically increased so that, by the time the first members of the genus Homo appeared, around 2.5 M.Y.A., brains had taken a big jump. It nearly doubled in size by 2 M.Y.A. At least by 1.5 M.Y.A., hominid brain size was into the lower end of our modern range; by 500 K.Y.A., it was right about at our average brain size of today.

> ### Paleoquest
>
> This trend of increasing hominid brain size was a costly affair in terms of how much more energy and how many more calories an animal had to expend. The energy cost must have been offset by the advantages of a bigger brain. And this means asking what the brain was doing, and what kinds of behavior were developing.

Stone Tools Back on Stage

Now we can introduce stone toolmaking to the picture. The first stone tools are dated at 2.6 M.Y.A., and we track some of the refinements and developments in tool making with the increase in brain size. The fit is not one-to-one, and some have argued that it wasn't so much the actual increase in size that was important, but the modification of the organization and functioning of the brain. That may well be true. But reorganization and brain function do not preserve in the fossil record, so we are left to infer what specific changes in the brain led to what specific kinds of behavior.

Talking Back in Time

One of those behaviors that will continue to be a focus is the origin of language. We argued that vocal communication formed a rudimentary language with the australopithecines. But then this basic language continued to evolve, probably along with brain evolution, and didn't reach what we would consider a modern level of expression until the Archaic *Homo sapiens*, of about 500 K.Y.A. There will be some debate on this. But what I don't think is debatable is that our modern ability to speak underwent a long evolutionary process that involved brain evolution, which, in turn, interacted with cultural and behavorial evolution. So it was a biobehavorial interaction. Here's another example of a trend that had biobehavorial links.

Better Bigger Bodies

We noted that Lucy and the later gracile australopithicines were about 4 to 4.5 feet tall and probably weighed well less than 100 pounds. The robust australopithecines were quite a bit heavier. Thereafter, hominid body size increased and more or less reached modern average size by about 2 M.Y.A.

What accounts for the trend toward increase in hominid body size? Here's a list of proposed explanations:

- ◆ It was tied to the increase that was taking place in brain size.

- ◆ It afforded early hominids more protection as they adapted to living away from forests into open grasslands.

- ◆ It was directly linked to cultural developments in subsistence activities such as in scavenging or small animal hunting. Increased intake of animal protein and fat could be implicated here.

> **Paleofacts**
>
> Humans have been undergoing an increase in height for the past several centuries. This is called a secular trend, and it seems to be mostly explained by dietary changes, not necessarily dietary improvements. The historical secular trend toward taller people more recently has been followed by excessive body weight gain and obesity in the United States.

It might be that adaptation to hot, dry climates in Africa would have benefited hominids to become taller and more linear in body build. We know that body size and build are connected with adaptation to climate.

> **Paleoquest**
>
> Along the lines of adapting to hot, sunny environments, there is a reasonable presumption that early hominids of Africa had high levels of skin melanin, which means that they would have been darkly pigmented. Ongoing research is attempting to find out why skin color varies from darkly pigmented populations near the equator and lightly pigmented populations away from the equator.

We should note that the trend toward overall body size in hominids, like the other trends we discussed and the next one to cover, are responding to behavioral causes. There's no chicken-and-egg quandary here. Behavior must have driven the biological change.

Trending Toward Smaller Faces and Teeth

Here's a trend that is sort of the reverse of the others. Instead of increasing in size, hominids evolved to have smaller teeth and upper and lower jaws, all of which was accompanied by some changes in the overall appearance of the face.

We focus on the teeth, or dentition, because this is probably where much of the evolutionary action was. Of course, teeth are housed in jaws. So, if we consider function or use, really the combination of the jaws and teeth is involved. What kinds of use are they involved with? Certainly, eating and chewing come to mind. But our jaws also perform some nondietary functions. Not generally with a dentist's recommendation, we sometimes use our jaws for holding, opening, tearing, and breaking nonfood items. I leave it to you to fill in the blanks on what objects are the subjects of these activities. Let's just say that at times we use our teeth as tools. That's in spite of the fact that our biobehavorial evolution has likely led to tools to replace the use of our teeth, for both dietary and nondietary purposes.

> **Paleofacts**
>
> The controlled use of fire, which appeared at least by the Middle Paleolithic, made some foods easier to chew. For example, cooking meat breaks down muscle fibers and thus requires less chewing before swallowing. So use of fire for cooking probably interacted with the reduction of jaw use and subsequent tooth reduction.

Early hominids, starting with the australopithecines, had very large teeth and appropriately large jaws to accommodate them. The robust form that we noted had especially huge molars that are thought to be adapted to a diet of small, hard objects of seeds and nuts. But even the gracile form had large teeth, as did the hominids that followed. There was the trend toward dental reduction, but it didn't really end until modern humans, or AMH.

Putting these fossil facts into a biobehavorial framework leads us to conclude that hominids were using their teeth both for heavy chewing and for nondietary use. The reduction in teeth trend then is partially explained by the development and increasing dependency on tools—for example, in cutting and crushing and otherwise preparing food before it was consumed. We might be able to alter that old saying "You are what you eat" to "You are what you eat with" or maybe, "Tools maketh the teeth smaller."

The trend toward smaller teeth and the reduced heavy use of the jaws was likely accompanied by an overall reduction of the facial area. Forces or pressures from heavy chewing and jaw use act on the entire facial area, from the forehead to the chin. Thus, as tools replaced heavy jaw activities, facial structures became less pronounced. That is, because the teeth and jaws got smaller, there was less prognathism or facial projection.

When the jaw receded, evolutionarily speaking, the chin became more prominent. On the other hand, with a reduction of forces acting on the forehead region, the browridges, which had acted as sort of shock absorbers, became less prominent. And these changes pretty much resulted in the face of modern humans. Of course, we must not lose sight of the biological variation that I spoke of earlier. After all, modern faces are wonderfully different—for someone who studies biological variation, this is a major delight.

We have reviewed the major trends in hominid evolution to show how biobehavioral interaction probably operated. Consider it a general outline rather than proof positive in every detail. Much more research needs to be done. This is a good lead-in to the next chapter, which covers the vexing two-headed question of where the Anatomically Modern Humans came from and when they arrived in Eurasia.

The Least You Need to Know

- Cro-Magnon was the first group of AMH in Europe.

- AMH may have originated in Africa and then spread throughout Eurasia.

- Although Cro-Magnon is sometimes thought of as the flagbearer for AMH, it should be noted that AMH outside of Europe are just as important.

- The biobehavioral approach is very fruitful for better understanding human evolution.

- With the appearance of AMH, the major trends of human evolution in terms of physical features are complete.

Chapter 14

Debating the Origins of AMH

In This Chapter

- ◆ Two major models of AMH origins
- ◆ Fossil clues to AMH origins
- ◆ AMH origins as seen from archaeology
- ◆ Using ancient genetics to assess AMH origins
- ◆ Explanation for why genetic variation changes over time

Cro-Magnon ushered in the AMH, or Anatomically Modern Humans, in Europe around 30 K.Y.A. But from where? That is the topic of this chapter. We cover two very different models that have been proposed to explain AMH origins. Adding to the information from hominid and archaeological remains, we include genetic evidence. So, we have three kinds of evidence and two explanatory models, all pointing to one question: What was the origin of AMH? This question, perhaps more than any other, has generated a tremendous amount of interest, debate, and controversy among prehistoric archaeologists and paleoanthropologists, as well as within the general public. This could be because we are talking about us, in a rather personally identifiable way. After all, it is pretty hard to identify with australopithecines or even other more recent hominids. I guess most people don't want to be referred to as Neandertals. But with the arrival of AMH, we might become more emotionally invested and charged. There is cause to see ourselves more clearly and to perhaps wonder, where do we come from? Let's look at the alternatives through the eyes of prehistory.

We begin by presenting major features of two *models*, or theories. Then we assess the evidence for and against each model. Finally, we offer some general comments on where matters stand at this time.

Out of Africa

The first model that we describe is usually called the Recent African Origin Model, but it also goes by the names of Population Replacement Model and, in a biblical vein, the Noah's Ark Theory. At times, even Out of Africa is the label of choice.

All of these model names sound like they deal with the population movement out of Africa—and they do. Here are the essential elements of the Recent African Origin Model:

Anthrolingo

A **model** refers to a theoretical construction that is offered to explain a natural phenomenon. For example, it would be used to account for the empirical evidence that AMH were in Europe at least by 30 K.Y.A.

- After originating in Africa, *Homo erectus* populations moved out of Africa and into Eurasia around 2 M.Y.A.

- Anatomically Modern Humans originated in Africa between 200 K.Y.A. and 100 K.Y.A.

- Portions of these AMH then moved northward out of Africa, first inhabiting Asia and then on to western Europe.

- These later arrivals from Africa replaced the existing Archaic *Homo sapiens* that had evolved out of the earlier *Homo erectus*.

- Replacement meant that there was little or no interbreeding of AMH with local Archaic populations of Eurasia.

- After some period of overlapping with each other, the existing Archaic populations went extinct.

- That left the AMH as our direct ancestors.

This model imposes additional conditions, such as the fact that replacement would have been abrupt. In addition, there shouldn't be any evidence of continuity or transition from the Archaic groups to the AMH groups.

For an opposing view, we now turn to the Multiregional Model.

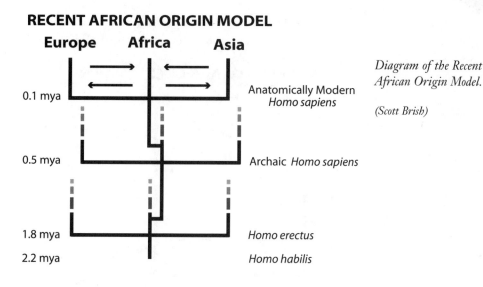

RECENT AFRICAN ORIGIN MODEL

Diagram of the Recent African Origin Model.

(Scott Brish)

Growing Up Local

Region is loosely defined here and could represent whole continents of Asia and Europe or portions of these. For the moment, we refer to whole continents.

Here are the essentials of the Multiregional Model:

♦ After originating in Africa, *Homo erectus* populations moved out of Africa and into Eurasia around 2 M.Y.A.

♦ Thereafter, the *Homo erectus* populations continued to evolve within each region, first to Archaic *Homo sapiens* and then to AMH.

♦ The continental regions were not cut off from each other; individuals were able to move between groups.

♦ This meant that interbreeding or *gene flow* took place to help maintain similarity of the genes of populations across Eurasia and back into Africa.

Some conditions also apply here. The Multiregional Model does not predict rapid and abrupt change from one group to the next—that is, between the Archaic and Modern populations. And it predicts regional continuity or transitional changes falling between the

Anthrolingo

Gene flow is an evolutionary process that involves individuals from one group mating with individuals from another group and, by producing offspring, transferring some of their genetic material. This is also called migration, but not all migrations involve gene flow.

groups. It also proposes that some traits that were present way back into time—say, back to *Homo erectus*—could be retained and seen even up to the AMH.

MULTIREGIONAL MODEL

The Multiregional Model.

(Scott Brish)

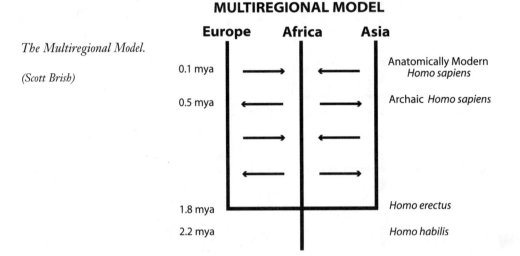

The basic distinctions between the two models are pretty obvious and marked. Either the AMH populations found in Eurasia were of long-standing with an unbroken history, or they were more recent and stopped the history of earlier groups by replacing them.

Fieldnotes

Perhaps because these two models were so far apart, modifications have been introduced to bridge them. The modifications generally allow for some traits of modern humans to have originated within Africa but then to have spread to Eurasia through gene flow, and eventually to replace the earlier Archaic traits. This would be a movement of genes, not individuals. Tongue-in-cheek, this might be called the "Make Love, Not War" model.

Now it is time to assemble the support—or lack thereof—for the Recent African Origin Model and the Multiregional Model. As you might anticipate, there is a quite a bit of uncertainty, if judged only by the amount of controversy that this topic has generated.

Stacking Up the Evidence

It would take a book itself to cover all the information derived from the fossil and archaeological records, along with the more newly developed genetic analyses. Short of that, let's look at summaries of what each of these lines of evidence show. Of course, some people who are strongly committed to one of the models would probably see things quite differently.

The Fossils Say Maybe This and Maybe That

The Recent African Origin Model uses the AMH skulls that we listed for Africa as support for a contention that the AMH appeared much earlier there than anywhere else in Eurasia—more than 100 K.Y.A. Thus, Africa is the presumed place of origin and time for any later AMH found in Eurasia.

The European Scene

This argument seems quite solid with regard to Europe, in that Cro-Magnon is claimed to sharply break away from the Neandertals whom they overlapped with in time. But earlier we noted that from Saint-Césaire (as a Neanderthal) to Combe Capelle (showing a mixture of Neandertal and Modern features) and then to Cro-Magnon (as a AMH), some regional continuity could be espoused by the Multi-regional Model. At the very least, these fossils could represent a high degree of biological variation present at the time.

Muddled Middle East

Shifting to the Middle East, the Recent African Origin Model again claims that local Neandertals were completely separated from the AMH. This could be true. Yet the AMH, such as the Skhul skull, has some facial features that make it less than fully modern.

Once more, the Middle Easterners at this time period show variability that might not fall within distinctly labeled categories, as Neandertals versus modern. Rather, they show grades of differences. This variability could, of course, be the result of gene flow from one group to the next. That is a prediction of the Multiregional Model.

> **Paleoquest**
>
> The question of whether the degree of variation between Neandertals and modern humans was so great that they couldn't or chose not to interbreed remains unresolved at this time. Yet, there seems to be a movement toward accepting as fact that some amount of gene flow between the groups occurred.

Eurasian Continuity

Moving on to Eastern Europe and Asia tends to shift the support away from the Recent African Origin Model and more toward the Multiregional Model. Why? Because there is evidence of regional continuity of local evolution and variability that would be expected under the process of continued gene flow.

Some of the best evidence for this comes from the Vindiya site in Croatia, which we described in the last chapter. Then there is the Liujiang skull from China, dated at 100 K.Y.A. or more—it is an AMH. This would place it at about the same time as AMH in Africa. So if the dating of this skull holds up—and there is still a good deal of uncertainty about that—then China, too, must have had some early AMH that did not come from Africa.

In a summation of the fossil record, the Recent African Origin Model is best supported in Western Europe and possibly the Middle East, and, of course, supports Africa itself. But the Multiregional Model is best supported in Eastern Europe, the Far East, and also Australia. Doesn't that sound like one model will not fit all situations? Let's now shift our attention to the archaeological record.

Archaeological Arguments Could Go Either Way

The crux of this argument is that either the archaeological remains, such as artifacts, show a sharp break from one level of tool technology to a later, presumed more advanced one, or there is continuity in technological development without any real breaks. What does the evidence show?

For Africa, there tends to be a continuation of stone tool technology, but tools made from bone show a higher level of sophistication at the time of the appearance of AMH. So here is some support for the Recent African Origin Model.

> **Paleofacts**
>
> Bone tools found in Africa show a highly sophisticated manufacture; some of them are even barbed. This looks like a break from earlier technologies.

But it doesn't look like any of the advancements in Africa are carried out of the continent. Asia basically shows regional continuity. And the Middle East, where there are reported to be both Neandertals and AMH, were all abiding by the Mousterian tradition. There's no support here for the Recent African Origin Model. But there are still some lingering questions for the Multiregional Model over what the connections were, if any, between the Neandertals and AMH.

Europe presents an interesting, if not befuddled, picture. First, Neandertals are practicing the Mousterian tradition, par excellence. But then, around 40 K.Y.A. there is the appearance of a definite change in tool technology. This change probably wasn't sudden and may have gone through some transitional development that led to the Aurignacian tool kit. You might recall from Chapter 12 that Aurignacian was listed as the second division of the Upper Paleolithic. And, of course, we associated the Upper Paleolithic with AMH. Could this be the evidence of the newly arriving AMH out of Africa and their breakaway from the Neandertals and their Mousterian manners?

Possibly, but there is a little problem: No hominid fossils have been found yet in association with the Aurignacian tools.

Then there is the site at Saint-Césaire that we have been mentioning. Recall that this is a Neandertal site dated at around 35 K.Y.A. Well, it appears to have a mixture of Mousterian and Aurignacian tool industries. This leaves two obvious questions. Did the Mousterian technology develop aspects of the Aurignacian? Or did Neandertals borrow some of this more sophisticated technology from the AMH? Perhaps this is best left as a "time will tell" kind of question.

In summing up the picture painted by archaeological remains, there once again is an overwhelming amount of uncertainty. Aspects of both the Recent African Origin Model and the Multiregional Model receive partial support. We follow this rather undecided position with additional clarification shortly. But next, there is genetic evidence to review.

Ancient Genetic Evidence

We have mentioned genes and genetic information a few times before. But here is the place to build a little clearer picture of what genetic information means and why it is important to the study of human evolution and prehistory. When looking at genetic material taken from fossils, this is referred to as *Ancient DNA*, or *aDNA*.

> **Fieldnotes**
>
> A proposal has been made that Neandertals and AMH living in the Middle East did not actually come into contact. Instead, they moved in or out of the same region in response to changing climates, without overlapping their stays in that region.

> **Paleoquest**
>
> Additional research needs to be done to find out the maker of the Aurignacian tools. For now, it is thought that they were made by AMH.

> **Anthrolingo**
>
> **Ancient DNA,** or **aDNA,** refers to genetic material that is extracted from bones or teeth of earlier hominids, such as Neandertals, and analyzed for similarity with Modern samples of DNA. The oldest hominid aDNA is at least from 40 K.Y.A. Animals, such as a bear, had aDNA from more than 90 K.Y.A.

We have already said that aDNA was successfully extracted from Neandertals of western Germany and that an analysis of this material indicated that Neandertals were very different from modern humans. A conclusion based on this evidence was that Neandertals were on a side branch of human evolution and did not contribute to our modern gene pool.

A more recent finding has thrown some doubt on the conclusion that Neandertals were not in our direct genetic ancestry. This comes from a site in Australia, which, incidentally, is where we will be going in the next chapter. The site is called Lake Mungo and is shakily dated at 62 K.Y.A. Some think that a more accurate date is in the 45–40 K.Y.A. range. The fossil that provided the aDNA is not considered to be a Neandertal, yet its aDNA did not differ from that of Neandertals. But it did differ from that of modern humans.

Here the conclusion is that both Neandertals and non-Neandertals differed genetically from us. This finding tends to support the Multiregional Model. It suggests that all of the ancient DNA was different than our modern DNA, regardless of what group it came from.

Up to now, we have been discussing Ancient DNA extracted from fossils. But another application in genetic research deals with modern DNA taken from living individuals.

The results of the DNA study are then used to reconstruct evolutionary history. We will discuss this evidence, but it might be helpful to lay a little groundwork of how modern genetic information is useful for reconstructing the past.

> **Paleoquest**
>
> Ancient DNA extracted from bones of a presumed Neandertal baby recovered from the Caucasus region dated at 29 K.Y.A. confirmed what the western Germany Neandertal showed. But there is a question of whether this is a Neandertal or an AMH. If it is really an AMH, then both AMH and Neandertals differed genetically from modern humans.

> **Paleofacts**
>
> It is not now possible and probably won't ever be possible to "bring back" Neandertals or any other fossil hominids by using the "Hollywood tricks" played in the *Jurassic Park* films. But it is an entertaining idea.

The Stuff of Heredity

Genes are the basic units of heredity. They are what we inherit from our parents. Genes play an important role in helping to determine our physical appearance. This applies to features on our bones and teeth, as found fossilized throughout the evolutionary record. We base our interpretations of evolutionary relationships upon this fact. Quite simply, the more similar fossils are, the more closely related we think they are. This is because they would share more of their genes that were inherited from some common ancestors in the past.

Looking at the question of why fossils do or do not have similarities has a quick answer: This is because of evolution. We take up this discussion again in Chapter 20. Here we can note that evolution can cause differences in genetic information due to four processes:

> **Paleofacts**
>
> Morphological similarity may be due to sharing common genes. But we do have to be aware that sometimes this similarity gives a false picture. Everything you see is not always what it seems to be. For example, sea mammals are not fish.

- ◆ Natural selection
- ◆ Gene flow
- ◆ Mutation
- ◆ Random genetic drift

It's a Natural

Natural selection is the process that Charles Darwin proposed, accounting for the modification of life forms. In sum, natural selection brings about successful adaptation and reproduction so that species can continue to change as the environment changed. Of course, the longer groups stay together, the more genetically similar they are. Conversely, if some groups split off, they continue to diverge and become genetically different. An example is when our earliest hominid ancestors split away from our common ancestor with the chimpanzee.

Mobile Genes

We have already defined gene flow as the exchange of genes from one population to another. Remember the argument of whether the Neandertals could or did successfully interbreed with modern humans. If they did, that would be gene flow.

We also mentioned that gene flow would serve to unify the genetic information from different groups. Their gene pools would remain more similar. The Multiregional Model depends heavily on the operation of this evolutionary process.

> **Paleofacts**
>
> We have noted that we shared a common ancestry with the chimpanzees some 5–7 M.Y.A. Genetic analysis of chimps and humans today has revealed that we still share more than 98 percent of genetic material in common. But that remaining 2 percent is profound in how it produces such different outcomes.

Mutating Genes

Mutation is a chemical change in genetic material. New genetic material is always being made in the cells of our body. During the process of making new material, mistakes occur. Indeed, "shifts happen." One form of genetic material can be shifted to another form. This is mutation.

Mutation increases genetic variation. The amount of mutational change depends on the amount of time elapsed. Thus, the longer two groups have been separated, the more different they will become as a result of mutational change. This forms the basis for the _molecular clock_.

Drifting Genes

Finally, there is random genetic drift, which also shifts genetic information. But it operates in the opposite direction to that of mutation. Rather than accumulating variation, which is the action of mutation, random genetic drift leads to a loss of genetic variation. This mostly happens when the size of the evolving population is very small. And the sizes of early hominid populations were very small. So we expect that random genetic drift would have been an active process.

Since the four evolutionary processes can all be operating at the same time, genetic variation can go up or down, or stay even for a while. But genetic variation forms the evidence that we now need to look at.

Genetic variation is measured by the amount of mutational difference that has accumulated in a particular kind of genetic material known as mitochondrial DNA, or *mtDNA*.

Three major statements concerning genetic variation affect the question of origins of AMH:

Anthrolingo

MtDNA is found in mitochondria, which are the energy providers of the cell. They are only passed down or inherited through mothers, but not fathers. Almost all of Ancient DNA is actually mtDNA. This is because it is much more plentiful than DNA found in the cell nucleus and because mtDNA holds together quite well over long periods of time.

- ◆ Compared with other primates, such as chimpanzee, humans have a lot less genetic variation.

- ◆ Modern African populations have much more genetic variation than either Asian or European populations.

- ◆ Studies of genetic relationships show that African groups tend to separate out from Asian and European groups.

The first statement essentially means that modern humans have not been around as long as modern chimpanzees. This tends to support the Recent African Origin Model. Recall that this is a model of replacement in which the older Archaic humans were replaced by modern humans who came out of Africa more recently.

The second and third statements indicate that modern African groups are the oldest because they have the most amount of genetic variation. Most of this variation came from accumulated mutational change over long periods of time. These, too, support the Recent African Origin Model.

Fieldnotes

The first AMH were collectively known as "Mitochondrial Eve." Later, when the Y-chromosome, which appears only in males, was studied, it joined Eve and they were referred to as "African Eve and Adam." This doesn't mean single individuals, but groups from which their genetic material came and was passed down through a very long line of succeeding generations.

All in all, the Recent African Origin Model is better supported by an analysis of genetic variation. But a little wrinkle might mess up this contention. Genetic variation is highly dependent upon population size. Simply stated, the larger the population is, the more genetic variation it is likely to have. We have already said that early hominid populations were very small in numbers. So perhaps the reason that African groups show the most amount of variation is that they are the largest, not necessarily because they are the oldest. And that's about where matters stand at the present time. Continuing research on more genetic evidence will likely lead to a resolution.

But considering that the fossil and archaeological lines of evidence are also up in the air, it looks like any resolution regarding the origins of AMH will remain undecided for some time into the future. Notice here that I used the plural *origins* because it might well turn out that there will be different sources of AMH for different world regions. In sum, part of both the Recent African Origin Model and the Multiregional Model could be blended to form the more accurate picture.

Now we are about to make our next big launch—no, not to the Moon or Mars, but to new worlds on Earth that had not yet seen humans. Actually, it will be two launches, one at the south side of the Pacific Ocean and the other at the north side. As is our custom up to now in human prehistory, we will still be walking. But boats and even sea-voyaging canoes will appear along the way.

The Least You Need to Know

- Anatomically Modern Humans were very variable and are not easily assigned to a single category.

- None of the existing models fully accounts for AMH origins.

- The Recent African Origin Model is best supported by evidence from Western Europe, and Africa itself.

- The Multiregional Model receives most of its support from Eastern Europe, the Far East and Australia.

- Ancient DNA will likely become increasingly important for investigating questions about human prehistory.

Part 5

Out of Asia

Having looked at alternative models for tracing the origins of Anatomically Modern Humans, the stage is set for examining the next great leaps in humankind. Populations that had extended their occupation to the limits of land in Southeast Asia continued on to the adjacent island chains. Having settled around the coasts and into interior Australia, there was an apparently planned set of voyages, leading to the occupation of Melanesia, Micronesia, and Polynesia. The expansion voyages didn't cease until the easternmost point of land in the Pacific, Easter Island, was reached. We then look to the far north of Asia, at those hearty folks who traversed the land bridge that connected northeast Asia and northwest America during the last Ice Age.

Chapter 15

Australia and Islands Across the South Pacific

In This Chapter

- ◆ Prehistoric archaeology down under
- ◆ Melanesian migrations
- ◆ Sailing and settling Micronesia
- ◆ Eastward expansion into Polynesia

Earlier I said a major underlying theme of this book is variation and change in human biology and culture. I think you will agree that a second topic of emphasis is human groups on the go. Certainly, for the past couple of million years, there is evidence of movement of hominids initially into areas uninhabited by other hominids and then later into already occupied regions. In this chapter, and also in Chapter 17, we will be looking at the first of these circumstances—that is, people moving into newly discovered areas and setting down roots that continue to grow and develop to this day. Here, we trace the movement into Australia and its neighboring islands of New Guinea and Tasmania. We then embark on a sea voyage that allows us to recount the fantastic feats of very ancient mariners in their deliberate quest to discover and settle nearly all of the habitable islands of the South Pacific. Of course, we also must account for their ocean-worthy vessels.

First Stop, Australia

Australia has received considerable media coverage due to the recently held Olympic Games in Sydney. Our interests here will broaden in both space and time. We will go back to the time when hominid groups first entered the region, established coastal settlements, and, demonstrating remarkable skills in adapting, moved into one of the driest, hottest areas of the world, the Outback.

Several times during the Pleistocene, Australia joined neighboring islands of New Guinea and Tasmania to form a land mass known as Sahul. This is also called Greater Australia. Likewise, the island chain extending out of mainland Asia, including Java, Sumatra, Bali, and Borneo, were connected into land area called Sunda.

Land connections were formed because of ice ages. When glaciers and ice fields were largest, this meant that a huge amount of water was locked up in them. And this resulted in a drop in sea levels—and not just a little drop of feet or yards. At the height of glaciations, sea levels declined between 300 and 500 feet. This would have exposed much more of coastal land shelves—and if the shelves were shallow enough, land bridges would have formed between islands. In Chapter 17, we also use Ice Age information in discussing the movements of people across the Bering Land Bridge and into North America.

Greater Australia with a land connection to New Guinea.

(Scott Brish)

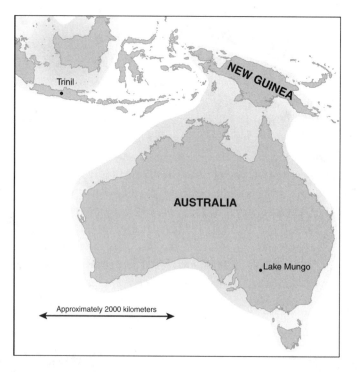

At four major times glaciers were at their maximum size: 65 K.Y.A., 53 K.Y.A., 35 K.Y.A., and 18 K.Y.A. The rise and fall in sea levels lasted for thousands of years. So, for any hominids moving along in this area, there would be plenty of time to carry on their journey. But they could not have walked all the way. Between the Sunda and Sahul land masses, there was a very deep sea trench that formed a watery gap between Australia and the islands extending out of Southeast Asia. This is the *Wallace Trench*, or *Wallace Line*.

Considering the Wallace Trench and other narrower gaps between islands, the widest span of water was around 50 miles, with many in the range of 10 to 15 miles. So movement of hominids out of Southeast Asia and into Australia would have required them to have built some form of watercraft to use the islands as stepping stones. This doesn't seem too far fetched, considering that hominids were living in the region for more than a million years, as evidenced by the Java *Homo erectus* that we described earlier. But to date, there is no direct evidence of what these original watercraft might have looked like. It could be imagined that the earliest built resembled the vegetative rafts we mentioned earlier.

Anthrolingo

The **Wallace Trench,** or **Wallace Line,** is a very deep 25,000-foot, channel that separated the Sunda and Sahul land masses. It is named for Alfred Russel Wallace, who proposed a theory of natural selection to account for the origin and development of species at the same time that Darwin did.

Paleofacts

K-Ar cannot date deposits much younger than 100,000 years old. This is because not enough time has elapsed for sufficient argon gas to form and be trapped in the volcanic rock.

So, now that we have some background, when did hominids first arrive in Australia? Unfortunately, as with many other areas, it has been difficult to get sound dates for Australian sites. K-Ar dating isn't available—at least, not for the prehistoric hominid sites. They are too recent to be dated by this method.

But carbon-14 dating has been done successfully, even though this stretched the upper limits of the process. When applied in Australia, the earliest archaeological materials were grouped around dates of 40 K.Y.A. Yes, there are some much earlier estimates. Earlier we mentioned the possible date of 62 K.Y.A. for Lake Mungo, but that still needs additional confirmation, as does a very early date of 120 K.Y.A. for another site in northern Australia.

And 40 K.Y.A. sort of fits into the lowest sea levels and largest land connections noted earlier. It's now time to review the proposals made in reference to the peopling of Australia.

Settling Greater Australia

When talking about the discovery and population of Australia, three major migration theories have been advanced:

♦ The three-wave theory

♦ Two sources of migrants

♦ A single homeland for all migrants

All three theories trace original Australian migrants back to somewhere in the areas of Indonesia or Southeast Asia. Following a more recent custom, we will refer to the original group or groups as Australoid. We should also recognize here that the living descendents are called *Australian Aborigines.*

Anthrolingo

Australian Aborigine is the term applied to the present-day descendents of the initial settlers in Australia. The Australian Aborigines have received considerable ethnographic study that has revealed a rich complex of social relationships and impressive expressions of art.

We have borrowed some of their language in our use of such words as *boomerang* and *didgeridoo.*

The theories differ in terms of how many groups there were and how many different times they migrated to Australia. The three-wave theory doesn't have much support today. So we can now turn to the fossil hominids that have been discovered in Australia, to test the two other theories.

The Fossils of Earliest Australians

The earliest dated fossils have been described as gracile. You might recall that label from its application to the australopithecines from Africa. But it doesn't mean that. It simply means that the skulls show features like those of modern humans, such as these:

♦ Thin braincase bones

♦ Rounded foreheads with moderately developed browridges

♦ Small lower jaws and teeth

For a different look, later dated fossils are described as robust. But a better label might be Archaic, which means they resembled the group we have described as Archaic *Homo sapiens*. A list of features are as follows:

◆ Thicker skull bones

◆ Sloping foreheads and prominent browridges

◆ Prognathic or projecting faces

◆ Large jaws and teeth

Thus, at face value, there would seem to be at least two different groups that made their way to Australia at perhaps different times. But this is countered with the argument that these aren't really two different *types* or different populations; instead, they fall at the ends of a range of variation within one group. And the difference in dates between the gracile and Archaic is said to be simply due to problems in securing accurate dates. The two forms may, in fact, overlap in time.

The matter is pretty much at a standstill, except that the archaeological record shows no real evidence for the replacement of one group by another. New genetic analysis may well shed some light on Australian and South Pacific population origins and migrations.

> **Paleoquest**
>
> It is not clear why skulls of earlier hominids are thick. This is considered to be a primitive condition and was replaced by later thin-walled skulls. Continuing research may provide answers.

> **Anthrolingo**
>
> **Type** is mostly an outdated term that viewed fossils as idealized forms and did not recognize that they could vary a great deal from one to the next. Type or typological thinking has been replaced by the notion of variable populations.

Artifacts of the First Australians

Some Australian sites have yielded large numbers of artifacts and associated cultural remains, such as the following:

◆ Core and flake tools

◆ Scraperlike tools

◆ Axes

◆ Fire-cracked stones

◆ Fireplaces

- Burnt emu (flightless bird) eggs

- Cremated burial

- Hematite (yellow) and ochre (red) pigments

- Rock artwork

You probably can fill in many of the blanks on what these items tell us about prehistoric Australian lifestyle.

Thus far, there have been no definite ties made between the Australian tool technology and cultural development to anything in Asia, except in general terms. Let's have a closer look at what the archaeological remains tell us about Aboriginal Australian culture.

Glimpses of Aboriginal Culture

There are some significant points to make. First, the early Australians had controlled use of fire as evidenced by hearths at the Lake Mungo site. And in the finding of cremated burial at another of the Lake Mungo localities, this might be one of the earliest examples of this way of handling of deceased individuals. At the same site as the cremation, which was the cremation of a woman, there was a second burial of a man. The intentional burials establish the likelihood of some ritual connection and development of a spiritual life in Australia some 30,000 years ago.

Artistic expression also is apparent. This refers to the rock artwork that has been found at a couple of early sites. One, in particular, is impressive: It consists of petroglyphs (rock carvings) of geometric figures.

As to how the earliest Australians lived, in general terms they were primarily adapted to living along the coasts, and they followed out a maritime way of life. This means they lived partly from sea food, such as reef fishes, but they also had access to wild plant foods. And the marsupials, such as kangaroos, would have been on their menu.

The original coastal dwellers came in from the north, settling mainly along the east coast, but also inhabiting the west coast of Australia. There was a human settlement of New Guinea in the range of 35 K.Y.A. to 30 K.Y.A. Tasmania, the island located below the far southeast corner of Australia, was probably settled somewhat later. Around this time there would have been a land connections, or only a short spans of shallow water, to cross.

The living descendents on New Guinea are called Highland Papuans. None of the aboriginal Tasmanians survived into the twentieth century; they all died out in the middle of the nineteenth century.

It looks like a human group—or, more likely, two groups—had moved into Australia, perhaps not all at once, but in a steady flow of fewer numbers. After successfully establishing communities on the coastal area, Australian Aborigines moved up major rivers to settle the interior, or Outback. Earliest interior archaeological sites date from 25 K.Y.A. to 20 K.Y.A. Certainly, living in these very hot, dry regions would have commanded strong adaptive skills.

Paleofacts
A tragic end of aboriginal Tasmanians came under the rule of colonial administrators who initiated extermination policies. Of some 2,000 aborigines present in 1847, all but 44 were killed. By 1876, all remaining survivors were gone, having succumbed to disease and alcohol abuse.

People on the move invite researchers to ask the question of why? We said earlier that movement out of Africa could have been unplanned. Perhaps there was opportunistic traveling, but not with directed purposes. It has been proposed that people moving out of Southeast Asia and into Australia, New Guinea, and islands far out into the Pacific Ocean were planned migrations. That statement is perhaps best supported in the later sea migrations that carried voyagers all the way across the eastern Pacific Ocean.

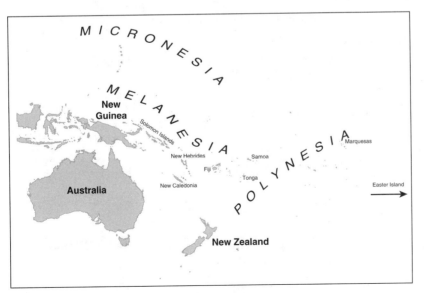

Oceanic culture areas of Melanesia, Micronesia, and Polynesia.

(Scott Brish)

We will be discussing these voyagers shortly. For now, let's just say first that precise motives for migrating are not known. But then, to make successful long-distance sea voyages, a level of preplanning must be done. And that is what the next major prehistoric migration into the South Pacific was all about.

Island Cultures of the South Pacific

We will be describing the three main culture areas found in the South Pacific—namely, Melanesia, Micronesia, and Polynesia. These are sometimes collectively known as Oceania. And, of course, we will be primarily dealing with the prehistory of these areas—that is, their original migrations and settlements.

Our first stop in Oceania is Melanesia.

Fieldnotes

The South Pacific is the setting for several well-known and widely acclaimed books and films. Herman Melville's *Moby Dick,* Robert Louis Stevenson's *Treasure Island,* and James Michener's *Tales of the South Pacific* are just three prime examples of the former. And who can forget *The Mutiny on the Bounty* for an epic film?

Paleofacts

It was once thought that somehow African migrants had populated Melanesia. But more likely the similarity in skin color is due to a similar adaptation to sunlight.

Eastward to Melanesia

Melanesia ("Black Islands") contains such well-known places as the Solomon Islands and Bougainville. Unfortunately, they are too often remembered for the fierce battles of World War II. Today they show a considerable amount of language diversity that would indicate that aboriginal groups were separated for long periods of time. Biologically, Melanesians have been termed Negroid based on darkly pigmented skin color.

If the present is a guide to the past, then Melanesians who originally settled the islands lived by planting gardens and probably kept domesticated animals. Yams became a major staple. And pigs were raised, eaten only at important feasts; otherwise, they were counted as wealth.

Archaeological work has indicated that early Melanesians were not struggling for existence or barely making a living. In fact, they were very adept at finding and making maximal use of their resources.

Austronesian Speakers

Around 5,000 years ago, a new wave of migrants moved into the South Pacific. They came out of coastal southeast China and probably Taiwan. These are known as

Austronesians, the designation for their language. There is a possibility that some mixing took place between Austronesians and Papuans. But then, other Papuans could well have been displaced to more isolated regions of New Guinea and neighboring islands within Melanesia.

Austronesians were noted for a distinctive pottery style called Lapita, which they probably brought with them as they moved out of Southeast Asia. The Lapita pottery style spread widely, from New Guinea in Melanesia all the way to western Polynesia, which we will be discussing shortly. For unknown reasons, the making of Lapita pottery in Polynesia ceased, but the distinctive geometric patterns can still be seen on *tapa cloth* being made today.

Then, roughly 4,000 years ago, navigational skills were developed, along with ocean-going canoes, that allowed voyagers to travel to the far-flung islands that make up Micronesia.

Fieldnotes

You will notice that I have shifted to giving dates by spelling out the years. This seems to be a little more appropriate than using the K.Y.A. designation for these more recent time periods.

Anthrolingo

Tapa cloth is made from the bark of the paper mulberry or breadfruit trees. It was made by peoples of both Melanesia and Polynesia. The principle decoration was geometric forms of plants and fish. Tapa cloths were used as everyday items, but special ones were made for ceremonies or to commemorate significant events.

Micronesian Voyagers

Micronesia ("small islands") extends north of Melanesia. As the name implies, most of its islands are rather small and widely separated. Parts of Micronesia have also reached well-known status, this time because of the nuclear weapon testing sites in the Marshall Islands, notably Bikini (France) and Eniwetok (USA) atolls.

As you look at the map of Micronesia, dare to dream of hopping into a large open canoe, stabilized with two hulls, powered by sturdy paddlers, or driven by wind in its sails, out into the South Pacific. The canoe could hold scores of people, as well as an assortment of animals and plants. People would, of course, mean families, although some of the early island discoveries could have been made by fishermen as they searched for new fishing grounds.

Paleofacts

There is documentation that one of the largest of these doubled-hull canoes was long enough to accommodate 140 paddlers.

Now, where are you going and how do you get there? This is the place to tell you of the mariner skills of South Pacific islanders, particularly those from Micronesia and Polynesia.

A canoe of Oceania.

(NOAA Library)

These expert navigators did have maps, partly mental but probably also laid out in shells on the sand, as was done up to fairly recent cultural history of the area. But they also had a simply ingenious set of navigational aids to help guide them on their oceanic treks. The following were some of their navigational aids:

- Star positions and patterns
- Wind directions
- Cloud formation, along with weather prediction
- Wave direction and shape
- Current direction and ocean swells
- *Seamarks*

Anthrolingo

Seamarks are observations made on birds, fish, or sharks. Their behavior might indicate direction and proximity of islands.

Now, some of these navigational aids are not very reliable. Thus, seamarks might be used only in dire straits, as when lost or without orientation. But others can be fine-tuned. For example, observing the little ripples on swells or the steepness of a wave could indicate the direction an ocean current was moving.

And these seafarers learned to read currents like modern sailors read navigational charts and compasses. Well, maybe not quite so successfully, but how else do we account for the ability of Pacific peoples to not only have initially reached these far-flung specks of land, but to move back and forth among islands that are hundreds and even thousands of miles apart—and on a regular basis? The exception might be Easter Island, which we cover in the next chapter.

Canoe hulls were carved out from large tree trunks with stone tools. Smaller single-hull canoes had an outrigger attached for stability. Double-hull canoes were lashed together with cross braces. They had a deck with two sails (woven from coconut leaves) and a small thatch hut affording some protection against the elements.

In describing the feats of South Pacific seafarers, it seems only appropriate to call them colonists. Clearly, there was purpose to their travel. And while initial embarking meant they were not entirely sure of where they were going and had no clear destination, they apparently had the confidence to push off. Of course, there must have been some instances of being pushed off course or accidentally striking unknown lands by lucky chance. And what about not-so-lucky voyages? Well, the sea must have claimed a certain number of lives due to capsizing in heavy seas or a shortage of food and water.

What is not known for certain is whether population growth and strain on resources might have prompted some of the colonization of the South Pacific. It probably did. Again, looking at more recent cultural developments in the area suggests that there may have been some political unrest motivating those who lost the competition to move on to new lands, or in this case, new islands. And that's our cue to now head for Polynesia.

> **Paleofacts**
>
> These large double-hulled canoes were capable of making voyages of more than 2,000 miles, and were about 50 percent faster than the ships used by European explorers.

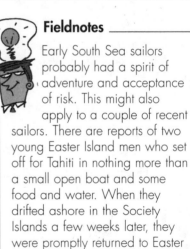

> **Fieldnotes**
>
> Early South Sea sailors probably had a spirit of adventure and acceptance of risk. This might also apply to a couple of recent sailors. There are reports of two young Easter Island men who set off for Tahiti in nothing more than a small open boat and some food and water. When they drifted ashore in the Society Islands a few weeks later, they were promptly returned to Easter Island.

The Polynesian Triangle

The Polynesian Triangle is certainly not the Bermuda Triangle, where allegedly planes and ships have been lost forever. Polynesians, possessing those superb seafarer skills seen in Micronesians, covered the largest amount of ocean area of the South Pacific islanders. And after initially discovering islands, they made return visits to distant islands on a regular basis. A common round-trip was from Hawaii to Tahiti.

Historically, three theories have been advanced to account for the origins of Polynesians:

♦ They moved out of Asia and did not mix with any groups along the way.

♦ They are the result of mixing with Australoids, Papuans, and Austronesians.

♦ They are a mixture of Melanesian and Micronesian peoples.

An updating of these theories would tend to support some variation of the third one. It is quite unlikely that they could have passed through straight out of Southeast Asia without interacting with at least Micronesians.

Polynesian physical appearance is quite different from that of the Australoid and Papuan peoples. They have somewhat less pigmented skin color and straight or wavy black hair, and they are taller and heavier than Melanesians.

Based on archaeological research, an approximate time line for the settlement of this astronomically sized area of Polynesia is as follows:

♦ About 2,300 years ago, voyagers from western Polynesia—notably, Tonga and Samoa—moved to the east to settle central Polynesia.

♦ About 1,600 years ago, Hawaii was discovered and settled by voyagers from the Marquesas, or possibly the Cook and Society Islands.

♦ About 1,400 years ago, Easter Island was settled by voyagers from Mangareva or possibly from the Marquesas.

♦ About 1,000 years ago. Cook and Society Islanders also populated New Zealand.

So, in something more than a thousand years, this vast expanse of island-dotted ocean had been discovered and occupied. Truly, a feat of this magnitude must stand near the top of human achievement—perhaps on the order of a prehistoric moon landing.

> **Paleofacts**
>
> Polynesia ("Many Islands") forms a rough triangular arrangement, with New Zealand, Easter Island, and Hawaii serving as the three points. This area constitutes about 10 million square miles.

> **Fieldnotes**
>
> The language of Polynesians is most closely related to Micronesians.

> **Paleofacts**
>
> Central Polynesia comprises the Cook and Society Islands (Tahiti) and also the Marquesas.

The fact that there is some uncertainty about the precise origins for these settlements speaks to how highly skilled they all were in navigating the high seas. It also says something about their interest in holding on to family and cultural ties, after moving off to distant islands.

Polynesians actively engaged in fishing, which might explain some of their impetus to travel. And they grew gardens and kept domestic animals. You might say that they had a mixed and balanced economy. And with economic success there might also have been population increase. Too many people for limited island resources means overpopulation. And here is one of those other explanations for seeking out new islands to occupy. Population expansion throughout Polynesia may have worked out quite well. This was the outlet to handle contin- ued growth.

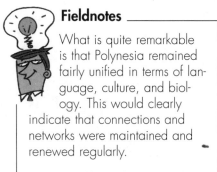

Fieldnotes

What is quite remarkable is that Polynesia remained fairly unified in terms of lan- guage, culture, and biol- ogy. This would clearly indicate that connections and networks were maintained and renewed regularly.

But one Polynesian island may have lost its ability to escape the consequences of overpopulation. At least, that is the story often told about Easter Island. We go to Easter Island, or Rapa Nui, in the next chapter.

The Least You Need to Know

- Greater Australia was settled at least by 40 K.Y.A.

- Melanesians migrated by both land and sea, with some form of early watercraft.

- Micronesians were the world's first great seafarers.

- Despite vast distances separating islands, Polynesians maintained regular contact with each other.

Chapter 16

Solving Mysteries of Rapa Nui (Easter Island)

In This Chapter

◆ How Rapa Nui was named, discovered, and settled

◆ Legends of Rapa Nui's past are tested by archaeological findings

◆ Rapa Nui experiences a glorious beginning but later crashes

◆ Now is a time of recovery and replanning the future for Rapa Nui

In the last chapter, we recounted the magnificent feats of Oceanic seafarers. They deliberately set out to discover new and distant islands in their highly sea-worthy double-hulled canoes. And their navigational skills had to be finely tuned to successfully settle nearly all habitable islands in the South Pacific. They were certainly *kahuna*, meaning "experts" in a Polynesian dialect. This chapter traces the relatively brief (in the overall coverage of this book) settling of one island, its rise to glorious artistic achievements, and its fall into disruption and destruction. This is the prehistoric story of Easter Island. But there is also Easter Island in present times, and we will cover some of this more recent history. Some have argued that what happened to Easter Island could serve as a broader lesson to what might befall whole nations unless they become better stewards of their natural and humanly produced resources. We will touch on this matter as well.

The Island: Its Names and Its Place in the Pacific

Easter Island received that name as a consequence of being "discovered" by Jacob Roggeveen on Easter Sunday, 1722. Of course, Easter Islanders weren't discovered at all, except from the perspective of a Dutch explorer.

Isolating a Name

The islanders had other names. One that is often cited is *Te Pito o Te Henua*, which has been rendered as "Navel of the World." This would seem to imply that they saw their little island centered in a vast body of water, perhaps not fully aware of the broader outside world.

> **Paleofacts**
>
> Rapa Nui measures only about 14 miles by 7 miles and covers a tiny drop of the Pacific Ocean, with an area of around 50 square miles. This would make the island smaller than the spread and sprawl of most metropolitan areas.

Going back to names, the one that seems to be most preferred is *Rapa Nui*, or "Great Rapa." This name was given by French sailors from Tahiti who thought the island resembled Rapa in French Polynesia. For the remainder of this chapter, we will use Rapa Nui.

Where in the World?

It is pretty much an understatement to say that Rapa Nui is isolated. To give some idea of distances, it is about 2,000 miles from the South American coast and about 2,000 miles from the Marquesas, which may well have been the point of departure for the original Rapa Nui settlers. Quite a bit closer, at roughly 1,200 miles, is Pitcairn Island. Pitcairn is notable for being the island of retreat for mutineers from the *HMS Bounty*. Otherwise, it is wide open ocean.

> **Fieldnotes**
>
> Thor Heyerdahl, a Norwegian explorer, demonstrated in his Kon-Tiki Expedition of 1947 that a balsa raft could successfully traverse thousands of miles of open ocean from Peru to the Tuamotos in eastern Polynesia. However, this exceptional feat of courage and skill has not convinced many researchers that it was actually done in prehistoric times.

The island is very small and very isolated. How could it possibly have been discovered by Polynesian voyagers? We said earlier that they deliberately sailed out with the intent to find new islands or new fishing grounds. They must have been fully aware of the ocean currents and prevailing winds. But the prevailing winds in the Eastern Pacific are, in fact, the trade winds known as easterlies.

Winds blow toward the west and against anyone wanting to sail out of central Polynesia toward Rapa Nui. Of course, experienced sailors could use zig-zag tacking maneuvers, but this would have extended the journey by thousands of additional miles.

Finding and Founding Rapa Nui

The clues to solving this particular mystery surrounding the Rapa Nui are a number of factors, some planned and some by chance, that happened to come together and allowed Rapa Nui to be reached and settled. Here's a list of these proposed factors:

◆ The usual easterlies shifted to westerlies. This would facilitate eastward sailing.

◆ A double-hulled canoe with families, food, plants, and chickens was on a planned voyage to a known island in eastern Polynesia.

◆ The most likely planned direction was south, but the canoe got off course or was blown off course.

◆ Navigational aids were used for orientation, and they possibly led the voyagers to an island.

◆ That island happened to be Rapa Nui.

That sounds a little too neatly packaged. But most of these factors are probably not unique to the Polynesian voyagers who discovered Rapa Nui. In various combinations, they likely entered into a lot of their deliberate expeditions.

There is an intriguing possibility that once on Rapa Nui the voyagers even continued eastward and reached South America. And then made a return trip. For some researchers, this is a more likely scenario than South Americans sailing to Rapa Nui.

Now that we have settlers on Rapa Nui, we can review the archaeology as it reveals how the islanders managed their affairs and managed to get into difficulties.

> **Paleoquest**
>
> Further research may help to work out the pattern of reversals of the trade winds. When the westerlies occurred in the winter, did they blow hard and long enough to push a canoe as far east as Rapa Nui?

> **Paleofacts**
>
> Thor Heyerdahl theorized that Rapa Nui was populated in part by Peruvian sailors from South America. Lack of genetic evidence has made this theory rather unlikely. The extraterrestrial theory of Erich Von Daniken doesn't have a smidgen of Earthly possibility.

Digging Rapa Nui

Pinning down the time of occupation of the earliest Rapa Nui sites has been aided by carbon-14 dating. These estimates place the beginnings probably no earlier than A.D. 600. The founding group likely brought with them the usual Polynesian fare of taro, bananas, sugar cane, and sweet potatoes.

Rapa Nui protein sources included chickens, stowaway rats, birds of the sea and land, and fish and porpoises from the sea. It was of great interest to find that porpoises constituted such an important item in their diet. Overall, there is archaeological evidence of dietary adequacy for many centuries. This could be called a flourishing phase in Rapa Nui cultural prehistory. It was the time when those huge stone artifacts appeared on the scene.

Fieldnotes

Sweet potatoes have been used to argue for a South American connection, possibly resulting from Polynesians initiating contact with South America, rather than South Americans carrying sweet potatoes to Polynesia.

Anthrolingo

Megaliths are large stone blocks, some carved to represent human figures, which are found in many cultures across the entire world. Perhaps one of the more widely known megalithic structures is at Stonehenge in Britain.

Paleofacts

There are almost 900 moai inventoried on Rapa Nui.

Stone Heads Plus

There is a widespread custom of carving out and erecting stone statues among central Polynesians. This custom was continued on Rapa Nui. In more formal terms, it is referred to as a *megalithic* tradition.

Rapa Nui stone statues, called *moai*, are more than a head. They also include roughly the portion of the body known as the torso. The reason they are sometimes considered just heads is because of soil buildup around their bases.

The stone implement for making the statues was shaped like a crude hand-ax, but more rounded with a sharpened point. This tool was used in a pecking fashion. With repeated blows, the head-plus-torso figure emerged out of the stone block. Yes, it took enormous effort and time. But the volcanic stone is relatively "soft," and headway could be seen blow by blow. The stone is still rather heavy, weighing in at about a ton per linear foot of statue.

Moai tended to be relatively small at the beginning, but toward the end of the megalithic tradition, they got increasingly larger. The largest is about 70 feet long and silently rests in its quarry crypt.

Moai statues partially submerged.

(Robert J. Meier/Scott Brish)

A large unfinished moai and the author at the Rano Raraku quarry.

(Robert J. Meier/Scott Brish)

Megalithic Gravestones

Why were the statues made? The clearest answer seems to relate to their placement on ceremonial or temple platforms called ahus. The ahus were constructed in honor of extended families or lineages. The ahu had a stone crypt or burial place for deceased ancestors, and the moai statue stood on top, possibly serving as a rough equivalent to what we may think is a headstone on a grave. The ahu would be the place for families to then carry out their religious or ceremonial activities.

Paleofacts

Some of the ahus are very well made, with precise masonry work. The perfection of joints between large stone blocks has been wrongly attributed to South American stonemasons who had reached the island. More likely, this was the skilled work of Polynesian islanders themselves—another mystery resolved.

Ahus are located away from the interior and on the coastal areas. The moai were placed on them facing inward. Some had an additional block of red volcanic rock, called scoria or pumice, balanced on top of the head. These are referred to as top-knots. They sort of resemble top hats with disproportionately large brims. It's truly an impressive sight.

The precise fit of stones at an ahu temple.

(Robert J. Meier/Scott Brish)

Heavy Hauling

The next two obvious questions are these:

- How did the moai megaliths get to the ahus?
- How were they erected on the ahu platforms?

Perhaps it would be easiest to just accept the oral tradition that they "walked" there. Ahus are located in some cases miles away from the quarry site. Several theories have been advanced. These have been tested using stone replicas, exacting engineering logic, and computer simulations.

The soundest possibility comes from Jo Anne Van Tilburg, from the Institute of Archaeology, UCLA. She proposes a sledgelike device. Two large logs were lashed together in a V shape. The moai was then placed lying down on the sledge, and the sledge was pulled over a series of log rollers, with the V end up front. Ropes for lashing and pulling were made from tree fibers. Once at the ahu platform, the sledge with the moai still resting on it was tilted into position on the stone base. The topknots could have been rolled up stone ramps that were then removed.

As part of the mysterious lore surrounding Rapa Nui, it puzzled some that trees could have been available on this island. When it was observed by visitors in the eighteenth century and later, it appeared completely barren of larger trees. It required more recent pollen analysis to establish that when the islanders arrived and for some centuries ahead, the island was forested. That's another mystery shot down.

> **Paleofacts**
>
> As with the excellent stonework on the ahus, it has been asserted that the Polynesian Islanders were not capable of making, hauling, and erecting the moai. But they were and they did. There's no mystery here, except in the details.

Population Goes Up, Trees Go Down

But there's tragedy lurking behind that new discovery. Here was a once-forested island that was later completely deforested. The pollen analysis reveals the facts. By A.D. 800, the island forest was shrinking, and it pretty much disappeared a few centuries later, probably due to overuse and clearing for farming. This would indicate a growing population that needed more food provided through a larger crop base.

Starting with the founding group, which could have been in the neighborhood of 100 persons total (men, women, and children), growth of the island population was likely rapid and steady.

Certainly a large and growing population would seriously tax the limited resources and any ability to procure a stable food supply. Recall that the safety valve in other Polynesian situations similar to this is voyaging to new islands. Apparently, Rapa Nui didn't have that option. Perhaps they no longer had seaworthy canoes and no trees left to build them.

 Fieldnotes

At its peak, around the fifteenth century, conservative estimates place the Rapa Nui population in the range of 6,000 to 7,000. But some would go as high as 20,000.

Legends Tell a Grim Story

It's here that life on Rapa Nui takes a devastating downturn. Politics or social unrest on the island may have played a role. Stories and legends recounted through the years tell of two factions on the island. One was called Long-Ears and the other was the

Short-Ears. The difference between the two groups relate to the practice of distending the earlobes, which you can readily see on the moai statues. Earlobe distention may follow a Polynesian practice of wearing disc-like earlobe ornaments. But did the Long-Ears make the moai statues? There is no clear answer to this.

> **Paleofacts**
>
> In a final reference to what seems to be unsupported claims, Thor Heyerdahl believed that the Long-Ears were the original settlers from South America and the Short-Ears were Polynesians who arrived later. The archaeological record does not bear out this claim.

> **Anthrolingo**
>
> **Refuse pits** are sites associated with living areas that contain garbage or discarded food and other items. They are very useful to prehistoric archaeologists for reconstructing aspects of ancient lifestyle, including dietary patterns.

Legends, as oral tradition, have not been backed up with desired documentation and verification. That's the case of the Long-Ear/Short-Ear story. It does goes on to say that a battle took place during which all but one of the Long-Ears was killed. Here there is fairly good documentation from the archaeological record that around A.D. 1500, the population was going through a drastic reduction. The upper layers of the *refuse pits* no longer contain bones of the staple food item, the porpoise. Also, the pollen analysis shows there were no more large trees.

Back to the legend, in which it is reported that food had become so scarce that cannibalism was practiced. The appearance of human remains in the upper strata of the refuse pits also seems to substantiate that unfortunate portion of the story. In sites, and strewn near to their place of manufacture, were hundreds of spear points called mataa, which were fashioned from obsidian in huge numbers, setting up what seemed to be a weapons stockpiling. They probably figured into violent conflicts. Human skeletal materials bear evidence of injuries that could well have been the result of spear attacks.

By the end of the eighteenth century, moai statues had been toppled off their ahu platforms. And ahus were destroyed, with bones of the ancestors scattered about. Mataa armed conflicts erupted. Terrible times were ravaging Rapa Nui.

In shorthand notation, Rapa Nui people went from scarcity to famine to warfare. Could matters have gotten any worse for the struggling survivors? They certainly did. Some European visitors arrived to witness the internal strife, but later outside exploiters actively participated in Rapa Nui's decline.

Outsiders Add to the Decline of Rapa Nui Culture

Slave raids began slowly on the Rapa Nui in 1805, but they intensified during the second half of the century. And in a particularly cruel twist of fate, some ill slaves were released and returned to the island only to spread deadly smallpox among their remaining families.

At this time, missionary census estimates record a total of about 1,000 islanders remaining. Depending on what peak population size is used, this would already represent a loss of around 80 percent. But before the turn of the twentieth century, further declines were brought about by large numbers of islanders leaving for Tahiti and other points in central Polynesia. They were apparently seeking refuge from the deteriorated living conditions.

A Rebounding Population

Reliable census estimates record well less than 200 survivors in the late nineteenth century. This was the lowest number since Rapa Nui's founding some 1,500 years earlier. It went from a peak population size of more than 6,000 to only about 150 people. But the story of Rapa Nui certainly doesn't end there.

The population began to grow again around the turn of the twentieth century. There were only about 300 people living on the island in 1922, but by the year 2000, there were around 3,000. This is a very rapid increase— a tenfold increase in less than 100 years. Just as the devastating decline meant a tragic end for much of an earlier cultural expression on Rapa Nui, a very rapid increase in population is now presenting a new set of problems and concerns. We will discuss these shortly. First, the cultural decline on Rapa Nui raised some red flags.

Fieldnotes

It is reported that between 800 and 1,000 islanders were captured and transported to work the guano fertilizer islands off the coast of Peru between 1859 and 1862.

Fieldnotes

Census counts during the late nineteenth century were taken by missionaries. The accuracy of these numbers is probably much higher than when reports from explorers such as Captain Cook, who briefly visited the island. Those explorers likely did not actually see many of the people; reports are that they hid in caves from fear of the outsiders.

Drawing Lessons from the Past and the Present

It does seem somewhat strange that a little island in the big Pacific could have become so significant in setting off an alarm, at least for those who listened. Perhaps Rapa Nui is the little canary in the vast world mine.

Rapa Nui as a Microcosm

The prehistory and history of Rapa Nui have been used as a warning to the larger world that bad things can happen under adverse conditions. One of those conditions might well be unchecked population growth that exceeds finite resources and a capability of securing enough food.

But in the case of Rapa Nui, it is also possible that the very smallness of the island contributed to its decline. Perhaps there were periods of drought that did not allow natural resources, such as trees, to recover. Adverse weather conditions combined with intensive exploitation would be deadly.

> **Paleoquest**
>
> It might be that continued pollen analysis will pinpoint any major shifts in rainfall patterns, such as periods of drought, that contributed to the loss of Rapa Nui's forest.

> **Fieldnotes**
>
> The Natural Resources Defense Fund has reported that about 40 percent of all tropical rainforest has been cut down, and it is being lost at the rate of an acre per second.

Whatever conclusions might be drawn from Rapa Nui, it seems only prudent for the large nations and governments to gain some insight from this knowledge. We started this book by saying that one reason prehistory is done is for the lessons it contains. Well, here's a lesson: It doesn't have to exactly fit the high-tech modern world.

And do we really want to wait and watch a collapse happen before we learn from the past? How much more of a loss of the world's rainforests will convince us that bad things can happen?

Rapa Nui doesn't really provide clear answers, but it surely raises the proper questions. Now Rapa Nui faces a new set of problems connected with its rapid recovery of population numbers over the past century.

Growing Pains

As noted, Rapa Nui has undergone expansive population growth over the past century. To be sure, it has not approached the level seen in prehistoric time. But there are several signs on the figurative and literal road that Rapa Nui is again struggling with population issues.

Here's a list of such problems and concerns:

- Lack of adequate farmland and room for keeping animals
- A huge influx of tourists

- Too many fast-driving automobiles

- Planned major developments of a new seaport, air base, and markets

These are growing pains like those experienced in many places. What makes it so much more difficult for Rapa Nui is that there likely are fewer options. Perhaps the speed and the number of cars could be curtailed. In 1998, there were about 2,000 cars on the island. Possibly these have replaced the many horses from early days. Here is another option under consideration: Rapa Nui is within Chilean authority, and the Chilean government has ownership of around 80 percent of the land. Apparently, there will be a release of ownership to the islanders at some point following negotiations.

Then there is the tourist industry. In 1997, there were about 10,500 visitors to the island, and this number grew to 17,000 in a couple of years. That's both good and bad news. The good news is obviously in terms of the economic benefits. But the not-so-good news is that there are increased demands to build a larger seaport for cruise ships.

Fieldnotes

A few years ago, a law was passed whereby island property could be acquired only by members of the Rapa Nui ethnic group.

This could have a consequence of impinging upon and destroying archaeological sites. And, of course, it's the archaeology that draws so many visitors to the island. Also on the plus side of tourism is that the crafts business is stimulated. There is a high demand for small wood and stone carved statues.

Beyond crafts for the tourist trade, there appears to be a strong interest in maintaining artistic and musical traditions. A yearly ceremony is held to celebrate Rapa Nui's cultural heritage. Beyond their tumultuous and turbulent past, Rapa Nui does have much to celebrate. They have survived a brush with extinction and are now poised to build another glorious future, without ever leaving the island.

Join a Dig

The University of Hawaii offers an Archaeological Field School on Rapa Nui. Participants are trained in all aspects of prehistoric archaeology as they recover artifacts and study ancient sites such as where the ancient islanders lived, the moai stone statues, and the ahu ceremonial platforms. This fieldwork includes the training of Rapa Nui high school students. These are good hands into which to place the past and the future of the island. Website information regarding the dig can be found in Appendix C.

A moai kavakava statue said to represent akuaku, a supernatural being.

(Scott Brisb/Robert J. Meier)

Now we bid Aloha to the balmy, palmy South Seas and head to the blustery far northern end of the Pacific Ocean. A land bridge was ready for migrants to cross and begin an epic-making journey that would take them throughout all of the New World.

The Least You Need to Know

- Rapa Nui was settled by Polynesians around A.D. 400.

- The founding population flourished with such developments as a megalithic tradition of large stone statues.

- About a thousand years ago, growing problems of overpopulation, overuse of resources, perhaps periods of drought, slave raids, and diseases all combined to decimate the people to the brink of extinction.

- Since the turn of the twentieth century, there has been a rapid recovery of population, but this now has presented new problems of lack of farm land, too many cars, and too much development.

- Rapa Nui has become a major tourist attraction because of its archaeological treasures.

Chapter **17**

North America Is Now Open

In This Chapter

- ◆ From Siberia to America
- ◆ Modeling migrations
- ◆ Clovis big-game hunters
- ◆ The megafauna extinction
- ◆ The look of first Americans

Recall that the two underlying themes of this book are variation of human biology and culture through time and place, and movements of human and prehuman groups. It all started in Africa, proceeded to Eurasia, and then moved on to Australia and across the South Pacific. Now we are at the threshold of the last major launch of humans on the surface of our planet. That's perhaps exceeded only by our relatively recent landing on the moon, which obviously required a rocket launch from our planet. We are talking about the migration of walking humans into what thousands of years later would be called the New World, and their eventual expansion all the way to the tip of South America. We are talking about thousands of miles in a surprisingly short amount of time.

These migrating humans were, of course, walking, with possibly some coastline boating. The important questions to be addressed are these:

◆ When did the migration or migrations take place?

◆ What lines of evidence are used to trace the migrations?

◆ What sort of life did the earliest migrants pursue?

We will also take up two special topics:

◆ The disappearance of a large number of large North American mammals

◆ Scientific research that conflicts with Native American beliefs

Setting Up the Ice Stage

Once again, we bring back glaciers to this portion of human prehistory. The time period is at the end of Pleistocene, when glaciers were advancing and retreating, with no apparent regularity. Of course, what they were doing, in addition to making the world's environment colder and dryer, was freezing up large amounts of the Earth's finite water supply. And the consequence of this was to lower the sea level. Seen from our present perspective, we are looking at the region that shows an extension of northeastern Siberia approaching a westward extension of North America. They don't quite touch, but they are probably within sight on clear days. Yet, back in the days of glacial advancements and lowered sea levels, this area formed a broad grassy platform known as *Beringia*.

Anthrolingo

Beringia is the name for the land bridge connecting northeast Siberia and northwest America. At times it was a 1,000-mile-wide expanse of grassland that would have supported large herds of grazing animals.

If you had been there at that time, you would have seen the Bering Straight as the Bering Valley. And this is what formed the Bering land bridge. There would be animal life, perhaps a lot of animals. Were there human groups? Let's go to the archaeology of northeast Siberia to answer that.

Siberian Roots

At the present time, northeast Siberia has a number of more or less settled groups. Most have been there for some time, but none goes all the way back into the days of the Bering land bridge. For various political and cultural reasons, there has been some shifting around. So their presence won't be of any assistance in answering the question just asked.

But archaeological research will. And it shows that humans have been in the area for a long time. There is a claim that they go all the way back to a million years ago, but that is under serious dispute. What is known with good reliability is that occupation of the region had occurred at least by 35 K.Y.A. Now we are setting down a solid foundation.

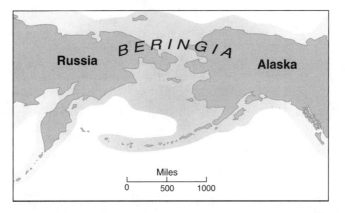

The Bering land bridge.

(Scott Brish)

This happens to be around the time that the Bering land bridge would have been formed, or possibly there were short spans of water—no real barriers, really. Now we have people and we have a bridge—what next? How about a crossing? Okay, but there is a little problem we now have to face. The archaeological record on the North American side of the bridge is a bit slim for this early time period and doesn't show that any of these Siberians actually made the trip. Let's establish some more of the foundation for the peopling of the New World, and then we will return to this vital issue.

The First Americans Were Asians

After the secondary discovery of the New World by Europeans, there were all sorts of sources attributed to the native inhabitants they encountered. But reason and the basics of science replaced earlier fanciful notions.

It became generally accepted that Native Americans had originated in Asia. We will discuss the various lines of evidence marshaled to support this contention, but for now here's a list of physical traits that are commonly shared by Native Americans and Asians:

Fieldnotes

One of the more popular notions was that Native Americans were the Lost Tribes of Israel.

- ◆ Straight, black hair

- ◆ Sparse body hair

- ◆ Less pronounced browridges

- ◆ Broad cheekbones

- ◆ Little facial projection

- ◆ Presence of an *epicanthic eyefold*

Anthrolingo

Epicanthic eyefold refers to a small fold of skin that covers the inner corner of the eye and may extend toward the outer margin of the eye.

In keeping with our theme of human variation, we want to emphasize that this list does not say that all features will be seen in all persons. And their degree of expression also varies among people.

Assuming that the sharing of these traits is due to a sharing of ancestors, we should now take a look at how and when early Asians made the crossing into North America.

Modeling Migration

The timing and number of migrations into the New World have undergone historical renovation. In other words, earlier proposed models have been either torn down or upgraded as new evidence comes in.

Fieldnotes

It should be mentioned that reasonable researchers can and do differ in their interpretations even if they use the same lines of evidence. Some would say that this freedom of expression is what makes the study of human prehistory so exciting.

There are currently two major models to discuss:

- ◆ The three-wave model proposes entry into the New World at the earliest possible date of about 12 K.Y.A.

- ◆ A multiple-migration model claims that the first migration was 30 K.Y.A. or more.

The principal point of difference between these two is that of timing. Let's first have a look at the three-wave model.

Three Waves, Three Lines of Evidence

The three-wave model attempts to integrate evidence derived from studies in language, dentition, and genetics. Obviously, if all three agreed on what they show, this should lend strong support to the proposed model or theory. Language categories tend to lead the construction of models.

Wave One

The first wave to arrive in North America were people who spoke an Amerind language. They are the ancestors to the great majority of later Native Americans. They came to occupy all of North America except Alaska and northwest Canada, and they also expanded into Central and South America.

Wave Two

Then a second wave contained those who spoke a language called Na-Dene. They stayed mostly in the interior of Alaska and into Canada.

Wave Three

Finally, the third migrant group, which spoke languages known an Eskimo-Aleut, crossed Beringia and settled along the coasts of Alaska, including the Aleutian Island chain, northern Canada, and Greenland, especially on the western coast.

As I mentioned, the language categories sort of drive this model. The other two lines of evidence of dental and genetic information play supportive roles.

Fieldnotes _____

Two tribes of the original Na-Dene later migrated into the southwestern United States: These are the Navaho and the Apache.

Fieldnotes _____

Genetic evidence is mostly seen as capable of supporting the three-migration theory, and it also could be used for different models and even for earlier times of entry for the first Amerind speakers.

The matter of Amerind speakers raises most of the criticism of the three-migration model. There is strong objection to the claim that this one category could possibly account for all of the language diversity seen from Canada to the tip of South America. Beyond that, 12,000 years does not allow enough time for all of this diversity to develop. In sum, there must have been more and earlier migrations.

The three-wave model does receive some pretty solid support from archaeology. Here's where that stands.

Archaeology and the Three-Wave Model

Several archaeological sites are located in Alaska and Canada, with artifacts of small stone blades and wedged-shape cores that are very similar to those found widely throughout Asia. Their dates, reliably estimated by the carbon-14 method, cluster around 11 K.Y.A. This timing would fit pretty well with the three-wave model that starts the first wave at 12 K.Y.A. But then the water starts to get a little murky.

That's because there are sites in present-day Pennsylvania (at the Meadowcroft Rockshelter), at Cacus Hill in Virginia, and in Chile, South America (Monte Verde site), that have been dated with carbon-14 well before 12 K.Y.A. As always, these dates would benefit from confirmation. But if they do hold up, then for these sites to exist at the time they do, there must have been a much earlier migration.

Thus, it would seem that the three-wave model doesn't stand up very well in terms of timing, although in number of migrations, there is continued debate. We then have to search for evidence for earlier entries to the New World.

> **Paleofacts**
>
> It would have required several thousand years for small groups of people to move through all that ground between Alaska and distant points in eastern North America and South America—perhaps 7,000 or 8,000 years. Power-walking probably was not yet in vogue.

Multiple Migration Model

Let's start with the archaeology. There aren't a lot of sites, unfortunately.

Dig This

In the Yukon Territory, Canada, not too far from Beringia, there is the site of Old Crow. It produced dates between 43 K.Y.A. and 22 K.Y.A. There is some question of reliability for these dates. In addition, that's quite a large range in estimates.

> **Anthrolingo**
>
> Glottochronology (literally "tongue time") is a formula for determining how different two languages are and how long ago they diverged from one another.

Language Clock

Although some question the reliability in using changes and restructuring of language in a clocklike fashion, there is some basis for accepting it. Several methods are available for assessing degrees of relationship. One is called *glottochronology*.

Language evidence suggests that the first migrants could have arrived at least 20,000 years ago. In fact, with as much language diversity as is found, that date might be pushed back to 30 K.Y.A. to 40 K.Y.A.

Genetic Clock

Some of the same cautions just expressed with regard to language also apply in using genetic change and diversity to measure time. But on face value, this line does indicate that New World migrants split off from their Asian counterparts around 25 K.Y.A. to 20 K.Y.A. Or, in the minds of those highly accepting of genetic evidence, estimates could go back even further, to, say, 30 K.Y.A. or, once again, even 40 K.Y.A.

While there is considerable uncertainly regarding just how far back this earlier peopling process of the New World started, there is growing confidence that it must have been well before the many absolutely dated sites clustering around 12 K.Y.A. Here we want to describe what these sites reveal with regard to way of life.

> **Paleoquest**
>
> Genetic analysis is still being developed. As more studies are done, it seems fairly certain that the picture of peopling of the New World will begin to clear up.

The Clovis People

North American prehistoric archaeologists have given the earliest and most clearly defined level of cultural development the label of Paleoindian. Closely associated with the Paleoindian is a tool technology known as Clovis. While literally hundreds of sites have Clovis-type tools, the name is derived from an important site in New Mexico. What is a Clovis tool?

Applying the terms we introduced earlier, this is a stone spearpoint that is made initially by percussion and then followed up with pressure flaking. But there is one more delicate and significant step before the spearpoint is finished.

A Paleoindian fluted spearpoint from Bone Bank site, Posey County, Indiana.

(Cheryl Munson. Courtesy of the Glenn A. Black Laboratory of Archaeology)

The base or broad end of the spearpoint is struck, which, if all goes right, removes a flake and leaves a channel or flute about a quarter or third of the way up. Hence, this is often called a *fluted* point. Mistakes usually mean that the point was ruined, and some of these artifacts are also found at sites.

Anthrolingo

Fluted points are finely made spearpoints that require special skill in producing a channel or flute. Clovis points have a flute about one third of the way from the base, while later and generally smaller Folsom points have flutes extending nearer to the point end.

It appears that the fluted area helps to make a more secure attachment when the spearpoint is hafted to a wooden shaft. The Clovis point was developed in the New World; none is found in Asia or elsewhere. But they appear in sites from Canada to that tip of South America, Terra del Fuego. Wherever they are found, the dates for the sites fall in a fairly tight cluster around 12 K.Y.A. to 10 K.Y.A. Now, there are two major points to make with regard to this point:

- If it developed in one place, which seems likely, the technology spread very quickly.

- If it spread very rapidly, there must have been a decided advantage over earlier technologies.

Advantage here means in terms of hunting efficiency, for that is what the spearpoint would be used for. Clovis points are commonly found in association with large mammals. Hunted mammals included the following:

- Mastodons

- Mammoths

- Bison

- Horses

- Caribou

- Musk oxen

- Giant beavers

- Giant ground sloths

Clearly, there must have been hunting efficiency and proficiency. Small mammals were also hunted. As we will discuss shortly, many of the large animal species went extinct by 9,000 years ago. Did the hunters have something to do with their extinction?

Paleoindian hunting scene. The hunter is using an atlatl or spearthrower.

(Chase Studio. Photo Researchers, Inc.)

Clovis people were not exclusively hunters. They also gathered roots, seeds, and berries. As glaciers shrunk, there was increased dependence on foraging for food. And even though the hunting-gathering package put together by the Clovis people was apparently very successful, it wasn't the way of life for all at this time.

There is evidence from Brazil that a very different kind of adaptation worked better in the rainforest of the Amazon River Basin. This site is dated more than 10 K.Y.A. Recovered remains indicate that their diet consisted of small game, birds, fish, mollusks, and fruit.

Could these rainforest dwellers be from a different group of migrants than the Clovis people? Or were they from the same group but doing what humans are very adept at? That would mean modifying their lifestyles to fit the different environmental and ecological situation. A highly adaptable culture would permit such modification. Apparently, the big-game animals listed earlier didn't have that ability. At least, there was a major episode of extinction. Let's review that topic.

Fieldnotes

The Brazilian Amazon site of Caverna da Pedra Pintada may have the earliest evidence of cave art in the New World. On the walls are paintings of circles and handprints in red pigment. The site is dated around 10 K.Y.A.

Where Did All the Megafauna Go?

Paleoindians were accomplished hunters. An abundance of large animals or megafauna likely provided a well-stocked larder. Beyond that, from what we learn of more recent Native Americans, they probably used all parts of the animals—certainly for food, shelter, robes, and carrying devices. Tanning of animal hides would have been a common activity.

Woman tanning a hide in a Paleoindian scene.

(Chase Studio. Photo Researchers, Inc.)

There is the notion that megafauna had not been under any great predator threat before the appearance of humans. That means that initially they would not as likely have run off when approached by hunters. This situation has suggested to ecologist Paul S. Martin that Paleoindians, with their highly efficient hunting skills, carried out an "overkill" that resulted in the extinction of many species. The ecological obituary included the magnificent mammoth and mastodon.

Fieldnotes

One report states that megafauna in North America dropped from 79 species to 22 species following human migrations to the New World. Some extinct forms were the mastodon, mammoth, and giant beavers and ground sloths.

But, as you probably guessed, the overkill hypothesis is not fully accepted by all. There isn't very much archaeological evidence. Butchering sites of megafauna don't have anywhere near the numbers of skeletons that would be predicted if massive kills were taking place. Then, too, many of the extinctions of species occurred before the time of the Clovis hunters.

In place of the overkill hypothesis, it is argued that environmental conditions following the retreat of glaciers were rapidly changing. There would be loss of habitat with the rising sea level. And the warming trend could have been so fast that the cold-adapted forms could not make the necessary modifications. In short, evolution was outrun by changing climate. Some species were able to readapt, as evidenced by the continued existence of caribou and musk oxen.

We have described the Paleoindians in terms of their Clovis fluted points, their way of life, and just now the possibility of their interaction with megafauna extinctions. Next, we will have a look at the human skeletal materials from this time period. They happen to be even more rare than the skeletons of mammoths.

Rarity has been exceeded by heightened controversy over one skeleton, Kennewick Man.

> **Paleoquest**
>
> A possible third outcome could be a combination of heavy hunting practices and a prolonged and steep warming trend. There has also been a proposal that a major viral infection took place among the big mammals. Future studies could shed some light on this matter.

Fossilized First Americans

Decades of extensive archaeological research in the New World have resulted in good documentation of ancient cultural practices and a fairly complete mapping of the distribution and dating of these first Americans. But there has been a paucity of recovering human skeletal remains from this early time period, and what has been found is widely scattered across the country. Here's a list of the more prominent finds:

- Santa Rosa Island, California, dated 13 K.Y.A.
- Midland "Man," Texas, dated 11.6 K.Y.A.
- Marmes Skull, Washington, dated 11.5 K.Y.A.–10.5 K.Y.A.
- Minnesota "Man," Minnesota, dated 11.5 K.Y.A.–10.5 K.Y.A.
- Tepexpan, Mexico, dated 11.5 K.Y.A.–10.5 K.Y.A.

There continues to be uncertainty about dating of these finds, although there is a rather tight clustering. With regard to physical features, some of the material is not preserved very well, but what can be seen is consistent with referring to them as Native Americans. It should be recognized that biological variation is expected,

> **Paleofacts**
>
> Both Midland "Man" and Minnesota "Man" were later determined to be females.

especially in the widespread distribution of the recovered materials. But other skeletal materials have been found that begin to raise questions of who they are and where they came from. Here's that list:

- Luzia, Brazil, dated 11 K.Y.A.

- Spirit Cave, Nevada, dated 9.4 K.Y.A.

- Kennewick, Washington, dated 9.3 K.Y.A.

The last two of these are said to have physical features that do not resemble Native Americans or Asians. The traits that come into play are a flatter face and a more pointed jaw, as compared with more facial projection and a squared-off jaw. In fact, with regard to Kennewick, labels such as Caucasoid and European have been introduced to the discussion. Discussion has sparked controversy and conflict among various interested parties.

On one side are American Indian tribal representatives who claim that Kennewick is Native American by virtue of the fact that it predates the arrival of Columbus to the New World. Several affiliated tribes have requested that Kennewick be released for proper reburial.

On another side is a group of researchers who are seeking access to the skeletal material. They want the material studied with the expectation that further research might shed some light on the skeleton's population identity.

The eventual decision regarding Kennewick is currently involved in a court case set up to resolve the dispute. For now, it appears that additional study of Kennewick will be permitted. What then happens will depend on the research findings.

Fieldnotes

A public law governs disposition of recovered skeletal remains identified as Native American. This is the Native American Graves Protection and Repatriation Act, or NAGPRA. NAGPRA may come into play in the case of Kennewick.

Some physical anthropology research is beginning to show that the first migrants to the New World did not look like Asians or Native Americans as usually defined. But this does not mean that they weren't of Asian origin. What is being proposed is that the initial crossing of Beringia was made by Asians from a much earlier time period before physical features of more recent Asians had developed, such as more rounded heads and broader cheekbones. Once again, it should be pointed out that every population is variable, and individuals can and do differ from what is considered to be typical physical appearance.

We have mentioned that archaeological evidence indicates an earlier migration, one that occurred before the Clovis people. The language and genetic clocks also suggest this.

One proposal is that the first crossing of Beringia was made by people from Asia before they developed their more recent physical appearance. These people would have traveled along the coastline. Then a second migration, possibly through the interior ice-free corridors, involved later Asians, with their changed physical features. And these were the ancestors of present-day Native Americans. But as we have seen numerous times throughout this book, this proposal must be treated as tentative and certainly subject to more research.

This chapter described the big-game Paleoindian hunters, known as Clovis. In the next chapter, we continue on this topic to present the whale hunters of northern Alaska.

> **Paleoquest**
>
> Continued research is being done to determine the timing and routes for New World migrations. It is now believed that one favored route was down the western coastline of the Americas. Then there is an interior route. But this has to be considered in light of glacial advances and the possibility of travel between glaciers in ice-free corridors.

The Least You Need to Know

- Solid evidence indicates that the New World was settled at least by 12 K.Y.A.

- Evidence is mounting of a much earlier migration beyond 20 K.Y.A.

- Clovis big-game hunters were very efficient, but it is not clear that they played a major role in megafauna extinction.

- An ongoing dispute centers on the disposition of the Kennewick skeleton and, in general, on the question of what the earliest settlers to the New World looked like.

Chapter 18

Northern Hunters, Survivors of the Ice Age

In This Chapter

- ◆ Eskimo-Aleut and Na-Dene settlement in Alaska
- ◆ Island, coastal, and inland contacts among Alaskan natives
- ◆ Inupiat whaling culture
- ◆ An application of ethnographic analogy

In the last chapter, we traced the human settlement of the New World via Beringia. While in place, Beringia offered both humans and animals easy access across two juts of land. One is called the Chuckchi Peninsula, which extends out on the Asian side. The other is the Seward Peninsula, extending westward from the North American side. Animals and humans went back and forth across Beringia.

In this chapter, we focus on the human groups that at some point settled on the North American side in an area now known as the state of Alaska. Eskimos are the particular group we look at, and their whaling activities draw our special attention. Consider this a use of ethnographic analogy.

We can gain some insight to the earliest migrants to the New World. And as we noted, these may be well in excess of 20,000 years ago. Ethnographic analogy is not proof of what once was, but it does suggest possible past behaviors that otherwise are not preserved. Our time line for looking at Eskimos is about at the time of European contact in the late eighteenth and early nineteenth centuries. Mention will also be made of major changes in Eskimo culture that has taken place since that early contact period.

East of Beringia

In the last chapter, we talked about the three-wave migration model and its use of major language divisions. Here we are interested in the two-later arriving divisions, namely, the Na-Dene and Eskimo-Aleuts. Their time of entry to North America is about 5,000 or more years ago. Here's where these groups ended up in present-day Alaska.

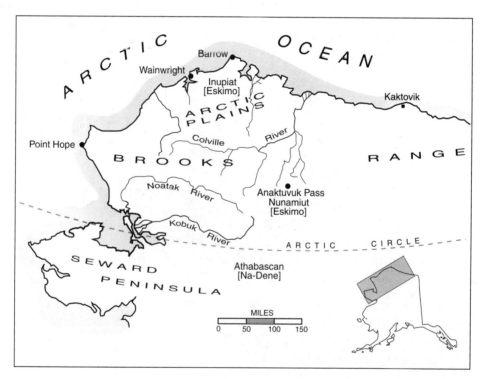

Eskimo and American Indian localities in Alaska.

(Scott Brish)

Over Land and Up Rivers

The Na-Dene occupied the interior portions, traveling the river valleys, and for the most part, stayed in tree-covered areas. They also settled in the coastal region in southeast Alaska. Their language group is Athabascan, and today some are known at Gwich'in, who live in the general vicinity of Fairbanks.

Island Hopping in the Arctic

In a way, the Aleuts resemble their counterparts in the South Pacific, except that the conditions are much harsher and the sea voyages distances are not quite so long. But strong navigational skills still came into play as they settled the Aleutian Island chain, island by island heading west.

A rare three-hatch kayak.

(Robert J. Meier/Scott Brish)

Open sea travel was done by kayak. A kayak is somewhat canoe-shape and very effective for speed and maneuvering.

The Aleuts are closely related to the inhabitants of Kodiak Island, the Koniags. The Kodiak Island chain, or archipelago, was also settled by this group.

Chirikof Island in historic times was occupied by Russians, who may have used the island as a penal colony or kept natives there to hunt sea lions that had a rookery on the island.

Caribou Corridors

Certain Eskimo groups also settled the interior. They generally lived north of the Na-Dene. This interior group is called the Nunamiut, and today they live in the Brooks Mountain Range. Their subsistence was partly based on migrating caribou herds that traveled the mountain passes on their way to and returning from their breeding and calving groups on the North Slope of Alaska.

Fieldnotes

The Koniags, or perhaps Aleuts, made it all the way to Chirikof Island, a tiny speck of land isolated in the North Pacific. Chirikof might be considered the "Easter Island" of the north, very small and treeless, but also stone statueless.

Paleofacts

Eskimos of Canada are generally referred to as Inuit.

Going Coastal

Then there are those Eskimo groups that settled the western and northwestern coasts of Alaska. We concentrate on those who lived roughly from present-day Point Hope to the Point Barrow area. These are established communities today and have been occupied for thousands of years. Their language is called Inupiaq; likewise, the name of the people is Inupiat.

Next, we want to outline some of the more important interactions that took place among and between these groups.

Keeping in Touch

Although settlement occurred in certain areas, these groups were also highly mobile—and had to be to survive. Game animals and fish, their primary food items, were not always sufficient in the same area year after year. This meant traveling in search of food. And traveling meant contacts. But traveling was also done for social and economic reasons. People desired to keep in touch with their relatives and friends. And there were advantages when trade items could be exchanged. Next we discuss the principal contacts that took place.

Siberian and Alaskan Eskimos

It is hard to say that Siberian and Alaskan Eskimos actually separated, except with respect to the dominant nations involved today. It is clear that families on both sides of the Bering Straight maintained their connections. The rather narrow straight, 50 miles or less, presented no barrier to kayakers, and during winter there was solid ice to travel across. There are also a couple of small islands about halfway in the journey.

Aleuts and Koniags

We mentioned that Aleuts and Koniags are closely related. There are accounts that kayakers made the trip back and forth. In one instance, it was to transfer a woman from the Aleutians to Kodiak for the purpose of marriage. A special three-hatch kayak was used for the trip.

Inupiat and Nunamiut

Contacts between the coastal and inland Eskimos were regular. Travel generally followed major rivers such as the Colville and the Kuk. These were for trade and also could involve the exchange of women for marriage. The interior was also a much less reliable caribou-hunting area. Sometimes it was a matter of the caribou passing through a different mountain pass than the one where the Nunamiut had set up camp. Thus, famine and starvation depleted the Nunamiut occasionally. This might have been followed by coastal Inupiat moving into the interior to build the population back up.

> **Paleofacts**
>
> The Diomede Islands are located about midway in the Bering Straight, with the International Dateline passing between them. Little Diomede is owned by the United States, and Big Diomede is owned by Russia. It's likely that some human contact still takes place between these two islands at this time.

Nunamiut and Athabascans

The southern reaches of the Nunamiut and the northern extent of the Athabascans crossed at times. While there may have been hostilities, there were also friendly relationships. These contacts took place along rivers such as the Kobuk. Today there are Nunamiut and Athabascan villages located across the Alatna River from each other. Once again, early contacts were for trading and socializing, although marriages also occurred.

The variety and extent of contacts between groups can be used to think about the past of all hominid groups. Although prehistoric connections for the earliest migrants to Asia or Europe were not the same as we see here, we do gain some perspective of how they could have looked. We now shift to a hunting activity that

> **Paleoquest**
>
> There is a proposal that Nunamiut and Athabascan ancestors were actually much more closely related. In fact, they could have been basically the same group that entered the New World and then split into two groups. Additional research may clarify this issue.

also provides a model of how things might have been in the earlier days of big-game hunters in other parts of the world.

A Whale of a Job

Inupiat Eskimos developed a way of life that ensured survival under extreme environmental conditions. We will look at some of these developments shortly, but here we concentrate on hunting of the whale.

Location, Location, Location

Whales migrate along the western coast of North America and head all the way to the Arctic Ocean and the Beaufort Sea. Some places along the coast of Alaska bring them closer to shore. One of these locations is Point Hope. The Inupiaq name is *Tigara*, which means "pointed finger." That describes a narrow strip of land jutting out into the ocean. Tigara is already situated on a peninsula-like extension of land. And that would give the whale hunters closer access to their migrating meals.

Another prime location was Point Barrow. Point Barrow is also situated on a land projection and is on a corner of land that requires whales to turn sharply right as they leave the Arctic Ocean and enter the Beaufort Sea on their spring migration.

These favorable spots were joined by a number of others throughout the prehistory of whaling activity along the northwest coast of Alaska.

Let's take a look at what this meant some time into the past.

> **Paleofacts**
>
> Both Point Hope and Point Barrow, are active whaling communities today.

Hunting the Bowhead

The usual whale species hunted was the bowhead. It provided food, *baleen* for making items, and bones for building shelters.

Other kinds of whales were also sometimes hunted. Quite often this was the small beluga whale, which travels in large pods or groups. These pods might be driven into small inlets where it was easier to harpoon the beluga.

> **Anthrolingo**
>
> **Baleen** is hard, plastic-looking plates with hairy edges that whales use to filter out small sea food items such as zooplankton. Many plates, about 7 to 8 feet long, hang from the upper jaw of the bowhead whale.

The Boss or Captain

Whales were hunted by a crew of about six men, well organized, as you imagine, since this was a high-risk enterprise. The crew was headed by a boat captain or *umialik*. He was wealthy enough to have a boat and the necessary tools of the trade. The boat used was a rather large open vessel, called an *umiak*, which was made of walrus hide. It didn't leak, but it needed to dry out periodically.

A crew and its umiak whaling boat.

(Robert J. Meier)

The umiak was dragged over sea ice to open leads of water. At times the hunters could remain at the edge of the ice, but otherwise they used the boat to increase their chances of intercepting a big bowhead.

A Whaling Tool Kit

The necessary equipment beyond the boat was simple but highly efficient and effective. Tools included a detachable toggle-headed harpoon point and its shaft, a line and bladder float, lances, and *ulus*.

This is the equivalent of high-tech equipment in the prehistoric world. The toggle-headed harpoon was especially innovative. After it struck the whale, the shaft fell off and the harpoon head rotated sideways with the line and float attached. Remember when we introduced the innovation of composite tools? Here is the height of such. In its rotated position, the harpoon point was less likely to pull out as the injured whale sped off. The dual purposes of the line and the bladder float were to tire out the whale and help the hunters keep track of where it was heading.

Anthrolingo

Ulus are crescent-shape knives traditionally made from slate. The curved surface extended its cutting action.

This hunting method, as said, is both simple and effective. Few whales that were struck were lost. It might have taken hours or even days, but nearly all whales were retrieved. The success rate today is not as good as it was in the past.

Paleofacts

Modern whaling gear involves aluminum boats and bomb darts, or explosive charges. The success rate in retrieving struck whales using this equipment is not as high as with the traditional method.

Fieldnotes

Modern equipment includes snowmobiles for hauling. Snowmobiles may have more power, but it has been said by wise old-timers that if it breaks down and you are caught in a big snow storm far from home, you can't eat it like you could with dogs.

Paleofacts

It was the practice of some Eskimos and Athabascans to allow breeding between their dogs and wolves. This might have added back certain desired traits that had been removed by selective breeding of the domesticated dog.

Soon after the whale was retrieved, the Inupiat thanked the whale spirit for allowing it to be caught. The Inupiat were ever mindful that proper appeasement was essential to their hunting success. The next step in the retrieval process was to haul the whale onto the ice, or begin to butcher it from the ice edge. Long-bladed lances were used by hunters to open the whale, and ulus cut big pieces into smaller pieces. Pieces of what?

The Inupiat term for whale skin and fat (blubber) is *muktuk* or *maktak*. These pieces were several inches thick, and once removed, whale meat was carved off the carcass. As you imagine, a load of muktuk and meat is heavy. Getting it back to shore meant loading it in the umiak and dragging that back, or loading up a sled and letting the dog team haul it back.

Who Let the Wolves In?

Dog teams have been an important element in Eskimo survival across the Arctic. How long they have been around is not known for certain. Dog bones and wolf bones look very much alike. Recent genetic studies indicate that wolves were domesticated to dogs in Asia around 15,000 years ago. It appears that some wolves might have hung around people to gain access to an easier meal of handouts.

In this sense, wolves domesticated themselves. And after centuries of breeding, they are apparently the best able of all animals to "read" human behavioral cues. Many dog owners can attest to that.

A Whale of a Feast

Under the direction of the umialik captain, distribution of the muktuk and whale meat followed an orderly pattern. Usually every family received some. Excess whale could be placed in underground caches dug out of the permafrost. No need for refrigerators here.

Some meat was stored inside, and even though it "turned" or underwent fermentation, it usually could be eaten without harm to the person, as long as the pot was regularly stirred. Unfortunately, in some reported cases, stored meat and juices produced botulism in the air-deprived bottom of a container, with fatal consequences to those who ate it.

Tossing a Celebration

A successful whale hunt or season was cause for celebration, in a ceremony called *nalukataq*. First, there was the distribution of whale just mentioned. Then running games and other athletic activities took place. One of the more exciting was the blanket toss. Persons were placed on the center of a hide blanket and repeatedly tossed higher and higher.

A skilled "tossie" could perform acrobatic moves in midair, and that person also hoped that the "tossers" didn't toss him off balance so that he missed the blanket and landed on the much firmer ground. Paleopathologists might be on the lookout for a high frequency of arm and leg fractures.

Dancing and Drumming

There were also occasions for dancing and drumming. The drum instrument was walrus gut tightly stretched across a frame. When struck, it gave a sharp, resonate thud. Several drummers beat in unison while the dancers danced.

Drummers at a dance.

(Robert J. Meier)

Men performed a stomplike step as they might re-enact a hunting story of stalking and harpooning a seal. Women were a quite a bit less active and swayed in rhythm to the beat.

Let the Games Begin

Eskimos engaged in many kinds of athletic contests. Many of these were tests of strength, perseverance, and endurance of pain. These are some of the traits that were important to survival, and games were an outlet for practicing and perfecting them.

Performing these athletic contests was carried up to modern times when Eskimos and Athabascans came together each year at the Native American Olympics held in a gymnasium in Fairbanks. This was also a time for contesting in other traditional skills such as seal skinning with ulus or keeping a seal-oil lamp burning. There might also be singing, dancing, and drumming competitions. In this way, the past is relived and rekindled. And for those who watch, it is an opportunity to observe what it might have been like in some earlier time and place. Here we want to return to that earlier day to describe more of traditional Inupiat way of life.

Not by Whale Alone

As important as it was, whale hunting was not the only subsistence activity the Inupiat engaged in. They carried out a number of other hunting and fishing activities. Gathering was rather limited to berries. There is clear evidence that they made extensive and possibly wise use of their environmental resources.

Here's a list of other kinds of hunting and food-gathering activities engaged in by Inupiat Eskimos:

> **Paleoquest**
>
> It has been said that Eskimos practiced a form of conservation based on an understanding of ecology and finite supply. This could be so, or possibly they simply didn't have a technology that would allow overuse or heavy depletion of resources. More research is needed on this topic.

♦ Seal and walrus hunting

♦ Caribou hunting

♦ Polar bear hunting

♦ Duck and ptarmigan netting

♦ Fishing, especially salmon runs

♦ Berry picking

As you can see, this diet is heavy on animal protein and fat. But as a source of calories and required dietary components, these are much better than carbohydrates.

One item on the menu apparently did cause problems at times: the polar bear liver, which concentrates high amounts of vitamin A. There have been reports of vitamin A toxicity leading to death, and also a possible nonfatal case. In this latter instance, it was said that the person's skin and hair turned white. In the great scheme of things, this was probably minor in comparison with actually hunting the polar bear. In fact, it has been said that the role of hunter and hunted is often interchanged. The score may actually be in favor of the polar bear.

Feast or Famine

Certainly, there were times when food was plentiful. It was at these times that large amounts were eaten. With a high food intake, one side effect is to generate a lot of body heat. And that is good if you live in the arctic. Said a little differently, the Eskimo diet would not be very adaptable if you lived in the tropics.

On the other side of the coin, there also were lean days, periods of famine and starvation. These episodes were likely local, involving small groups, and more often were inland rather than on the coast.

Large caribou herds didn't always migrate through the mountain passes where people had settled. That would mean a short supply of this important food item. Then, too, the more vulnerable babies and elderly were more likely to die during times of food shortages.

The sharing of food ethic mentioned earlier helped to smooth out the good and bad times, and for that the Inupiat overall benefited. Now we can take a deeper look into Inupiat culture.

> **Paleofacts**
>
> Some decades ago, it was a puzzle why Eskimos didn't suffer from vitamin C deficiency, leading to scurvy. Or why they didn't have high rates of heart disease. They got vitamin C from raw meat and consumed large amounts of heart-friendly fish oils.

> **Fieldnotes**
>
> Inland groups lived, and some still live, in an area now designated as the Arctic National Wildlife Refuge. The U.S. Senate blocked an attempt of the current administration in 2002 to open ANWR to oil drilling. It's likely more attempts will be made.

> **Paleofacts**
>
> Eskimos are said to practice "abandonment of grandparents." More often it was the grandparents who recognized that they could no longer keep up with a group on the move, and perhaps on the move to find food. So they voluntarily stayed behind rather than become a burden.

Spirit of Community

Inupiat settlements along the northwestern Alaskan coasts were permanent; at least a few were like Point Hope and Point Barrow. This meant that with good times, population tended to grow. But conditions were probably never so plentiful that population growth went out of control and led to overuse of the resources. This gives a very different view in comparison with Easter Island.

The community thrived on promoting values of cooperation and sharing. But competition and autonomy or independence were also extolled virtues. This combination could account for successful survival—that is, these values along with the Inupiats' uncanny ability to develop a technology for extracting a living from a tough and unforgiving environment.

Family Ties

The Inupiat had basic family units composed of members from both the father and the mother's sides. So this would be a double-extended family. If the community was large enough, there was a marriage practice of *endogamy*. Otherwise, there might be a requirement to select a partner from another community. This is where the trading meetings and fairs could play a role.

Dad Stays Home

When marriage partners did come from another community, most often the wife moved in from elsewhere. This is called *patrilocality*.

 Anthrolingo

Endogamy refers to a set of marriage rules that require choosing eligible partners from within a specified boundary, such as a village or community. Exogamy sets up rules that require marriages to take place with partners outside certain boundaries, again such as a village, or degree of relationship.

Patrilocality is a residence rule that specifies that the husband remain home, at the place of his father, with his wife moving to his locality.

One of the reasons given for patrilocality in the case of the Inupiat is that men would be familiar with their father's hunting and fishing areas. And familiarity could help to ensure success in subsistence activities. Success was also highly dependent upon the efforts of women. Women were essential to the economic well-being of the family.

They were the ones responsible for preparing and cooking, say, a seal, after it was brought home.

There is also the recognition that Inupiat respected geographic boundaries and would not willingly encroach on someone else's territory—at least, they wouldn't without a threat of being beaten or worse.

There were ways of joining with other communities in friendly relationships. One of these was in setting up hunting partners. These partners were not related or very distantly related, but they acted toward each other as if they were close relatives.

And as mentioned earlier, the coastal Inupiat at times migrated inland, either by choice or to replace those lost through starvation. These moves tended to cement relationships across communities.

In the end, violence did break out at times between groups, but mostly it was avoided by following some well-understood rules of conduct. We have mentioned the harsh living conditions of the Arctic. That might make many of us think of housing and clothing. Here's some information on these topics.

> ### Paleofacts
>
> The Eskimo engaged in a practice referred to as wife swapping. This was based more on the need for assistance of a woman than on sexual liaison. Hunting partners exchanged wives, for example, if one man's wife was pregnant and could not safely go on a hunting trip.

Shelter and Clothing

No one would be surprised if I said it got cold in northwestern Alaska. But many might be surprised to learn that this area does not receive a lot of snow. It is virtually a desert in terms of annual precipitation, with around 6 to 8 inches. This is less than that received in the Mojave Desert. Of course, whatever snow came down in the fall pretty much stayed around until spring thaw in April or May. This lack of good snowfall in the tundra area of the North Slope of Alaska restricted the construction of what is widely known as an Eskimo *igloo*.

Igloos were built for temporary housing during hunting trips inland. But on the coast there just weren't the right snow conditions. And that

> ### Anthrolingo
>
> **Igloo** is the native term for "house," but generally has come to refer to a dome-shape structure made from blocks of snow. These are very efficient for maintaining heat and, with the traditional seal oil lamp, could raise the internal temperature to 90°F. That's quite warm but also quite smoke-filled.

shelter so prominently used by prehistoric peoples, the cave, was not very available in the flat tundra and coastal regions of Alaska. So other forms had to serve the purpose.

Home in the Earth

One kind of construction made houses out of chunks of sod. These might be piled against an embankment, or could be supported with whale rib bones or driftwood. Stone walls also were used at times.

Sod houses were built by the inland Nunamiut as well. In modern times, when they received materials to build wood-frame houses, it was quite noticeable that the sod houses had been more warm and comfortable.

Who Is Your Tailor?

If you recall from way back in Chapter 12, Upper Paleolithic peoples started the trend of fitted or tailored clothing—for good reason, it appears. This was likely warmer than loose, robe-like garments. Inupiat Eskimos perfected the making of tailored clothing in pants, parkas, and boots, called mukluks. Of course, animal skins and furs were the raw materials. Generally, seal skins made the bulk of the clothing that was then trimmed in wolf or wolverine fur. Eider duck down was also used for insulation. Mukluks were likewise made from seal skin.

Fieldnotes

A story is told that if two hunters were out and one fell into the water, the other one would share some of his clothing with the dunked one, after he stripped off all of his wet clothing. The moral is that two quite cold men were better than one dying from exposure and the other remaining dry.

How efficient in maintaining body heat were these? Probably as good as or better than any manufactured clothing, up to the invention of materials that wicked away moisture and "breathed."

If someone in Eskimo-style clothing started to exercise too much, sweating would begin. And sweating is bad since once the person stops any strenuous activity, cold sweat begins to freeze. To prevent this from happening, Eskimo clothing had chimneys or vents that could be opened to release some of the body heat. That's a rather ingenious solution.

Ethnographic Analogy

These brief accounts of the Inupiat Eskimo help to fill out some of the picture of what it might have been like in earlier periods of time. To be sure, the details are expected to differ. But in broad terms, some of the problems they faced and some of the solutions they made are likely to be similar. That's what ethnographic analogy is all about. It gives us a clearer perspective of what might have been.

The Least You Need to Know

♦ Eskimos and Aleuts mainly settled the islands and coastlines of Alaska.

♦ Na-Dene groups are mostly found in the interior of Alaska.

♦ The Inupiat culture of northwestern Alaska was closely tied to the hunting of whales.

♦ Ethnographic and historic accounts of Inupiat are helpful in offering a perspective into prehistoric cultures.

Part **6**

Issues in Human Origins

Having looked at a good deal of the scientific methodology of human pre-history, we now dig a little deeper into the nature of science to address some of the challenges to evolution. We lay out the basics of Darwinian evolution, followed by an update of Darwin's work, and then respond to creationism and intelligent design.

In the final chapter, we look at the various strategies that humans have at their disposal to direct our future. We are indeed the captains at the helm of this great enterprise. What will be our destination?

Chapter 19

Science Driven by Questions

In This Chapter

- ◆ Questions drive scientific inquiry
- ◆ The past as experiments
- ◆ The importance of being theoretical
- ◆ Challenges of and techniques in prehistory
- ◆ Questions, questions, and more questions

Human prehistory is a fascinating area of study. Perhaps this book has given you a sense of what prehistory covers, how it covers it, and what remains to be uncovered from the past. These might be considered the positive aspects of the science. But the study of human prehistory also has been subject to harsh criticism. It has been criticized in terms of its methods and findings. And possibly most controversial are those who think that the questions investigated by human prehistorians are not really scientific and can't be studied using the scientific method. The focus of this chapter is to present the nature of science and the way in which human prehistory conforms to scientific principles. Examples have been selected from earlier chapters. In this way, highlights of human prehistory can be reviewed.

Keeping in Step

Most school children are trained to apply the scientific method when they work on their science fair projects. They know that they must follow certain steps, mostly agreed on by scientists around the world. Here are the basic steps of the scientific method and their equivalents in human prehistory:

1. State a hypothesis or pose research questions.

2. Describe methods, which is the same step in human prehistory.

3. Conduct an experiment or *survey* sites, and collect hominid fossils or archaeological remains from the sites.

4. Analyze results or do a laboratory study of bones and stones and other information collected at the site.

5. State conclusions or interpret fossils and reconstructions of past cultures.

6. Repeat step one: Restate a new hypothesis or pose new research questions.

Anthrolingo

Survey refers to the preliminary work done at a site to determine both the presence of prehistoric materials and, if there, what their distribution at the site is.

Have you ever heard of going around in circles? This is not what science is, at least not intentionally. Hopefully it is more like, *start here* and you will end up *back here*, but all the more wiser! The circularity of the scientific method recognizes that, except in very limited instances, the results and interpretations are never final. There will always be later improvements and modifications to be made. In short, science marches on, and advancements rest on already accumulated knowledge.

Science Driven by Ignorance

Most definitions of science include a reference to the accumulation of knowledge, usually gained through systematic observations. But what is the opposite of knowledge? Ignorance.

The Power of Ignorance

Unfortunately, ignorance has taken on derogatory connotations, when, in fact, it basically means lacking in knowledge. It does not mean lacking in intelligence. Scientists understand that they conduct research on problems or questions on which there is currently a lack of understanding and knowledge.

When scientists begin any research project, they are ignorant of the specific knowledge they might gain, even though they expect the newly discovered knowledge will advance their science discipline. It could be said that if knowledge is the road to wisdom, then ignorance drives the vehicle of science forward. We take a little detour here to consider ignorance from the standpoint of educating children, our budding scientists, and all other career destinations.

Fieldnotes

Stupid might be the word that seems interchangeable with *ignorant*. It isn't. *Stupid* could be defined as not using the knowledge a person has in an appropriate manner. Following a stupid act, you will often hear, "You know better than that."

Ignorance in School

Science education could be solidly based on the principle of ignorance. Much of current educational effort is directed toward imparting scientific knowledge. Certainly, this is important. We couldn't function very well if we didn't possess a good deal of understanding of how the world works. But if we want students to begin to discover the world for themselves, then they must start by asking questions. More precisely, they need to maintain questioning minds. This is essentially what the buzz phrase "critical thinking" is all about. Critical applies not only to thinking, but also to speaking, reading, and doing.

Very young children seem to naturally have questioning minds. They are full of questions. "Mommy, why is this?" "Daddy, why is that?" For some parents, these endless questions can reach a point of impatience. The inquiring mind seeks answers and enjoys discovery. Have you seen the joy a child shows in having figured something out? It's about the same kind of enjoyment experienced by the adult scientist whose experiment just yielded a wonderful result: *"Eureka!"*

Unfortunately, in many schools, the questioning mind of the young child is formed into the vessel-to-be-filled mind of the older student.

Paleoquest

It could be the natural outcome of brain evolution for children to seek knowledge through their questions—knowledge that could well have had survival value later. This could be a promising area of research.

Anthrolingo

Eureka is the appropriate exclamation for having found something, or for exclaiming, "I've got it!"

A lot of the awards and rewards, including grades and contest prizes, are based on knowledge. Students receive prizes for their answers more so than for their questions. But there are increasing efforts of teachers to keep that spark of inquiry alive in their students' heads.

While this argument on questioning and discovering minds may seem to best fit science topics and classes, it could be applied across all of the usual subjects offered in our schools. Moments of "eureka" discoveries can come in many forms, in music and art as well as in the laboratory. And speaking of the laboratory, that is where experiments usually take place, except in the science of human prehistory.

Prehistoric Experiments

Step three in the scientific method is to perform experiments. This doesn't directly apply to human prehistory. Obviously, we can't go back in time to control any of the conditions or events that were then present.

In a way, human prehistory is one huge experiment that has already taken place. Extinction of species and loss of cultures and civilizations could be seen as experiments that, for whatever reasons, failed. Others flourished to become ancestors of modern forms. It is the prehistorian's job to go out in the field to find the results, good or bad. Of course, the prehistorian must be prepared with and guided by the right questions. What this kind of research lacks in control, it makes up for in surprise of discovery. I am pretty sure that when Don Johanson found the Lucy material, there was boundless excitement—one of those "Eureka!" moments.

Fieldnotes

We covered experimental toolmaking and tool use in Chapter 8. These efforts are carried out in a laboratory type of setting. They are very helpful in determining how tools could have been made and used in the distant past.

Back here in the more mundane world, we all carry a little science in our brain bag of tricks. The scientific method is used to make decisions in our daily lives. Sure, we don't make it a formal procedure, but science serves as a guideline that tends to work some of the time.

Fieldnotes

One of our common uses of scientific information applies to weather forecasting. We are given probabilities or chances that certain weather events will occur. Then we are able to see the outcome of that prediction, and base our future expectations on its success or failure. With weather forecasting, we are essentially using theory testing in our daily lives.

Of all the notions in science, the one that seems most troublesome to get across to those not working in science is theory.

It's Only a Theory

Counting the plethora of detective, lawyer, forensic, courtroom dramas on television, there is a fairly steady stream of theorizing going on. How did he die? Who is the father of that child? Aspects of the scientific method are employed in the service of seeking justice. Is this what scientists mean when they refer to a *theory*? Probably not.

Certainly, researchers don't regard their theories as mere guesses or hunches, as defined popularly. The following are some examples of famous theories:

◆ Theory of relativity, al a Albert Einstein

◆ Big Bang theory, for the origin of the universe

◆ Theory of evolution, for the origin and development of life

◆ Theory of gravity, for what goes up must come down

Actually, the last one is usually considered a *law*.

We will take up the theory of evolution in the next chapter. Here we want to consider what theories are and how they apply to the study of human prehistory.

A theory expresses our current understanding of how nature works or what happened in the past. One measure of a good theory is how well it predicts the future. Other criteria for good theories are that they must first be testable and then be subject to being modified or even discarded if new evidence contrary to the existing theory is found.

Theories are advanced, tested, and then kept or discarded, depending how well they hold up under testing. Many competing theories can be

Anthrolingo

A **theory** is a tentative explanation for natural phenomena based on verified observations or evidence. A theory is constructed to explain facts; the more facts a theory explains, the better it is. A **law** is a theory with a very high level of predicting what will happen under certain circumstances. Gravity is a pretty good law.

Fieldnotes

As examples of competing theories, we covered several possible explanations for the origins of human bipedalism and the alternative models for the origins of AMH. These are subject to continued research and possible verification or rejection.

Paleofacts

Sometimes you hear the question, "Is that a theory or a fact?" The question seems to equate *fact* with *truth*. Facts, to scientists, refer to empirical evidence or data that they observe. Facts are what theories attempt to explain. "Just a theory" hardly diminishes scientific research. In fact, good theories are the hallmarks of good science.

Anthrolingo

A theory is composed of a set of connecting **hypotheses**. For example, the theory of evolution is tested by hypotheses stemming from the fossil record, from embryology, from comparative anatomy, and from other lines of evidence. Some scientists use *theory* and *hypothesis* interchangeably.

posed for a single natural event. As long as they all are testable and modifiable, and not yet disproved, research continues on.

Perhaps over time, one theory will prevail over the others. And if a theory is repeatedly tested and found to consistently explain a natural phenomenon, then it could be elevated to a law. Few theories in any branch of science reach law-like status.

Step one of the scientific method is to state a *hypothesis* or, as applied to prehistoric research, pose questions. In broader and more formal terms, prehistoric study begins with a research plan or program.

We have gone over the entire sweep of human prehistory, from the origin of hominids millions of years ago to the expansion of human groups into the New World barely thousands of years into the past. This was an immense research plan generally seeking answers to many questions concerning human origins.

Challenges to Prehistory

Here it might be useful to lay out some of the difficulties and challenges faced by prehistorians. We can also provide examples from the fossil and archaeological records described in earlier chapters.

What's Left?

It's obvious by now that the fossil and archaeological records are incomplete. But more than that, they are selectively incomplete. What's preserved are objects least likely to decay, dissolve, or erode—things like teeth and stone tools. So there are bits and pieces of only some of the total picture to work with.

Unfinished Business

Paleoanthropological and archaeological research certainly has not been extended to all potential sites in the world. How much has been recovered of the total amount that could be discovered? There's no answer here. But you can bet that what is yet to be found will modify what is currently known about human prehistory. Optimistically, the best sites are yet to come.

Reading Bones and Stones

Next, bones and stones from human prehistory are there for the reading. By reading, we mean making inferences about either the species represented by the bones or the cultures reflected in the stones.

Inferences are the prehistorian's way of bringing facts back to life. Footprints, like those found at Laetoli from 3.5 M.Y.A. are about as close prehistory can get to actually preserving behavior.

If the Evidence Fits

Of course, if it is treated similar to a forensic case, then an archaeological or fossil site can be investigated for the evidence that it provides. Since no one was there to directly observe what was going on, this is circumstantial evidence.

The American system of justice is largely based on circumstantial evidence. Shouldn't this make it also acceptable for science? Yes, on the same condition that it has to be used with due caution and founded on sound reasoning. In science, that means interpretations and conclusions must use the natural world as a point of reference. The notion of extraterrestrial beings somehow connecting with Easter Islanders to assist them in megalithic statue building does not qualify.

Fieldnotes _____

Inferences applies to the biobehavorial approach we spoke of earlier. For example, from the biology or morphology of the teeth, certain kinds of inferences can be made about the diet. Or the shape and other features of bones lead to interpretations about locomotor behavior, such as bipedalism.

Paleofacts

As we will note in Chapter 21, circumstantial evidence is not well received by the creationists. Yet, a lot of history, including much of what happened yesterday, rests on circumstantial evidence—that is, the events were not directly observed or taped by seemingly omnipresent video cameras.

Mirrors of the Past

Persuasive argument and clear reasoning also guide the prehistorian's use of ethnographic and primate analogy. We mentioned applications of analogies in several places in this book. Although they do not establish proof, these analogies lend support to interpretations. What analogy does is run by some tapes of behavior that allow the mind to consider possibilities. Applied properly, ethnographic and primate analogy do provide insights to what might have happened in the past.

Fieldnotes

We might never have known to ask certain questions without previous research. Recall that the scientific method cycles from asking questions to finding answers that lead to posing better questions.

Having met these challenges and employed these various techniques, prehistorians and paleoanthropologists have conducted their research. They have accumulated a wealth of knowledge and, by that definition, have advanced the scientific field called human prehistory. But their greatest contribution was to formulate the best of questions to ask about our prehistory.

What's ahead for human prehistory? As usual, it's the past.

The Really Big Questions

These are the questions that we covered in this book but that continue to drive prehistoric research:

♦ When and where did hominids originate by splitting off from the common ancestor with the chimpanzee?

♦ Why did major trends in biological evolution, such as bipedalism and the increase in brain size, occur?

♦ What factors led to first crude efforts in toolmaking and eventually resulted in spectacular cultural development and spoken language in the Upper Paleolithic?

♦ What accounts for the spread and migration of groups, initially out of Africa and later out of Asia and into Australia and the islands of the South Pacific, as well as across the Beringia land bridge and into the New World?

If this book has heightened your interest in human prehistory, then it might be good to keep your eyes and mind open for the latest fossil and archaeological finds and their likely attendant controversies. Who knows? One or more of the questions just mentioned might mark a breakthrough. I will enjoy that moment, and I hope you will, too.

The Least You Need to Know

- ◆ Human prehistoric research follows the scientific method.

- ◆ Ignorance, or lack of knowledge, drives prehistoric research.

- ◆ Prehistorians read the past as already conducted experiments.

- ◆ Major theoretical questions concerning human biological and cultural evolution have tentative answers, but they also guide ongoing research.

Chapter 20

Darwin's Evolution, Then and Now

In This Chapter

- ◆ Leading up to Darwin
- ◆ The theory of natural selection
- ◆ Marshalling evidence for evolution
- ◆ Darwin looks at human evolution
- ◆ Updating Darwinian evolution

In the preceding chapter, we discussed what theories are, and in most of the earlier chapters, we described the evolution of humans. In this chapter, we join them. First, we present the theory of evolution as proposed by Darwin. Then we consider changes in the theory that have taken place over the more than 150 years ago since Darwin's publication of *Origin of Species*. Recall that we said that good scientific theories are subject to continual testing and modification as needed. Darwin's theory is no different. While it basically stands correct as he proposed it, there has emerged substantial new evidence regarding the genetic sources of variation, time depth for life to evolve, and the speed or rate of evolutionary change. We discuss each of these updates. But first let's look at some history just before Darwin's theoretical breakthrough.

Before Darwin

Darwin's ideas concerning evolution did not exist in an intellectual vacuum. And the very idea of evolution did not originate with him. Many others made furtive attempts at explaining how the great diversity of life had originated. Of course, up into the nineteenth century, the answer to that question rested in the Bible. Here is one major historical figure who presented in no uncertain terms what the creator had in mind for planet Earth and its living inhabitants.

Paley's Purpose

William Paley was a natural theologian, meaning that he interpreted the natural world with respect for the work and purpose of a creator. Not a bit surprising, his major written contribution to the topic was entitled *Natural Theology* and appeared in 1802. Herein he portrayed the workings of the universe and life as a carefully designed machine or device. In fact, a watch was his metaphor for nature. And just as he argued that the complexity and fine-tuning of a watch had to spring from a designer, nature in its complexity had to be designed by the creator.

> **Paleofacts**
>
> A favorite example of this complexity is the eye. Indeed, Paley saw the eye as designed for vision. We return to this example in the next chapter, when we take up recent attempts to apply the notion of design in nature.

It should also be stated that Paley subscribed to the idea of fixity of species, since that would conform with the work of the creator. Remember that this essentially means that no new species had been formed or had gone extinct since the time of creation. In Chapter 2, we mentioned some pioneers in prehistory who began to question biblical accounts and the fixity of species idea. Here are two others who played close roles in the life of Charles Darwin.

> **Fieldnotes**
>
> The title of the poem, *The Temple of Nature*, might be a little misleading, but there is little doubt that Grandfather Darwin was on the right evolutionary track.

Evolution in Verse

Erasmus Darwin was Charles Darwin's grandfather. He was a physician and naturalist, and an accomplished poet. As sort of a coincidence, the same year that Paley published his work on *Natural Theology* in

1802, Erasmus Darwin produced a poem that told of the evolution of all kinds of life, from plants to fish, to animals, to birds.

Erasmus Darwin was even aware of the various lines of evidence for evolution, as in embryology and comparative anatomy, which were to become so prominent in Charles Darwin's argument.

Lamarckian Inheritance

Around the same time, at the turn of the nineteenth century, another naturalist had gained prominence. This was Jean Baptiste Lamarck. His specialty was zoology, and his scientific research led him to formulate principles or regularities on how animals responded to their environment. One of these was that parts of the animals that were used a lot would be strengthened and parts that were not used at all would eventually be lost. This was his notion of "use-disuse" principle. It basically described what we now know as *adaptation*.

But there was a fundamental flaw in the principle. Lamarck connected use-disuse with the notion of inheritance of acquired characteristics. This meant that whatever happened to animals in their lifetimes would somehow be transmitted to their offspring. This is not possible, but it was pretty ingenious thinking at the time.

Lamarck's research was well ahead of any clear understanding of the rules of inheritance. That was about a century away. In a classic example, this is how Lamarck's "inheritance of acquired characteristics" worked. Say that a giraffe ate leaves from trees. And over the years the giraffe had to eat leaves from higher and higher branches. By stretching its neck to the fullest, when it died, it passed along to its offspring a trait for growing a longer neck. And that next-generation neck could also be stretched. Many generations of stretched necks explain this particular anatomy of the giraffe. By using its neck to the fullest, or longest, that body part got strengthened and lengthened.

Charles Darwin also subscribed to this notion of inheritance of adaptive characteristics, as we will shortly see. But he did add some ingenuity of his own. Now let's turn our attention to

Anthrolingo

Adaptation is the process of successful interaction of either biological or cultural systems and traits to a given set of environmental conditions.

Paleofacts

One of the defining experiments showing the fallacy of inheritance of acquired characteristics was done by August Weismann, a developmental anatomist. In 1889, he cut off the tails of mice for 22 successive generations. Yet, mice in the twenty-third generation continued to grow tails.

some background on Darwin, and then recount the incalculable contributions he made to our understanding of evolution.

Darwin on a Journey

Charles Darwin was born on February 12, 1809. This would place his birth within the midst of the three historical figures we just discussed. Later, when it became necessary for him to make a career choice, he opted to go into the ministry. That probably was not his first choice. He spent his years at Cambridge not so much hitting the theology books, but pursuing his naturalist interests in beetles, botany, and geology.

With his degree in hand, at the barely ripe age of 22, he was invited to serve as a naturalist aboard the exploring frigate HMS *Beagle.* That invitation was accepted, and the *Beagle* journey lasted five years. Initially, the *Beagle* traveled to South America, went up the west coast, and then headed out into the Pacific and stopped by the Galapagos Islands.

> ### Paleofacts
>
> Being a minister and naturalist was a common combination at Cambridge and elsewhere in Britain. So Darwin was a conformist in this regard.

That stop proved to be highly significant for Darwin: He developed his ideas of how closely related forms diverged from each other acquired their own adaptations. Three species that especially caught his attention were finches, iguanas, and tortoises. Due to the continuing richness of the Galapagos for investigating evolution, a research station was established there and named in honor of Darwin.

Fieldnotes

More recent studies of "Darwin finches" have discovered that more than a dozen species of these birds are derived from a single common ancestor from South America. But their history of divergence is more complicated than first proposed. The finches became different in their beak size and shape as they adapted to different diets of insects and seeds.

After leaving the Galapagos, the *Beagle* traveled along the southern coast of Australia around the tip of Africa before making a second stop on South America. Finally, it headed back to England, landing there in October of 1836.

This was truly a journey of mind, body, and spirit for Darwin. Unfortunately for his body, Darwin apparently contracted a disease on the trip, most likely when stopping off at South America. He suffered the rest of his life with some sort of physical ailment. One report indicated that he had Chagas' disease, caused by the bite of a bug, the "assassin bug" that carried an infectious protozoan. His condition went downhill in later life, and he spent months unable to do any research. The disease may have contributed to his death on April 19, 1882.

Shortly after his return from the *Beagle* voyage, Darwin's illness did not seem to hinder his prodigious efforts in doing things naturalists are expected to do. He distributed his specimen collections to appropriate researchers, carried on correspondences with them, and read.

> **Paleofacts**
>
> There is no truth to the claim that Darwin renounced evolution on his deathbed, or at any other preceding time.

Eureka!

After reading one piece in particular, he had what might be called an "eureka" experience. Whatever it was, it helped to put into proper place the huge set of empirical observations he had amassed. The book that was to be so instrumental for Darwin was Thomas Malthus's *An Essay on the Principle of Population.*

Malthus declared that the human population had the potential for growing much faster than its ability to feed itself. But shortages of food and disease would act as checks on population growth. In the course of checking growth, the human population would suffer misery and want. This thinking was a key piece for Darwin.

It was in September 1838 that he had an "I've got it!" moment. What he had was a theory of evolution that he called natural selection. His extensive observations had thoroughly convinced him that closely related animals changed from one location to another, and that they modified and diverged over time. From a common ancestor there would be an *adaptive radiation* of new forms or species.

This is what evolution is and what origin of species meant to Darwin. Now he had a theory to explain just how speciation took place. Let's set up some background that will help to clarify what the theory of natural selection is.

> **Anthrolingo**
>
> **Adaptive radiation** is the process of several forms splitting off from a common ancestor to form new species. An example would be "Darwin's finches" that adapted to different kinds of diets and habitats.

It's a Natural

Darwin's theory of natural selection expands on Malthus's postulate that populations struggle for their existence when food supply becomes short. Here are the basic steps in Darwin's argument:

- More offspring are born than can survive.

- Individuals vary in certain traits.

- Some of those traits are inherited.

- Over time, those individuals with favored traits will survive and those with less favorable traits will not.

Hence, *natural selection* in Darwinian terms is the retention of favorable traits possessed by those individuals who are better adapted to survive. They are able to outcompete for food, shelter, and mates.

In rather direct terms, nature selects the parents of the next generation. And to the degree that parents are able to live and to successfully reproduce, their traits will begin to replace the traits of those who were not quite so successful. Please note how important variation in traits is here.

Anthrolingo

Natural selection is the increased likelihood of survival of individuals that possess adaptive traits. Of course, surviving must also be accompanied by successful reproduction of offspring when they mature.

Fieldnotes

Darwin's formulation of natural selection was based heavily on his familiarity with what is called artificial selection. Artificial selection had been extensively used by plant and animal breeders, who determined who the parents would be based on desired traits they wanted to promote. Darwin was aware of selective breeding of race horses and show dogs, and he bred domesticated pigeons.

By 1838, Darwin had compiled large amounts of evidence for evolutionary change, and now he has a theory to explain how this change came about. But apparently he wasn't anywhere near ready to publicize his findings. Perhaps this was due to his reluctance to face the challenges that surely would come from the general public, some of his colleagues, and most especially from religious officials who would denounce Darwin for replacing their creator with natural causes.

So Darwin continued to build and bolster his case for another 20 years. Here's a list of the lines of evidence that he so thoroughly assembled:

- **Morphology**—This which covered observable physical traits that were compared for different living species. Similarities implied that the species had once shared a common ancestor.

Land tortoise from one of the Galapagos Islands.

(Robert J. Meier)

♦ **Embryology**—Developmental traits likewise could be compared for similarities among different species. This also implied development from a common ancestral plan.

♦ **Rudimentary and vestigial structures**—These structures still occasionally appeared even though they seemed not to have a functional purpose as they once had in an ancestor. However, they had not yet been completely selected out.

♦ **Biogeography**—The distribution of closely related forms suggested a single common ancestor for all.

♦ **The fossil record**—Fossils were observed to change through time, or in Darwin's terms, there was "descent with modification," again from a common ancestor.

> **Paleofacts**
>
> Darwin did some excavation at a fossil site on South America. He observed morphological differences between ancient and modern armadillos. Here was documentation of "descent with modification."

We will return to discuss more thoroughly some of these lines of evidence shortly when we consider Darwin's thoughts on human evolution. But for now, let's complete the story regarding Darwin's theory of natural selection that was yet to be publicly announced.

Out of the Tropics

Darwin was busy preparing his "big species book" when, out of the blue, in 1858, he received a manuscript from Alfred Russel Wallace. Remember the Wallace Trench

Fieldnotes

Like Darwin, Wallace incorporated Malthus's thinking on competition for survival due to limited food supply, along with that key element for natural selection to operate, variation among individuals.

separating Greater Australia from Southeast Asia? It's that Wallace. Wallace had been working in Malaya long enough to come down with an illness. He would recount that in a fit of fever he came up with a mechanism or theory that would explain how an original species could give rise to new varieties. Does that sound familiar? It was indeed the same idea that Darwin had. It is not clear whether having a fever had anything to do with Wallace's flash of insight.

The Right Time

Probably Wallace's manuscript, along with the urging of his geologist friend, Charles Lyell, prompted Darwin to go public. He did so when he and Wallace jointly presented their ideas before the Linnean Society in London in 1858. In the next year, Darwin's book *The Origin of Species* was published.

Given the rather large book sales, it must be inferred that an impact was being made. *Impact* is a neutral term. The book placed Darwin in the middle of a firestorm of controversy. He did have a group of close colleagues who faithfully defended him to the public. They probably gave him the encouragement that he needed to sustain the barrage of hostility that he received from all walks of life, including fellow scientists. As we will see in the next chapter, the fact that Darwin has long since died has not extinguished the firestorm that rages in certain circles to this day.

> **Paleofacts**
>
> In its first year of publication *The Origin of Species* sold 3,800 copies, and 27,000 copies were sold before Darwin died in 1882.

It is safe to conclude that *The Origin of Species* is the bedrock of all later work in evolution and that it profoundly influenced the history of biological research. It is worth speculating that if Darwin had left out humans from his theory, perhaps there would have been a reduced level of controversy. And *The Origin of Species* almost does this. It makes vague reference to human evolution near the very end. But Darwin filled that gap. In 1871, he published his human species book, entitled *The Descent of Man*. Let's take a closer look at this book and some of its contents.

Darwin Deals with Humans

The careful, methodical, and thorough observations and comparisons that Darwin devoted to *The Origin of Species* carried over to The *Descent of Man*. The kinds, numbers, and significance of examples and areas of human evolution that he covered are simply astounding. From anatomy to emotions, and from secondary sex characteristics to wiggling ears, Darwin compiled a fascinating evolutionary history of humans. Here are a couple of examples of the lines of evidence he used.

Darwin's Origin of Species, The Descent of Man, *and some of his other works.*

(Scott Brish)

The Leg Bone Is Connected to the Hip Bone

For morphological evidence, he compared bones and other parts of anatomy with those of other animals and primates, including the Great Apes. His conclusion was that we humans had indeed shared a common ancestor with the apes. Furthermore, he correctly predicted that our origins would be found in Africa.

Wiggling Ears and Other Vestiges of the Past

Our domestic pets allow us to observe muscles in action that not many of us have. One is the ability to move our ears. Darwin saw those rare instances in which ear wiggling is possible in humans, as evidence of its retention from some distant ancestor. It's a rudimentary or vestigial feature. Likewise, other persons seem to retain the ability to move their scalp area. And of course, all of us are able to move our eyebrows and wrinkle our forehead, as evidence of some earlier, broader skin-twitching capability.

Beyond these and many other examples, Darwin made some insightful comments on evolutionary trends in *The Descent of Man.* Earlier we discussed several of the major trends in hominid evolution.

Here's a listing of some of the trends we followed in earlier chapters, but this time as interpreted by Darwin:

♦ Origin of bipedalism was gradual and occurred to free hands and arms for throwing stones and clubs for defense or for hunting.

♦ A reduction in the size of canine teeth took place as tools—stones and clubs—were used as weapons.

♦ An increase in brain size occurred as humans became more intelligent.

♦ Humans have a "naked" skin because it is attractive to members of the opposite sex.

Each of these do require a bit of tinkering to make them fit modern thinking. Or, as in the case of loss of body hair, it is not much better understood today than in Darwin's day. But the fact that Darwin proposed them at all underscores the uncanny ability he had to see both the details and the broad pictures of human evolution. Not many of today's scientists have this facility. Speaking of tinkering, it is now time to update certain aspects of Darwinian evolution.

Neo-Darwinism

As we have said, Darwin's theory of natural selection is still basically sound, even though some changes have been made. There has been a continuing stream of books and articles discussing nuances of how and where natural selection applies.

We won't be taking up those issues. But here we look at aspects of Darwin's work that have been updated

---

Paleofacts

Human babies occasionally are born with a tail that is surgically removed, with no lasting effect. This fact, as recognized by Darwin, implies that humans sometimes revert to an ancestral condition. He does not speculate that selection could make us once again a tailed primate if we so desired.

Fieldnotes _____

Adaptive trends are explained by Darwinian evolution as the result of natural selection operating in the same direction over a long period of time. For example, the trend toward increasing brain size in hominids was adaptive and resulted from the selective advantages it gave to the survival of hominids.

Paleoquest

One active area of research is investigating at what level natural selection operates. Is it at the level of the individual, or maybe a group of relatives, or even the whole species? Arguments have been advanced for all of these, especially the first two levels.

with the discovery and major advancements in genetics, dating methods, and new insights to the fossil record. This updating is called neo-Darwinism, or the *Modern Synthesis*.

Genetic Revolutions

Beginning at the turn of the twentieth century, with the rediscovery of Gregor Mendel's rules of inheritance, there was a rapid development of genetic information.

We had said that Darwin subscribed to a Lamarckian brand of inheritance of acquired characteristics. That is, traits acquired during the lifetime could be passed on to the next generation. The unknown element was how? Darwin, in his brilliance, provided a mechanism. His idea was called *pangenesis*, and it proposed that every organ and minute part of the body, from top to toenail, had specific hereditary units that Darwin called *gemmules*.

Darwin proposed that gemmules from all over the body traveled to the gonads (ovaries and testes), where they could be passed along at the time of fertilization. You might realize that baby giraffes born later could have longer necks than their older siblings because they would have benefited from having gemmules for developing longer necks. Well, that's pretty good thinking on Darwin's part, but it's not correct.

Anthrolingo _____

The **Modern Synthesis** refers to the incorporation of principles of genetics with Darwinian principles of evolution.

Fieldnotes _____

At the present time, we seem to be in another genetic revolution. Gene therapy is gaining increasing medical attention. Even claims of human cloning fill the air but must at this time, be treated as highly suspect, if not outright hoaxes.

Anthrolingo _____

Pangenesis ("whole origin") is Darwin's mechanism for transmitting traits from parents to offspring via hereditary units called gemmules that were found in all parts of the body.

Fieldnotes _____

The discovery of the gene toward the end of the nineteenth century and, shortly thereafter, the rediscovery of Mendel's rules of inheritance for genes started the first genetic revolution. We now know, of course, that genes don't respond to environmental effects in the manner proposed by Darwin, nor do they travel from all body parts to reside in the gonads.

So, Darwinian evolution gets an update, with genes being the fundamental units of inheritance, not traits that could be observed. The next area of updating has to do with variation, one of our favorite themes in this book.

A Sporting Chance

In his breeding experiments with pigeons, Darwin observed the sudden appearance of traits in the offspring. He called these sports. Well, they couldn't possibly be called mutations because Darwin didn't know about genes. But his sports sort of did what mutations do. They expressed new variation, and once introduced, they might be selected for and become more common.

So, even though it was not correct by current knowledge, Darwin had an explanation for how new variation might arise. Today we know mutations to be the ultimate source of new genetic variation.

Paleofacts

In his breeding experiments, Darwin occasionally observed traits that he called sports, controlled by "hidden" genes that were not expressed in the parents but that were later expressed in their offspring.

Anthrolingo

Genetic distance measures the degree of evolutionary relatedness between different forms or species.

Mutations Make a Difference

Genetic material, such as mtDNA, does become altered through mutation. And as we pointed out earlier, mutations increase variation over time. Or when applied to evolutionary studies, this means that the amount of mutational difference that has accumulated between two species depends on how long ago they shared a common ancestor. This is called *genetic distance* when it measures the closeness of evolutionary relatedness.

Earlier, we used the comparison of ancient mtDNA as a means to determine that Neandertals from Germany and elsewhere, and an Australian fossil were very different from modern humans. There is great genetic distance between the fossils and us, due to accumulated mutational changes.

Genetic distance analysis is becoming very powerful and precise, and will lead to exciting new insights to revealing evolutionary histories and relationships. Had he known, Darwin probably would have made extensive use of this molecular method of demonstrating evolution. He did know something about the final area that we will update.

Gaps in the Fossil Record

Darwin was quite aware that there were major gaps in the fossil record. In *The Origin of Species*, he spends a good part of two chapters discussing how these gaps cause difficulties to his theory. Well, back then, the search for fossils had barely begun. Yet from the little he knew, changing fossils through successive layers of time would be a strong argument for establishing the fact of morphological change. And, very important, changing fossils could demonstrate that natural selection accounted for the descent with modification over long time periods.

Missing Fossil Transitions

But there were gaps in the fossil record. To Darwin, there should be a sequence of transitional changes between evolving species. His idea was that evolution acted as a gradual, steady process.

Continual change should leave behind in the fossil record a succession of transitional or intermediate forms. But there were those gaps. Darwin troubled over this and reasoned that a lack of fossil preservation was due to imperfections in the geological record. So the fossils had been there once but were later destroyed.

Rapid Speciation

Within the past three decades or so, Darwin's view of gradual, steady evolutionary change has been modified, some would say markedly so. What is being proposed is that at times the rate of evolutionary change rapidly speeds up and then goes back to a more steady pace. When it is in its rapid phase, the transition to new forms or speciation is occurring. This relatively rapid phase is called *punctuated equilibrium* (PE).

Thus, rapid change means that there will be relatively fewer individuals who could become fossilized and potentially recovered by researchers. In essence, the gaps in the fossil record are there because that is how evolution proceeded. Evolutionists continue to debate how far and wide PE applies; it certainly isn't universal.

Some forms, such as species of sharks, have pretty well remained unchanged for hundreds of millions of years. Yet others, such as hominids, have undergone significant changes in just a few million years. And, yes, periods of

Anthrolingo

Punctuated equilibrium (PE) proposes that evolution has alternating short bursts of rapid evolution and speciation that is then followed by long periods of little change. Change in the geological clock that relatively rapidly would mean that it still takes tens of thousands of years or more for speciation to take place.

more rapid changes in hominids, such as brain size increase from early *Homo erectus* to modern *Homo sapiens*, has been considered to be a PE event by some paleoanthropologists.

This herky-jerky view of evolutionary change is a modification of Darwin's gradual model. It probably explains some of the scarcity of fossils, and it is no longer necessary to expect to find a continuous, unbroken stream of transitional fossils.

As you see from this updating, there has been both modification of Darwin's evolution, but there is also retention of much of what he initially proposed. That's the hallmark of a good theory.

The Least You Need to Know

- ◆ Darwin's theory of evolution, natural selection, has been thoroughly tested and supported through multiple lines of evidence.

- ◆ The publication of *The Origin of Species* in 1859 caused an uproar, but it eventually became the foundation for all later work in evolution.

- ◆ With the publication of *The Descent of Man* in 1871, Darwin offered many insightful adaptations in humans that were verified later with more sound scientific methods.

- ◆ Darwin's evolution has been modified and updated with the development of new areas of science, especially that of genetics.

Chapter 21

Challenges to Evolution

In This Chapter

- ◆ Science and religion—compatible or combatable?
- ◆ Creationism and its stand on origins
- ◆ Irreducible complexity portends intelligent design?
- ◆ Battles in the courtroom for the schoolroom

As we noted in the last chapter, Darwin drew a lot of criticism following the publication of *The Origin of Species* in 1859. But after roughly 150 years, the theory of natural selection that he proposed, and much of the description of evolution he provided, continues to be supported and verified. Newly developed areas of genetic research are especially exciting to watch unfolding. But also at this time, attempts from different directions are being made to discount either science or evolution or both. In this chapter, we review two of the more prominent of these attempts: creationism and intelligent design. We start off with a broader topic of science and religion, to clarify their respective roles in acquiring and handling knowledge regarding human origins and prehistory.

Science Versus Religion?

Discussions of science and religion often pit one against the other. Either an explanation for human origins is scientific or it is religious in nature. Obviously, this sets up a conflict in some peoples' minds. Can't there be accommodation of both? Well, there can be and are for many of the mainstream religions.

Fieldnotes _____

Many major religious organizations have supported evolution, including the Catholic Church, the United Presbyterian Church in the USA, The Lutheran World Federation, The General Convention of the Episcopal Church, the Central Conference of American Rabbis, and the Unitarian Universalist Association.

Paleofacts

Evolution and religion are well accommodated under the label of theistic evolution. One form of this accepts evolution and natural selection as the manner of God's creation.

Accommodation comes from an understanding that science and religion deal with different kinds of knowledge. Science, by its explicit intent, handles only knowledge that comes from the natural world around us. It is nature that can be empirically observed, about which theories can be tested and, when needed, modified or discarded.

On the other hand, religion deals with the supernatural. This is an area beyond the bounds of scientific inquiry. And it is an area that science has no right to deny or affirm. It can't do either because it doesn't have the means or tests to do so. Thus, there is no necessary conflict between science and religion.

Religion and science simply operate in two different realms. And that means that people who want to can hold both scientific and religious explanations for human origins. Other aspects might help to further clarify the distinction between religion and science.

Questions and Answers

As we have stressed throughout this book, the science of prehistory is based on questions. And when answers seem at hand, new evidence could force new questions to be addressed. It might be said that science is constantly dealing with unanswered or partially answered questions. As another generalization, religion is founded on dogma that sets forth unquestioned answers. These are beliefs that are accepted on faith and are not subject to revision. They are absolute truths.

Science doesn't have any absolute truths, nor does it seek to discover any. Remember, laws are simply statements of prediction that have a high degree of being correct—at least, under specified conditions.

Even the law of gravity can be exceeded at times. Science does strive to know and better understand the natural world, as large as the universe and as small as the genes of a fruit fly. Different orientations and destinations send religion and science along noncolliding pathways.

Science doesn't have absolute truths, but it does have testable theories. Keeping these points in mind perhaps will help as we now look at the first challenge to evolution: creationism.

> **Fieldnotes**
>
> A basic tenet of science is that the universe and all contained within, including life, have order, can be investigated, and may in time be fully known and understood.

In the Beginning ...

I chose these words for opening this section only to emphasize that creationism is essentially a religiously based movement that adheres to strict biblical interpretation.

We will discuss creationism with particular reference to the Institute of Creation Research (ICR), located in El Cajon, California.

Faculty and students at the ICR are required to accept a set of tenets of scientific creationism. Certainly, that seems in order for a religiously oriented organization. What makes the ICR a focus of this discussion is that it claims to be doing research that bears on questions of evolution and human origins.

What we will do next is list a set of statements, based on the tenets mentioned previously, that allows us to compare creationism with evolutionary science. Then we can proceed to look at how the lines of evidence that we used to support evolution are challenged by creationism.

> **Paleofacts**
>
> Creationism also goes by the labels of scientific creationism and creation science.

The following are statements regarding origins attributed to creationism, countered by statements based on evolution science:

Supernatural versus natural:

> **Fieldnotes**
>
> By no means will we bring into this discussion another of ICR's stated missions, which is to educate Christians.

◆ Creationism: There was sudden, supernatural creation of the universe and life within six 24-hour days.

◆ Evolution science: Naturalistic processes account for the origin of the universe and life over an immense period of time.

Micro- and macroevolution:

◆ Creationism: Mutation and natural selection are not sufficient to account for anything more than small changes in genes, or *microevolution*.

◆ Evolution science: Mutation, selection, gene flow, and random genetic drift combine to account for *macroevolution*, or large changes, as well as microevolution.

Anthrolingo

Microevolution refers to smaller evolutionary changes that take place within a species, while **macroevolution** refers to larger changes, including the origin of new species.

Within and beyond species:

◆ Creationism: Change occurs only within fixed limits—that is, within each kind, as in birds, bees, and bats.

◆ Evolution science: Evolutionary processes have resulted in the origin of new species and higher taxonomic categories, such as the genus.

Human and ape ancestries:

◆ Creationism: There was a separate ancestry for humans and apes.

◆ Evolution science: Humans and apes shared a common ancestor before their evolutionary lines diverged from one another.

Catastrophic and uniformitarian geology:

◆ Creationism: Catastrophic geological processes, including a worldwide flood, that occurred in the past led to rapid formation of such features as the Grand Canyon.

◆ Evolution science: Uniformitarian geologic processes occurred that are mostly steady and gradual but that occasionally are dramatic, such as earthquakes and volcanoes.

Young and very old:

◆ Creationism: There was a recent special creation origin of the universe, of the Earth and life, around 10,000 years ago.

◆ Evolution science: The origin of the universe occurred 12 billion to 14 billion years ago, the Earth was created at least 4.6 billion years ago, and life emerged around 3.5 billion years ago.

You may recognize many of these statements on evolution science from earlier chapters. We will follow up here in considering evidence that relates to three particular areas of dating methods, genetic information, and fossils.

Where's the Evidence?

Each of these three lines of evidence has been contested by creationists. The ICR produces considerable amounts of written, audio, and videotape materials. It also conducts workshops and engages in debates with evolutionists.

Young or Old Earth?

Creationists rely on the Bible, as they do for all of their statements about origins, for claiming very recent origins of the universe, the Earth, and life. Originally, the date used was around 6,000 years ago, but that number has crept up to around 10,000 years.

We have noted carbon-14 dates exceeding this limit four or five times for archaic *Homo sapiens* and Neandertals. And, of course, we have cited potassium-argon (K-Ar) dates for sites and associated fossils in the millions of years. Creationists have criticized these dating methods as inaccurate and unreliable; they are neither.

Their accuracy and reliability have been thoroughly established, not by evolutionists, but independently by nuclear physicists. It would seem quite unlikely that these scientists would somehow distort their findings just to conform to evolutionist thinking. What about genetic evidence?

Fieldnotes

Apparently, research projects at the ICR are testing established dating methods or setting up new methods that purport to demonstrate a young Earth. No results of this research have appeared in any scientific journals to date.

Common Genes, Common Ancestry?

Although relatively recent in terms of some kinds of genetic analysis, information pertaining to genetic materials and evolution extends back more than five decades. Early comparisons of humans and nonhuman primates began to show similarities in their genetic makeup or *genome*.

These same similarities are appearing in the most recent of genetic comparisons of primates. Beyond genetics, the same set of similarities has been found in comparisons of embryology and morphology of monkeys, apes, and humans. What does this mean?

For creationists, it means that a creator used a common plan when creating primates. For evolutionists, it means that the degree of similarity, in genes and in embryonic and adult anatomy, reflects their degree of evolutionary relationship. Testing of a creator's common plan is not scientifically possible. Theories regarding the degree of evolutionary relationships are testable. For example, in the last chapter, we mentioned genetic distance, which provides the results of such testing. And now to the fossils.

Missing Links?

One of the most persistent of claims made by creationists is that there are no transitional or intermediate forms in the fossil record. There are many. The hominid fossil record happens to be especially useful for demonstrating transitions.

The australopithecines themselves are, in many respects, intermediate to apes and hominids. Some have called them bipedal apes, and in early reports they are referred to as "man-apes," because of their small brains and large faces, combined with their hominid adaptation of standing erect.

Then came the range of Homo species, including *H. habilis*, *H. erectus*, and *H. ergaster*. These forms moved the transition even closer to our modern forms. Finally, there were the archaic *Homo sapiens* that connected an unbroken chain from australopithecines to us.

Fieldnotes

Other transitions are well established in the fossil record, including landforms leading to whales, and reptiles evolving into birds.

This is a rich fossil history, hardly the picture portrayed by creationists. The major outlines of human evolution and prehistory are in place.

Hoax Alert

Earlier we noted an attempt to use the Piltdown discovery as a legitimate hominid fossil. While it may be appropriate to say that it took a while to correct the situation, the hoax was exposed. And it was exposed by scientists.

This is an example of the self-correcting nature of scientific theories. Introductory textbooks and

Paleofacts

The fact that australopithecines possess a combination of ape and hominid traits establishes solid evidence that humans and apes once shared a common ancestry.

courses dealing with human evolution continue to use Piltdown as a cautionary lesson. The ship of science remains righted and continues to sail forward. Now let's turn to a second, and more recent, challenge to evolution.

Intelligent Design in the Universe?

In the last chapter, we noted that William Paley, an early nineteenth-century natural theologian, viewed nature as designed by a creator. There was a purpose and plan for all life forms. Paley proposed his notion of design in nature based on the argument that, just as a complex time-keeping device as a watch had to have a watchmaker, the complexity of nature could be explained only by a creator.

Fieldnotes

The authenticity of Piltdown was questioned because it did not fit the predominant theory that emerged after the hoax was perpetrated. An earlier faulty theory involving Piltdown was discarded in the process.

Whose Design?

This basic classic notion of design in nature is currently enjoying a revival. The proponents don't directly attribute design in nature to a creator, but as we shall see, their claims would not allow anything other than some form of supernatural intervention.

The current view is labeled as intelligent design (ID), presumably to distinguish it from any design or creative order that might develop within natural processes of evolution. One expression of ID starts with the observation that certain biochemical systems have many interacting parts. Then it is claimed that if any of the parts that are vital to the system functioning properly is removed, the system would fail. This is called irreducible complexity.

Fieldnotes

An example given for an irreducibly complex system is the blood-clotting mechanism. For blood to clot normally, a number of proteins and products need to be in place and must appear in the right sequence—at least, that is what is claimed by one proponent of ID.

The general claim is that irreducibly complex biochemical systems could only be the work of an intelligent designer or agent. And they cannot be explained through natural processes. The complex had to be designed as a whole and could not function by simply adding part after part.

But claims are subject to scientific testing. And that has been done with regard to the blood-clotting system. In using a mouse as the experimental animal, it was found that not all of the proteins were needed for clotting to occur. Sure, you could get into a continuing argument that this wasn't really the vital protein anyway. Wouldn't it be more direct to say that the blood-clotting mechanism is continually being studied and, through better understanding, whatever would have been a mystery before is now being solved? No need to resort to an ID. The same is true for the favorite complex structure of ID, the eye.

The Eyes Have It

William Paley and Charles Darwin were both intrigued by the complexity of the eye. They marveled at its anatomical structure and functioning. And not surprisingly, the eye came under evolutionary scrutiny. For Paley, that eye was the product of a creator designer. For Darwin, after he studied the anatomy of eyes from worms to animals, he concluded that evolution left a trail of evidence.

Darwin's theory of natural selection could account for a progression of increasing complexity in the development of vision. Recent work has essentially confirmed Darwin's view: It shows that the eye, just as with all other complex biological systems, has evolved through natural processes.

ID Is KO'ed

In sum, when tested, intelligent design theory is not supported by the evidence. More accurately, continuing research has consistently and convincingly shown that complex systems have evolved.

For no matter what the designer is claimed to be, it must be supernatural and, hence, beyond the investigation of science. The proponents of ID have not shed much light on the identity of the intelligent designer.

> **Paleofacts**
>
> There is also an evolutionary trail of vision in primates. Lower primates, such as lemurs, have a reduced ability to see in three dimensions and in seeing color. Higher primates, which most likely evolved out of lower primates, have more highly developed visual abilities.

> **Fieldnotes**
>
> It really is more appropriate to say that the theory of complex structures is being tested and supported, since ID is not a good scientific theory because it can't be directly tested.

Teachers and Textbooks

The challenges to evolution that we just covered are more than academic: They are *very much* academic, if you consider public high schools to be the academy.

Much of the initial efforts of creationism were directed toward changing the high school curriculum. Various tactics were in the air. One sought to prevent the teaching of evolution, and another wanted to require the teaching of both evolution and creationism; a third option was not to teach either one.

After initial court proceedings, some cases made their way up to the United States Supreme Court. Here's a list of major cases that forced the issue of including creationism in the science curriculum. First, though, we start off with a landmark decision regarding the teaching of evolution.

Teaching Evolution Is Legal

In 1968, in Arkansas, the United States Supreme Court invalidated a statute that had prohibited the teaching of evolution. At least now, no state laws prevented evolution from being taught. That law gained national prominence in the Scopes Trial of 1925.

But the 1968 ruling certainly didn't ensure that evolution would be taught across the nation's high schools. Textbooks continued to curtail coverage of evolutionary principles. Some of that curtailing is still going on.

> **Paleofacts**
>
> The tactic of requiring the teaching of both evolution and creationism became known at the balanced treatment, or equal time, proposal.

> **Fieldnotes**
>
> The 1960s were post-Sputnik, when it was realized that a surge in science education was badly needed to catch up with the Russians.

Off-Balance

In 1982, in Arkansas, a federal court determined that a balanced treatment bill requiring public schools to teach both creation science and evolution science was unconstitutional. Furthermore, the court stated that creation science was not a science.

Religious Act Denied

In 1987, in Louisiana, the United States Supreme Court ruled that a creationism act was unconstitutional because it endorsed a particular set of religious views.

Teaching Off-Limits

In 1990, in the New Lenox School District in Illinois, the Seventh Court of Appeals held that a public school district may prohibit a teacher from teaching creation science without violating free speech rights.

Disclaimer Allowed

In 1997, in Louisiana, a U.S. District Court rejected a policy requiring teachers to read a disclaimer about evolution. It also declared that curriculum proposals including intelligent design were the same as those that proposed the teaching of creation science. In effect, this decision assigned intelligent design to the category of a particular religious view.

The decisions also shifted the focus of those who challenged evolution away from the court system and to state boards of education and local school boards. Some successes, at least temporary, have been realized. For example, in 1999, the Kansas State Board of Education removed evolution as a unifying principle of science in a set of curriculum guidelines.

Fieldnotes

If evolution had been removed, this would have had a broad sweep across many sciences, including astronomy, physics, biology, and others that included evolutionary principles in their subject matter.

The next year, after an election of new members, the Kansas State School board overturned its earlier decision. These kinds of challenges continue to develop. Readers may stay informed on what is happening by going to the website of the National Center for Science Education, at www.ncseweb.org.

To be sure, there is still a lot to know about the workings of evolution, both in expanding lines of evidence and in testing and modifying current evolutionary theory. Today's mysteries or unknowns will be tomorrow's discoveries. And science marches on.

The Least You Need to Know

- ◆ Science and religion are not necessarily in conflict with one another because they deal with different forms of knowledge.

- ◆ Creationism and intelligent design are religious viewpoints—they are not scientific.

- ◆ There is no evidence against evolution—just many scientific questions that currently are being studied.

- ◆ In science courses, students should only be taught the scientific principles and research findings of evolution.

22

Challenges for Our Future

In This Chapter

◆ The ups and downs of evolutionary processes

◆ Natural selection is being replaced by cultural selection

◆ Strategies for directing and changing our future

◆ Babies by design

This chapter continues with a challenge theme, but of a very different sort. It deals with the evolutionary future of our species, *Homo sapiens*. Of course, the discussion presumes that we have a future and that we just might be interested in finding out what it could be. While our evolutionary past may give us some insight to our future, it by no means can serve as our "how to" book. We will have a look at what the present offers in the way of evolutionary processes because these act upon our genetic makeup. Then, three major strategies for planning and carrying out the future of our biological and genetic makeup will be discussed. We won't make reference to any weird morphs or monsters, but we will raise a few cautions.

Stock Market Quotations of Evolution

Earlier, we noted that no substantial changes in our physical makeup have taken place over at least the past 30,000 years.

That information should provide a clue as to how little change we would expect in the future. But then, beneath our biological and anatomical exterior, there lies the genetic core—well, not so much a core, but a biochemical formula. What changes might take place in our genes? One way to approach this question is to find out how our genes have been changing in recent time, as compared to, say, 100,000 years ago. Please note that "changing genes" is another way of referring to evolution.

We might express information on changing genes along the lines of stock market quotations—you know, what stocks are up, down, or unchanged. Using this stock market analogy, the four evolutionary processes of gene change or evolution at present in comparison with our past are as follows:

- Mutation is up.

- Random genetic drift is down.

- Gene flow is way up.

- Natural selection is down and up.

Let's fill in a little background on these evolutionary quotations.

> **Paleofacts**
>
> According to the Recent Africa Origin model, our biological appearance hasn't seen any major makeover in more than 100,000 years.

> **Fieldnotes**
>
> Mutation has two kinds of causes: those that might be called natural or present from the beginning of life, and those that are induced or introduced by human activities.

> **Paleofacts**
>
> Beneficial mutations do, of course, occur. These have been the basis for adaptive responses that usually are directed to a specific set of environmental conditions.

Manufacturing Mutations

Mutation today is higher than in the past simply because there are more agents that cause them to occur. Some manufacturing activities have been shown to have harmful side effects.

Two agents that are known to cause mutation are radiation and chemicals. The application of these has been extensive. And to the extent that their use is not controlled to prevent pollution and toxicity, they present harm to humans.

From a theoretical standpoint, mutation is the primary source of genetic variation. As we have discussed, genetic variation is vital for natural selection to operate. Mutation could be said to occur for better, for worse, or for neither. Most mutations are probably in the third category of being neutral and not acted upon by natural selection. Of those that are acted upon, the great majority turn out to be harmful to the survival or reproduction of the individual.

As we will point out shortly, not only does our species not need any new genetic variation produced by mutation, but the variation caused is likely to be harmful to us.

The total gene pool of our species has enough variation to carry us into about any future we can predict. In short, our evolutionary future will not be hindered by a lack of genetic variation. Thus, mutation as an evolutionary stock should be reduced to its lowest natural value by eliminating all inducing mutational agents. We now shift to drift and gene flow for their stock market rankings.

Fieldnotes _____

In our present real world, the increase in some forms of cancer in humans is probably due to increased exposure to cancer-causing mutagenic agents.

Drift and Flow Are Counterpoised

As we discussed earlier, random genetic drift is most likely to take place in small, isolated populations. That was the scene throughout human prehistory. Due to the massive increase and spread of the human species, especially since the Industrial Revolution, very few such human groups are present today. Our machines of mobility, whether boats, planes, or wheeled devices, ensure that no groups will ever be isolated again in the future. The genetic effect of drift is to reduce variation, but as drift goes down, gene flow between groups or *races* goes up.

Anthrolingo _____

Race is a taxonomic category based on the frequency of genes or biological traits that have a genetic basis. Races are statistically constructed units arbitrarily imposed on a broad and diverse genetic and biological background. Races are also defined in social and ethnic terms.

The process of gene flow is on the rise. As an evolutionary stock, it has accrued great value. Pushing that analogy even further, gene flow is trading at its highest prehistoric or historic level. And, as mentioned earlier, gene flow both adds variation to groups and also is a way to unite their gene pools. When I said that we really don't need any more mutation, I had in mind that a great storehouse of genetic variation already exists in the diversity of modern human groups.

Fieldnotes _____

According to U.S. Census Bureau statistics, rates of interracial marriages have been on a rapid rise in recent decades.

Gene flow leads to once different groups looking more like each other. They began to share biological characteristics. With continued and extensive gene flow among human groups, would that mean that our future will see a huge blended uniformity in physical appearance? Not very likely.

In the first place, that level of gene flow will not ever likely occur—that is, unless some dictatorial form of Big Brother gains control over our lives. Secondly, mate choice decisions tend to follow existing preferences, based on many physical features, such as skin color, height, and weight.

Of course, choosing a suitable partner involves much more than physical attributes. In fact, it might well be that social and cultural factors will continue to gain more significance in directing our future.

The Varying Faces of Selection

Darwin's theory of natural selection has stood the tests of time and remains the primary explanation for the range and diversity of life forms on the earth, including our own species. But there is good reason to question whether the action of natural selection continues to be very significant for our survival and whether it will have any major role to play in our future.

During our prehistory, natural selection was the directing force behind the major evolutionary trends that we covered, such as our increase in brain size. Our other adaptive changes, such as bipedalism, were vested in the natural selection process. But interacting with these biological trends were behavioral consequences and interactions. In Chapter 13 we talked about the bio-behavioral *approach* because this better reflected what human evolution was all about.

And because of this interaction, behavior actually began to replace biology as our primary means of adapting. In short, our cultural adaptation began to supplant biology and its underlying natural selection. Our ancestors established toolmaking, made shelters and clothing, and gained controlled use of fire.

Biological adaptation, especially of the brain, prepared the way for hominids to do all of these things. And having gained sufficient mental ability, our early ancestors no longer were so heavily dependent upon their biological adaptation or natural selection for survival. The term that has been used to describe this situation is *selection relaxation*.

Natural selection is likened to a force or pressure. And when cultural adaptation, noted previously, came into play, this pressure was relieved or relaxed somewhat. So, at the present time, at least some aspects for our survival are under less natural selection than they were in our prehistory. In our stock market analogy, some of the selection stocks have gone down. But could others be on the rise?

> **Anthrolingo**
>
> **Selection relaxation** refers to the decrease in pressure for biological adaptation due to the buffering or shielding effects of cultural adaptations. For example, culture provided the means for humans to survive in very cold climates; less important was their biological adaptation.

An Infectious Idea

Consider disease as a selective agent. During prehistoric times, contagious or communicable diseases probably were not a big threat. This was because groups were small and widely dispersed. That means that infections, caused by bacteria or viruses, just didn't have enough warm human bodies to keep spreading. Then, with enormous human population growth and regular contacts between groups, epidemics and pandemics broke out. SARS (severe acute respiratory syndrome) could be the latest of these outbreaks.

Enter medical science, which has contained and essentially eradicated the threat of many infectious diseases. Smallpox was one, and polio may be on the verge of eradication. But the threat is by no means gone. Other infectious diseases have arisen, such as HIV and SARS. And rising in the military mist is the specter of using infectious agents, such as smallpox, as biological weapons.

> **Paleofacts**
>
> One of the greatest medical concerns at present is controlling the worldwide spread of HIV infection and its clinical manifestation, AIDS.

In certain areas of the world, medical science and application have been strategically employed to ward off disease. For example, through vaccines and immunizations. And this probably has had an effect on our evolution. But this is not the only strategy available. Let's take a look at three kinds or levels of these strategies that will affect our evolutionary future. These clearly are packaged with ethical and economic challenges that will also need to be faced.

What's Your Choice?

We can control and alter the direction of our evolutionary future at essentially three different levels:

- Euthenics ("good environment")
- Euphenics ("good *phenotype*")
- Eugenics ("good genes")

We will expand on each of these, first to show what has already been done in applying the strategies and then to look ahead to what might be coming in the future. This would be gazing into the crystal ball.

Changes in the Neighborhood

Euthenics as a strategy is about as old as hominids themselves. It is what we have been describing as cultural adaptation when it pertains to improving the environment for human habitation.

Well, that's our prehistory of toolmaking, shelter and clothing preparation, and fire building. And, of course, it carried right into the future with building our comfortable personal surroundings with stoves, clothes, and air conditioners. But please note that only in certain parts of the world do humans live in high-tech creature-comfort environments.

Fieldnotes

Instead of strongly adapting to fit their environment, hominids modified their environment to fit their biological needs.

Anthrolingo

The **phenotype** consists of the observable features and traits of an individual. A companion term, the genotype, refers to the underlying genetic makeup of that individual. The genotype interacts with the environment to result in a phenotype.

So euthenics started with our earliest of ancestors, and there is no reason to think that it will ever be abandoned. But there are very sound environmental and ecological bases for curtailing and altering our current course of action regarding our future use of natural resources. Not many people likely want to return to ice-age conditions with ice-age technology. Short of that, proper stewardship of our environment is not only good for now, but it really is the only way to ensure our long-term presence on the earth.

Looking Good

Earlier in this chapter, we discussed our physical features, and in many of the earlier chapters, we described the physical makeup of hominid fossils. These observable traits are defined as the *phenotype*.

Our phenotype is partly under control of genes, and that is the genotype. But it is also dependent on the environment in which those genes are expressed.

Stature is part of our phenotype. What if a child didn't grow very well, even with an adequate diet? Could its phenotype be changed? Yes, administering growth hormone is one way of boosting the child's height.

Euphenics is the strategy of changing the phenotype to meet some predetermined standard of normality. Here's a partial list of euphenic types of bodily improvements:

Fieldnotes

As an example, our stature or standing height does have a genetic basis. However, we wouldn't grow at all, or would grow very poorly, without a proper diet.

- ◆ Eyeglasses to correct vision problems

- ◆ Dental fillings, crowns, and dentures to improve dental health

- ◆ Immunizations and vaccinations, to protect against diseases

- ◆ Organ transplants, to restore normal functioning

- ◆ Artificial body parts and prostheses to restore functions

Anthrolingo

Plasticity is the inherited ability for an organism to modify its phenotype. This ability comes in handy in certain environments. It also refers to physiological plasticity to adjust our heart rate or maintain a fairly constant internal body temperature.

The list could go on. And euphenics is very much connected with the development and progress in medicine. But, as with euthenic strategies, euphenic improvements are restricted to those areas of the world where this level of medical science is available.

During growth and development, the human body does have phenotypic *plasticity*. It can change in response to diet or even climatic conditions. Tanning of the skin is a plastic phenotypic response that occurs throughout the lifetime.

Probably no one disputes that this list shows humane improvements in a person's quality of life. For some reason, the phenotype falls short of what it could be for the person to live and act normally. And euphenics tries to restore normality. But what really is normal? Here's where ethics and a challenge for our future come in.

Say that a child with normal stature is given growth hormone, with the plan to enhance his or her height for opportunities in athletic endeavors. In this instance, if 6 feet is good, wouldn't 6 feet, 6 inches be better? Along this line, performance-enhancing drugs are available to athletes to extend their physical limits. And of course, the means to detect a banned substance's presence is under continued development.

Then there is the cosmetic surgery industry. Society may well establish standards of beauty. And for those who don't happen to conform to those standards, there already are numerous surgical and nonsurgical procedures (some quite radical) for making the necessary changes in pursuit of the perfect phenotype.

The demand for cosmetic correction or enhancement is currently here. Will it lessen in the future? Not likely. In fact, there is good reason to expect that euphenics will continue to grow as a means to relatively rapidly change phenotypes into whatever might be deemed the ideal.

Designer Genes

Justifiably so, eugenics has taken on negative connotations. Until the 1960s, some states in the United States had sterilization laws on the books that permitted reproductive rights to be surgically taken away from certain classes of people, such as those with mental illness. They were considered unfit, and the plan was to eliminate their possibility of having children. Presumably, the targeted conditions would then be gone in future generations.

Fieldnotes

Sterilization was criminally expanded to include persons with epilepsy, as well as black welfare recipients. Reparation is now being considered to compensate victims identified as wronged by this procedure.

Eugenics programs of this sort were badly mistaken on many grounds, and the offending laws have been purged from the books. So perhaps the term *eugenics* should then be expunged from our usage. For the most part, it has been. In its place are such terms as *gene therapy.* Hopefully they will not inherit the dark legacy of eugenics.

In a sense, gene therapy is even more directly involved with changing genes than the earlier eugenic programs. Gene therapy has methods for inserting different genes into a body, with the expectation that the new genes will restore a deficient or inadequate function.

Anthrolingo

Gene therapy involves medically based methods for replacing or altering the expression of genes for the betterment of an individual's health.

So far, the success of gene therapy has been positive, if somewhat limited, but its medical potential remains very high. And as we pointed out with the euphenics strategy, this gene-based strategy has made tremendous advancements in medical science. Right now, aided by results from the *Human Genome Project*, more progress has been made in the diagnosis and identification of the genetic disease, and less has been made in attempts to correct conditions through gene repair or replacement.

The future of our species does seem to be in the good hands of those working in the area of gene therapy, as long as it is directed toward reducing suffering and restoring or establishing a higher quality of life. Finding cures for genetic disease will take the high road for our evolutionary future. But here again, that measure called normality comes in. And where that term comes in, can ethical concerns be far behind?

The specific concern is whether these newly discovered and applied gene therapy methods can be used for nonmedical purposes. Well they can be, but should that kind of genetic engineering be encouraged and permitted?

The potential exists in the future for setting up catalogs of genetic features that people could choose for their unborn children. No, this is not possible now, and it may be a long way down the road. Designer genes and the cosmetic application of gene manipulation are but a dream—or nightmare—for now. But existing methods are beginning to make it possible to transfer genes from animals or plants into the human genome. That would certainly change the face of future humans.

The future could see tinkering with our genes in ways that evolution cannot. We have already rejected the intelligent design notion. But now humans are taking over the role once played by evolution and natural selection. A suggested term for this control might be *cultural selection*.

Fieldnotes

Cystic fibrosis is a genetic (actually chromosomal) condition that has been undergoing clinical trials using gene transfer on humans. Thus far, there has been limited success.

Anthrolingo

The **Human Genome Project** was a worldwide effort to map the entire genetic makeup, down to the level of precise DNA sequence. That goal has been effectively completed, and attention has now shifted to identifying the products of genes—proteins that, if faulty, are involved in causing genetic diseases.

Fieldnotes

Considering the concerns we expressed earlier with respect to intelligent design, "genetic engineering" is another term that should be expunged from our vocabulary, along with its unethical practices.

Because cultural selection would exist within the minds of human designers, it has far-ranging imagination coupled with no absolute limits—that is, none except those imposed by scrupulous researchers, bioethics committees, and a watchful public. From designer genes, we now go to designer babies.

Paleofacts

Gene transfer is of medical importance for correcting faulty genes, but a rogue researcher might find it humorous to insert the gene that controls the flash of a firefly, and produce a human who glows in the dark.

Anthrolingo

Cultural selection is the process by which genes are chosen for some desired outcome, either in the adult or in producing children.

Fieldnotes

Modern reproductive technology has made it possible to make babies from many combinations of sources of eggs and sperm, as well as with locations where fertilization and then gestation takes place. Applying this technology, there are around 32 ways to make a baby.

Designer Babies

It may seem a little odd that it is now possible to choose babies with more precision than it is to change the genetics of specific traits. In part, that has to do with the huge success in advancements in methods of human reproduction.

Many couples desperately want to have children and, for various reasons, are unable to. A number of procedures are available to improve their chances. And this application is generally recognized as a humane solution.

Speaking from the theoretical side, how does this relate to evolution? It is the very essence of what nature used to decide. Under natural selection, only some couples could produce offspring, and some could have more offspring than others. But at the present time, natural selection is very likely to be the least significant factor in determining whether a couple bears a child.

Under cultural selection, odds for having children have drastically changed. Even the roughly 50-50 chance of having either a girl baby or a boy baby has been largely removed. Sex selection for the next baby can now be done with nearly complete success of desired outcome. Some have worried that the sex ratio will become badly out of balance in the future. But it is also reasoned that if one sex becomes too rare, it will take on increased value. This could result in restoring an earlier sex-ratio balance.

Bring in the Clones

In human reproduction, people duplication hangs most precariously onto the slippery slope of ethical issues. Of course, duplication here refers to human cloning. Contrary to media reports, there have been no documented cases of human cloning.

There appears to be a strong sentiment against any efforts to produce human clones, registering from the scientific community and all other circles. Not the least of concerns is just how well clones fare in their lifetimes.

However the matter of human cloning turns out, it will not likely have any large impact on the future of our species—at least, not as long as cloning, if ever developed successfully for humans, is used in sporadic, isolated cases.

Of much greater concern from numerous perspectives is continued growth of the global human population. The discussions here regarding our future are focused on changing the quality of human phenotypes and genotypes. But this may well be trumped by the more pressing question of quantity and how to stem the tides of overpopulation.

Fieldnotes

Other methods of reproduction include in vitro fertilization and embryo transfer, and artificial insemination by sperm donor. These methods, along with fertility-enhancement methods, have received increased acceptance by society.

Paleofacts

Dolly, the cloned sheep, was put down recently because of health problems that may or may not be related to its cloned origin. Dolly also had shown apparent signs of premature aging that could signal warnings for cloning technology.

Returning to our focused purpose of this chapter, considering the overall arsenal of ways and means that cultural selection has to alter our phenotype and genetic makeup, it is safe to conclude that changes in humans will occur. What is unknown is whether these changes will be for better or for worse.

Evolutionary fatalism might argue that if we don't get it right, other species will take our place when we are gone. Cockroaches and gray rats seem to be pretty hardy cosmopolitan candidates.

But then, evolutionary optimism sees our future through the brightest colors of a prehistoric cave painting. Time will tell which view prevails.

The Least You Need to Know

- ◆ We continue to evolve, with gene flow as the predominant process.

- ◆ Causes of mutation, as from toxic chemicals and radiation, should be eliminated from our living environment.

- ◆ Natural selection has tended to become much less significant with the rise of our cultural means to determine both our survival and our reproduction.

- ◆ Our future, for better or for worse, is within our control.

Appendix A

Glossary

Acheulean   Stone tool industry characterized by biface hand-axes.

adaptability   The degree to which cultures or biological systems can change in the face of altered environments.

adaptation   The process of successful interaction of either biological or cultural systems and traits to a given set of environmental conditions.

adaptive radiation   The evolutionary process by which a single ancestor splits off to form several new species.

Ancient DNA   Genetic material that has been extracted from bones or teeth of individuals who lived from hundreds to tens of thousands of years ago.

anthropometry   The standardized set of methods for measuring the human body.

artifact   Any object that has been made or modified by humans or human ancestors.

Australian Aborigine   A living descendent of the first peoples to settle Australia.

australopithecine   Member of the genus Australopithecus.

baleen   Whalebone or plates that hang from the upper jaw of baleen whales, such as the bowhead, that screen out food while the whale swims.

Beringia A 1,000-mile-wide grassy bridge of land that connected northeast Siberia with northwest America during the Ice Age.

biobehavioral approach The recognition that biology and behavior interacted during human prehistory. This is the basis for making inferences about behavior from fossil remains.

bipedalism Mode of locomotion that involves the adaptation to habitually stand and walk on the hind legs.

biostratigraphy A dating technique that uses fossils that have been accurately dated at one site to date comparable species of fossils at another site.

blade A flaked stone tool that is at least twice as long as it is wide.

brachiation Mode of locomotion involving the repeated grasping of a tree limb with the hand of one arm, swinging the body forward to then grasp the tree with the hand of other arm—hence, arm-swinging.

braincase Part of the skull that houses the brain.

browridge The raised area of bone above the orbits.

burin A flaked stone tool that has a sharp angular point using for engraving.

canine diastema or **gap** A space between the upper canine and the first bicuspid (premolar), allowing the lower canine, which is protruding and cone-shape, space to fit in when the animal closes its jaw.

carbon-14 dating A dating method that is based on the radioactive decay of a carbon isotope. This method can be used to date organic materials up to about 75,000 years old.

cerebral cortex The highly folded outer layer of the brain, sometimes called the "gray matter."

cervical Refers to the region of the neck and the associated seven vertebrae or bones in humans.

chronometric dating Dating methods, sometimes called absolute, that estimate the precise year that a site or remains existed.

coprolite Feces or dung that is found in ancient sites and that may be useful in indicating diet and detecting disease.

cultural selection The process by which genes are chosen for some desired outcome, either in the adult or in producing children.

dendrogram A tree diagram that indicates the degree of evolutionary relationships among populations.

dental formula The specification of the number of incisors, canines, premolars, and molars.

derived trait A trait that evolved after splitting off from an ancestor. *See* primitive trait.

diffusion The process of ideas and cultural items transferring from one culture to another.

ecofact Natural items, such as animal bones, found at an archaeological site, that are used in the reconstruction of activities at that site.

endocranial cast or **endocast** A cast that forms on the inside of a fossilized skull as the brain is replaced with solidified minerals.

endogamy Marriage rules requiring that mates be selected from within specified boundaries, such as a clan. *See* exogamy.

epicanthic eyefold A small fold of skin that covers the inner eye area and may extend to the outside of the eye.

evolution A process of change over time in living forms.

evolutionary trend Discernible adaptive changes that show stages of development rather than appearing fully complete.

exogamy Marriage rules requiring that mates be selected from outside specified boundaries, such as a clan. *See* endogamy.

flint A favored raw material for making stone tools in the Paleolithic because it flakes in a predictable manner.

fluted point A kind of spear point that has a channel flake removed up from the base from both sides. Clovis and Folsom are fluted points.

gene flow An evolutionary process by which genes are transferred from one population to another.

gene therapy or **genetic engineering** Medically based methods for replacing or altering the expression of genes for the betterment of an individual's health.

genetic distance The measured degree of evolutionary relatedness between populations or species.

genome The genetic makeup that has now been specified at the DNA level.

genotype   The underlying genetic makeup of an individual. The genotype interacts with the environment that results in a phenotype. *See* phenotype.

gerontomorphic   Animal forms that grow up to look very different than when they were young. *See* paedomorphic.

heterodont   Having teeth that are different in shape and also in size. *See* homodont.

hominid   Member of the family Hominidae, which includes all human and prehuman forms.

homodont   Teeth that are similar in shape but may differ in size. *See* heterodont.

Homo sapiens sapiens   Modern humans.

humane   Possessing human traits, such as kindness, compassion, and consideration.

Human Genome Project   A worldwide effort to map the entire genetic makeup of humans down to the level of precise DNA sequence.

hyoid   A bone that supports the base of the tongue.

hypothesis   An explanation of observable facts that is subject to testing.

igloo or **iglu**   An Inupiat or Inuit Eskimo dwelling made from snow blocks. May also refer to other house types built from sod.

law   A theory that has been shown to have a very high level of predictability under specified conditions.

Levallois   A term for stone toolmaking that involves preparing the core before a tool is flaked off.

lithic   The term applied to artifacts or tools made from stone.

macroevolution   Evolutionary change that results in speciation. *See* microevolution.

magnetic reversal or **archaeomagnetism**   A dating method based on the periodic reversals of the earth's magnetic poles.

megafauna   Large herbivores, such as the mastodon and mammoth, that went extinct at the end of the last Ice Age.

megalith   Large stone blocks or statues, such as found on Rapa Nui, or Easter Island.

mental template   A plan in the mind for carrying out a specific task, such as making a stone tool.

microevolution   Evolution that takes place within a species. *See* macroevolution.

model   A theoretical construct offered to explain a natural process or phenomenon.

Modern Synthesis   The term for neo-Darwinism, or the combining of Darwinian evolution with modern genetics and other updates.

morphology   A term that refers to the shape and anatomic structure of animals.

mosaic   The notion that human evolution occurred in different steps, not all at once.

Mousterian   Stone tool industry associated with Neandertals.

natural selection   The fundamental theory of evolution that explains how species are formed and how species change over time.

New World   The continents of North and South America.

occipital bun   A pronounced rounded area at the back of the skull.

Oldowan Industry   The first recognized set of primitive stone tools found in East Africa, dated to some 2.6 million years ago.

Old World   The continents of Europe, Asia, and Africa, known to Europeans before the discovery of America by Columbus.

orthognathic   Having a relatively vertical aligned face. *See* prognathic.

osteoarthritis   Bone inflammation, most often occurring in the joints, that hinders normal activities.

osteodontokeratic culture   A name proposed by Raymond Dart for a set of presumed artifacts made from bone, teeth, and horn.

paedomorphic   Animal forms showing features of a young animal that are retained into the adult stage. *See* gerontomorphic.

paleoanthropology   The study of the biology and behavior of hominids from the Pliocene and the Pleistocene.

Paleoindian   Name for the first settlers in the New World.

Paleolithic   "Old Stone Age." Designation of the first stone tool industry, beginning more than 2.5 million years ago and ending about 10,000 years ago.

paleopathology   The science that studies ancient diseases and injuries from bones and teeth.

palynology   The study of pollen grains found at archaeological sites.

pangenesis   The theory that Darwin posed to explain how traits were passed down to their offspring. The theory has been discarded.

patrilocality   A residence rule stating that a newly married couple will live in the place of the father of the groom.

petroglyph   An etched or engraved pattern on a rock surface.

phenotype   The observable features and traits of an individual. *See* genotype.

physical anthropology   The study of the biological and genetic aspects of hominids, including modern humans.

pictograph   Painted figures on rock surfaces.

plasticity   The inherited ability for an organism to modify its phenotype during its lifetime.

Pleistocene   Epoch division of the Cenozoic era that began about 2 million years ago and extended to about 10,000 years ago. Time period of successive ice ages.

Pliocene   Epoch division of the Cenozoic era that began about 5 million years ago, followed by the Pleistocene, around 2 million years ago.

post-cranial   A term for designating all of the skeleton below the skull or head.

potassium-argon dating   A chronometric dating method that dates rocks of volcanic origin, such as ash, older than about 50,000 years.

prehistoric archaeology   The study of past cultures before the invention of writing.

prehistory   The time period before the invention of writing, about 6,000 years ago.

primitive trait   A trait that is retained from an ancestral stage into a later evolved form. *See* derived trait.

prognathic   Having a forward projection of the jaws and middle face. *See* orthognathic.

protoculture   The stage of social learning that is often applied to chimpanzees.

punctuated equilibrium   The theory proposing that after extended periods of little change (stasis), speciation occurs relatively rapidly. It is confirmed by evidence in the fossil record that appear to be gaps.

race   A taxonomic category based on the frequency of genes or biological traits that have a genetic basis. Races are statistically constructed units arbitrarily imposed on a broad and diverse genetic and biological background. Races are also defined in social and ethnic terms.

relative dating   A dating method that places events in their proper chronological sequence, such as younger/older, but that are "floating in time" without a more precise dating method.

refuse pit   An archaeological site that contains ancient garbage or discarded remains that are useful for reconstructing past cultures.

rock shelter   A shallow cave or rock overhang that served as a dwelling area during the Paleolithic.

sagittal crest   A crested ridge of bone along the midline of the skull to which lower jaw muscles are attached.

sagittal keeling   A raised area along the midline of the skull that does not serve for muscle attachment.

savanna model   A model that proposes that hominids became erect bipeds as their former homeland of trees was reduced by dryer climates and that they then took up residence in the large grassy savannas of East Africa.

seamark   Observations made as navigational aids in ocean voyages, such as the flight behavior of sea or land birds.

selection relaxation   A decrease in pressure for biological adaptation due to the buffering or shielding effects of cultural adaptations.

sexual dimorphism   Differences seen between the sexes, most obviously in those morphological traits related to the reproductive capability of females. It also can generally refer to other features that tend to separate the sexes in terms of overall size of the skeleton and degree of muscle development seen from bony landmarks on the skeleton.

site   An archaeological area that contains the remains of past cultures and peoples.

skull   The cranium plus the mandible, or lower jaw. If the cranium is missing its face and bottom portions, it is called a calvarium, or sometimes a skullcap.

sociobiology   The scientific study of the evolution of social behavior. This is applied to humans.

stratigraphy   Layers or strata (singular: *stratum*) in geologic and archaeologic sites.

subsistence   The activities devoted to making a living—how people get their food, what they eat, and whether divisions of labor between men and women are present.

survey   A field method employed by archaeologists to determine the presence and extent of a site.

sympathetic magic   Magic done by imitation of an act on the principle that "like produces like." An example is burning an effigy.

tapa cloth   Cloth made from the bark of the paper mulberry or breadfruit tree.

taphonomy   The scientific study of the history of a fossil and how an archaeological site was formed.

theory   An explanation of a natural phenomenon based on facts and subject to revision if new facts warrant it.

tree-dwelling model   A model proposing that immediate ancestors of hominids used a bipedal posture even as they still inhabited trees and could then expand on this behavior when they became more ground-living.

type   An outdated term when applied to describe fossils in very narrow limits, replaced by the notion of population variation.

ulu   A crescent-shape knife made by Inupiat Eskimos and used in butchering sea mammals.

uniformitarianism   A principle stating that the geologic processes that we see in action today are the same ones that operated in the past.

Wallace Trench or **Wallace Line**   A submarine channel, 25,000 feet deep, that separates Australia from Southeast Asia.

Books and Articles to Explore

Human Prehistory—Archaeology and Paleoanthropology

Agnew, N., and M. Demas. "Preserving the Laetoli Footprints." *Scientific American* 279 (3): 44–55, 1998.

Binford, L. *Bones: Ancient Men and Modern Myths.* New York: Academic Press, 1987.

Dettwyler, K. A. "Can Paleopathology Provide Evidence for 'Compassion'?" *American Journal of Physical Anthropology* 84:375–84, 1991.

Falk, D. *Braindance.* New York: Henry Holt, 1992.

Fegan, B. M. *Eyewitness to Discovery.* New York: Oxford University Press, 1998.

———. *Quest for the Past: Great Discoveries in Archaeology.* Prospect Heights, Illinois: Waveland Press, 1994.

Fouts, R., and S. T. Mills. *Next of Kin: What Chimpanzees Have Taught Me About Who We Are.* New York: William Morrow, 1997.

Johanson, D., and M. Edey. *Lucy: The Beginning of Humankind.* New York: Simon & Schuster, 1981.

Johanson, D., and J. Shreeve. *Lucy's Child: The Discovery of a Human Ancestor.* New York: William Morrow, 1989.

Klein, R. "Anatomy, Behavior, and Modern Human Origins." *Journal of World Prehistory* 9:167–198, 1995.

Larick, R., and R. L. Ciochon. "The African Emergence and Early Asian Dispersals of the Genus Homo." *American Scientist* 84:538–551, 1996.

Larsen, C. S., R. M. Matter, and D. L. Gebo. *Human Origins: The Fossil Record.* 3rd. Edition. Prospect Heights, Illinois: Waveland, 1998.

Leakey, M., and A. Walker. "Early Hominid Fossils from Africa." *Scientific American* 276 (6): 74–79, 1997.

Leakey, R. E., and L. J. Slikkerveer. *Man-Ape Ape-Man: The Quest for Human's Place in Nature and Dubois' "Missing Link."* Culemborg, The Netherlands: Maseland Grafische Vormgeving, 1993.

Leakey, R. E., and R. Lewin. *The Sixth Extinction: Patterns of Life and the Future of Humankind.* New York: Doubleday, 1995.

Lewin, R. *Bones of Contention: Controversies in the Search for Human Origins.* New York: Simon & Schuster, 1987.

McHenry, H. M. "How Big Were the Early Hominids?" *Evolutionary Anthropology* 1:15–20, 1992.

Morell, V. *Ancestral Passions: The Leakey Family and the Quest for Humankind's Beginning.* New York: Simon & Schuster, 1995.

Nitecki, M., and D. Nitecki (eds.). *Origins of Anatomically Modern Humans.* New York: Plenum, 1994.

Savage-Rumbaugh, S., and R. Kanzi Lewin. *The Ape at the Brink of the Human Mind.* New York: John Wiley & Sons, 1994.

Schick, K. D., and N. Toth. *Making Silent Stones Speak: Human Evolution and the Dawn of Technology.* New York: Simon & Schuster, 1993.

Schick, K. D., and N. Toth. "Paleoanthropology at the Millennium." In *Archaeology at the Millennium: A Sourcebook*. G. M. Feinman and T. D. Price (eds.). New York: Kluwer Academic/Plenum Publishers, 2001.

Shipman, P. *The Man Who Found the Missing Link: Eugene Dubois and His Lifelong Quest to Prove Darwin Right*. New York: Simon & Schuster, 2001.

Smith, F. H., A. B. Falsetti, and S. M. Donnelly. "Modern Human Origins." *Yearbook of Physical Anthropology* 32:35–68, 1989.

Solecki, R. Shanidar: *The First Flower People*. New York: Knopf, 1971.

Stanford, C. *The Hunting Apes: Meat Eating and the Origins of Human Behavior*. Princeton: Princeton University Press, 1999.

Stone, A. C., and M. Stoneking. "Ancient DNA from a Pre-Columbian Amerindian Population." *American Journal of Physical Anthropology* 92:463–471, 1993.

Stringer, C., and C. Gamble. *In Search of the Neanderthals: Solving the Puzzle of Human Origins*. New York: Thames and Hudson, 1993.

Stringer, C., and R. McKie. *African Exodus: The Origins of Modern Humanity*. New York: Henry Holt, 1996.

Tattersall, I. *The Fossil Trail: How We Know What We Think We Know About Human Evolution*. New York: Oxford University Press, 1995.

———. *The Last Neanderthal. The Rise, Success, and Mysterious Extinction of Our Closest Human Relatives*. New York: Macmillan, 1995.

Tattersall, I., and J. Schwarz. *Extinct Humans*. Boulder, Colorado: Westview Press, 2000.

Trinkaus, E., and P. Shipman. *The Neandertals: Changing the Image of Mankind*. New York: Knopf, 1992.

Walker, A., and P. Shipman. *The Wisdom of the Bones*. New York: Vintage, 1996.

Wolpoff, M. H., and R. Caspari. *Race and Human Evolution*. New York: Simon and Schuster, 1997.

Wood, B., and A. Turner. "Out of Africa and into Asia." *Nature* 378:239–240, 1995.

Rapa Nui (Easter Island)

Bahn, P., and J. Flenley. *Easter Island Earth Island*. New York: Thames and Hudson, 1992.

Englert, S. *Island at the Center of the World*. New York: Charles Scribner's Sons, 1970.

Heyerdahl, T. *Easter Island: The Mystery Solved*. London: Souvenir Press, 1989.

Martinsson-Wallin, H. "Early settlement of Rapa Nui (Easter Island)." *Asian Perspectives* 40:244–279, 2001.

McCall, Grant. *Rapanui: Tradition and Survival on Easter Island, 2nd edition*. Honolulu: University of Hawaii Press, 1994.

Van Tilburg, J. A. "Moving the Moai: Transporting the Megaliths of Easter Island: How Did They Do It?" *Archaeology* Jan/Feb: 34–43, 1995.

Peopling of the New World–Inupiat Eskimos

Binford, L. R. *Nunamiut Ethno-Archaeology*. New York: Academic Press, 1978.

Burch, E. S. *The Inupiaq Eskimo Nations of Northwest Alaska*. Fairbanks: University of Alaska Press, 1998.

Chance, N. A. *The Inupiat and Arctic Alaska*. New York: Harcourt Brace, 1990.

Crawford, M. H. *The Origins of Native Americans: Evidence from Anthropological Genetics*. Cambridge: Cambridge University Press, 1998.

Dixon, E. J. *Quest for the Origins of the First Americans*. Albuquerque, New Mexico: University of New Mexico Press, 1993.

Meltzer, D. J. *Search for the First Americans*. Washington, D.C.: Smithsonian Books, 1993.

Challenges to Science and Evolution

Natural History Magazine, April 111 (3) 2002. Several articles in this issue argue either for or against intelligent design.

Science and Creationism: A view from the National Academy of Sciences, 2nd edition. Washington, D.C.: National Academy Press, 1999. Available online at www.nap.edu.

Skehan, J. W., and C. E. Nelson. *The Creation Controversy and the Science Classroom.* Arlington, Virginia: NSTA Press, 2000.

Teaching About Evolution and the Nature of Science. Washington, D.C.: National Academy Press, 1998. Available online at www.nap.edu.

Human Prehistory Online

Here's a selected list of URLs or links that will assist you if you want to further explore human prehistory, cybernetically speaking. You will also find links for field schools and museums.

General

Human prehistory is well established on the Internet. Entering keywords such as paleoanthropology, archaeology, or human evolution into a search engine should bring up a number of interesting websites. Listed here are a few that will help you get started on what can be a fascinating, but hopefully not too addictive, pastime of surfing the web.

Human Evolution: The Fossil Evidence in 3D. Developed by Philip Walker and Edward Hagen, at UC Santa Barbara, uses Shockwave to rotate images 360°. The project has several images of primates and hominids.

www.anth.ucsb.edu/projects/human

The companion website to the PBS TV series on Evolution. Click Origins of Humankind; again with Shockwave, you can view hominid fossils. This site has a Search Evolution feature.

www.pbs.org/wgbh/evolution

Human Origins website of Jeanne Sept, Department of Anthropology, Indiana University, Bloomington, Indiana. This site has helpful course materials on human origins.

www.indiana.edu/~origins

"Investigating Olduvai," Indiana University. This is a CD-ROM on the archaeology of human origins, a multimedia teaching tool that is available for purchase.

www.indiana.edu/~origins/teach/Olduvai.html

"Prehistoric Puzzles." Also at Indiana University, this is a project under construction by Jeanne Sept that will tap into Internet archaeology sources.

www.indiana.edu/~origins/teach/puzzles.html

"Anthropology in the News," from Texas A&M. This site has breaking news from many fronts, including human origins and evolution.

www.tamu.edu/anthropology/news

Talk.Origins Archive. This newsgroup is devoted to the discussion and debate of human biological origins. It covers the evolution/creation controversy and has many links to related websites.

www.talkorigins.org

"Human Prehistory: An Exhibition." This website has excellent images—including Charles Darwin, Lucy, Lascaux cave paintings, and Venus figures. How's that for an interesting mix?

users.hol.gr/~dilos/prehis.htm

Archaeology on the Net. Here you'll find a large number of well-indexed topics.

www.serve.com/archaeology

Website of Yerkes Primate Center, with studies of chimpanzees in captivity. Listen to recordings of chimp and bonobo (pygmy chimp) vocalizations.

www.emory.edu/LIVING_LINKS/i/people/seres.html

Field Schools

Many active archaeological and paleoanthropological field school programs around the country provide opportunities for hands-on experience. Most of these are connected with universities, museums, and institutes. The following is a selected listing of such schools.

Paleoanthrology Society (with a listing of field schools from around the world)

> www.paleoanthro.org

University of Hawaii Field School on Rapa Nui (Easter Island)

> www.anthropology.hawaii.edu/projects/ppp/rapanui.html

Koobi Fora Field School in Kenya's Great Rift Valley

> http://www.rci.rutgers.edu/~mjr/index1.html

Paleoanthropology Field School in South Africa

> www.asu.edu/clas/iho/field.htm

Museums, Centers, Foundations, and Institutes

Museums and universities often have exhibits that relate to the general topic of human prehistory—too many to list them all here. If you live near a museum or university, call to see if any current exhibits are of interest to you. Most, if not all, of the museums have an Ask a Scientist feature, to answer any questions you have about human prehistory.

Center for Research into the Anthropological Foundations of Technology (CRAFT), Bloomington, Indiana. New research facility is under construction, with completion scheduled sometime in the fall of 2003. The center will feature an experimental tool-making laboratory.

> www.indiana.edu/~anthro/centers/craft.html

The Field Museum, Chicago. Go to Online Exhibits, The Anthropology Collection of the Field Museum, and click on any of the world's continents for information about materials housed and exhibited at the museum. This site has an Ask a Scientist feature.

> www.fieldmuseum.org

American Museum of Natural History, Division of Anthropology, New York. This museum is dedicated to the study of human biology and culture.

anthro.amnh.org

The Leakey Foundation, in San Francisco, has a mission to increase scientific knowledge and public understanding of human origins and evolution. The site carries up-to-date news on fossil discoveries and has an Ask a Scientist feature.

www.leakeyfoundation.org/foundation

Institute of Human Origins (IHO), Tempe, Arizona. This institute is devoted to research of recovery and analysis of fossil evidence for human evolution. It administers a field school in South Africa. Here are two excellent links.

www.asu.edu/clas/iho

www.becominghuman.org

Archaeological Institute at Arizona State, Tempe, Arizona. You'll find extensive links to archaeology on the Net. This site has an Ask a Scientist feature.

archnet.asu.edu

Smithsonian Institution, Anthropology Department, Washington, D.C. The Smithsonian has several programs of possible interest:

- Human Origins Program
- Arctic Studies Center
- American Indian Program
- Paleo-Indian Program
- Repatriation Office (deals with repatriation of Native American burials and cultural materials)

Its site also has an Ask a Scientist feature.

www.nmnh.si.edu/anthro

Index